PROGRAMMING WITH MOBILE APPLICATIONS: ANDROID™, IOS, AND WINDOWS® PHONE 7

THOMAS J. DUFFY

<tcr>COURSE TECHNOLOGY
CENGAGE Learning®</tcr>

Australia • Brazil • Japan • Korea • Mexico • Singapore • Spain • United Kingdom • United States

COURSE TECHNOLOGY
CENGAGE Learning·

Programming with
Mobile Applications: Android™, iOS,
and Windows® Phone 7
Thomas J. Duffy

Executive Editor: Marie Lee

Acquisitions Editor: Brandi Shailer

Senior Product Manager: Alyssa Pratt

Development Editor: Lisa M. Lord

Associate Product Manager:
  Stephanie Lorenz

Content Project Manager:
  Heather Hopkins

Art Director: Faith Brosnan

Marketing Manager: Shanna Shelton

Compositor: Integra

Copyeditor: Karen Annett

Proofreader: Suzanne Huizenga

Indexer: Sharon Hilgenberg

Cover Designer: Hannah Wellman

Cover image credit: Color Symphony/
  Shutterstock.com

Library of Congress Control Number: 2011944540

ISBN-13: 978-1-133-62813-2

Course Technology
20 Channel Center Street
Boston, MA 02210

Cengage Learning is a leading provider of customized learning solutions with office locations around the globe, including Singapore, the United Kingdom, Australia, Mexico, Brazil, and Japan. Locate your local office at:
international.cengage.com/region

Cengage Learning products are represented in Canada by
Nelson Education, Ltd.

For your lifelong learning solutions, visit **course.cengage.com**

Visit our corporate website at **cengage.com.**

Some of the product names and company names used in this book have been used for identification purposes only and may be trademarks or registered trademarks of their respective manufacturers and sellers.

iOS SDK, Xcode, and Interface Builder are trademarks of Apple, Inc., registered in the U.S. and other countries
Android is a trademark of Google Inc.
App Inventor: ©2011 Google Inc.
MOTODEV Studio: ©2011 Motorola Mobility, Inc.
Adobe product screenshots reprinted with permission from Adobe Systems Incorporated.
Visual Studio is a trademark of Microsoft Corporation.

Any fictional data related to persons or companies or URLs used throughout this book is intended for instructional purposes only. At the time this book was printed, any such data was fictional and not belonging to any real persons or companies.

Course Technology, a part of Cengage Learning, reserves the right to revise this publication and make changes from time to time in its content without notice.

The programs in this book are for instructional purposes only.

They have been tested with care but are not guaranteed for any particular intent beyond educational purposes. The author and the publisher do not offer any warranties or representations, nor do they accept any liabilities with respect to the programs.

Printed in Singapore by Seng Lee Press
Print Number: 03   Print Year: 2014

Brief Contents

Contents

CHAPTER 6   Apple iOS **166**

CHAPTER 7   Microsoft Windows Phone 7 . . . . **222**

Preface

Welcome to *Programming with Mobile Applications: Android, iOS, and Windows Phone 7*! This book is aimed at programmers—or those with some programming background—who want to move into the exciting world of developing apps for smartphones. The major platforms for mobile apps are Google Android, Apple iOS, and Microsoft Windows Phone 7, so this book focuses on developing apps for these three operating systems.

Approach

The approach used in *Programming with Mobile Applications: Android, iOS, and Windows Phone 7* is simple. You learn techniques applicable to smartphone development, and then apply these techniques in writing apps for Android, iOS, and Windows Phone 7. When possible, the apps created for each platform are identical so that you can use your newfound knowledge to help you decide which platforms you want to use. Each chapter begins with the traditional Hello World app and then moves on to more complex and useful apps. In addition, *Programming with Mobile Applications* includes coverage of writing Web apps as well as cross-platform apps by using the PhoneGap libraries.

The tools used in *Programming with Mobile Applications* are the standard tools developers use to create apps. Specifically, two tools are used for Android development: Google's App Inventor and Motorola's MOTODEV Studio. MOTODEV Studio is a branded version of IBM Eclipse with plug-ins for creating Android apps. Apple's Xcode 4 is used for iOS development, and Microsoft Visual Studio 2010 Express is used for Windows Phone 7 development. All these tools include an emulator for testing your apps, so you don't need a smartphone to run any of the apps covered in this book. In addition, all the tools used in this book are available free.

What This Book Is

This book serves as an introduction to writing programs for mobile devices. It familiarizes you with the software for creating mobile apps and the process of using the software development kit (SDK) for each platform covered in this book. You don't need actual phones because the apps you create in this book can run by using software emulators.

What This Book Is Not

Because this book is targeted to those new to developing mobile apps, it doesn't cover advanced topics, such as application programming interfaces (APIs) for each platform. Instead, it explains how to access the APIs you need so that you can develop that "killer app" you have in mind.

In addition, this book isn't an exhaustive information resource. You can find a wealth of information, tutorials, examples, and other resources for each platform online. You should learn enough from this book that you can modify and make use of code you find to fit your needs. There's no substitute for writing code, making mistakes, and learning how to fix them. Indeed, there's no better way to further your learning about programming.

Organization and Coverage

Chapter 1 introduces the smartphone landscape, reviews basic programming terms, and gives you an overview of the tools used to develop apps on each platform. You also learn about the history of the smartphone and the capabilities of the most current phones for each platform.

Chapter 2 covers platform architecture and app life cycle events and compares the three major platforms.

Chapter 3 covers best practices for developing smartphone apps. It includes a brief introduction to object-oriented programming concepts and describes the Model-View-Controller and Delegate design patterns in the context of smartphone programming. Finally, some optimization techniques that are useful for smartphone apps, including memory management, are discussed.

The next four chapters cover the three major platforms in detail. **Chapter 4** uses Google's App Inventor to create Android apps, and **Chapter 5** uses Motorola's MOTODEV Studio to create Android apps. **Chapter 6** covers Apple iOS, using Apple's iOS SDK, Xcode, and Interface Builder. **Chapter 7** covers Microsoft Windows Phone 7, using Visual Studio 2010 Express for Windows Phone.

Chapter 8 explains developing Web apps in the context of smartphones, using HTML, CSS, and JavaScript.

Chapter 9 covers cross-platform development with the open-source PhoneGap library. You develop native apps for Android and iOS by using HTML, CSS, and JavaScript.

Appendix A explains how to install and set up the software you need to work through the exercises in the book and describes how to create a project in each tool. You'll refer to this appendix often as a useful resource.

Features of the Book

Programming with Mobile Applications includes the following features:

- *Objectives*—Each chapter begins with a list of objectives as an overview of the topics discussed in the chapter and as a useful study aid.

- *Notes, Want More Info?, Programming Tips, and Cautions*—Notes offer additional information about programming concepts. The Want More Info? features give links that guide you to Web sites where you can explore topics in more depth or find useful resources. Programming Tips give advice on approaching problems from a programmer's point of view. Cautions warn you about situations that are easy to get into and likely to cause big problems.

- *Figures and tables*—Chapters contain diagrams to clarify programming concepts and screenshots to show the interfaces of tools you're working with. In addition, many tables are included to give you an at-a-glance summary of useful information.

- *Best practices*—You're encouraged to use programming and development techniques that follow industry-accepted standards and conventions. Because each platform uses an object-oriented programming language, you learn object-oriented design and programming techniques as well as the Model-View-Controller and Delegate design patterns. In addition, code optimizations for small devices are covered.

- *How-To exercises*—Starting with Chapter 4, each chapter includes boxed features called "How-To" exercises, which are hands-on tutorials that lead you through the development process step by step to create working apps.

- *Detective Work features*—Each How-To exercise ends with a Detective Work feature that challenges you to apply a concept you've just learned to a new situation, complete a task started in a previous exercise, or extend an app with additional features, for example.

- *Summaries*—At the end of each chapter is a summary list that recaps the programming concepts and techniques covered in the chapter so that you have a way to check your understanding of the chapter's main points.

- *Key terms*—Each chapter includes definitions of new terms, alphabetized for ease of reference. This feature is another useful way to review the chapter's major concepts.

- *Review questions*—Each chapter contains multiple-choice and true/false review questions, along with "Up for Discussion" questions for a review of key concepts in the chapter.

- *Programming exercises*—Each chapter includes programming problems involving concepts explained in the chapter to help students practice creating apps for each platform. Students are encouraged to work through the problems and have instructors check their work against the solution files.

- *Quality*—Every program example, hands-on activity, and case study was tested by the author in four major browsers (Internet Explorer, Mozilla Firefox, Google Chrome, and Safari) and again by Cengage Quality Assurance testers.

Student Resources

Source code and project files for the How-To exercises in *Programming with Mobile Applications* are available at *www.cengagebrain.com*.

Software Used in This Book

All software you use in this book is available free. With the exception of PhoneGap, you need to register with software vendors to download the tools. Most vendors have a marketplace, such as Apple's App Store and the Android Market, that charges a fee for posting your apps as well as a developer program you must enroll in to post your apps. Appendix A has instructions for installing and setting up all the software tools used in this book, but here's a list of tools, download locations, and guidelines for hardware requirements for each platform:

Google Android

Google App Inventor—App Inventor is a Web-based application. For information on system requirements and setup, visit *www.appinventorbeta.com/learn/setup/index.html*.

 At the time of this writing, Google is planning to turn over App Inventor to MIT Research Labs. By the time you read this book, the URL in Appendix A pointing to App Inventor might no longer work. Because App Inventor's new location is unknown at this time, look for updated information at *www.cengagebrain.com*. Search by ISBN for this book, select Access Now, and click Updates in the left navigation bar. Steps and screens might differ slightly from what's shown in this book.

Motorola MOTODEV Studio—Download from *http://developer.motorola.com/docstools/ motodevstudio/download/*. For information on system requirements, go to *http://developer. motorola.com/docstools/library/Installing_MOTODEV_Studio_for_Android/*.

Apple iOS

iOS SDK—Download from *https://developer.apple.com/xcode/index.php*. System requirements: an Intel-based Mac running OS X 10.3 to 10.7.

Note: This book uses Xcode 4. If you're using a Mac with OS X 10.5 or earlier, you need to install Xcode 3. Look for a section on the download page for the iOS SDK called "Looking for Xcode 3?." Apple will continue supporting Xcode 3.

Microsoft Windows Phone 7

Visual Studio 2010 Express for Windows Phone—Download the software and view system requirements at *www.microsoft.com/download/en/details.aspx?displaylang=en&id=27570*.

PhoneGap

Download from *www.phonegap.com/home/*.

For the Instructor

Programming with Mobile Applications is intended to be modular. The first part of the book covers concepts and techniques that apply to all the platforms. The second part covers each platform separately. Based on your students' experience, you can choose which chapters in the first part you want to include. If your students have already learned object-oriented programming principles and techniques, you might want to omit Chapter 3, for example.

In the second part, you can choose which platforms to target. If you don't have Macs available, for example, you could omit Chapter 6, or you might decide you don't need to cover two tools for Android development, in which case you could eliminate Chapter 4. Because the platform chapters cover the same apps, your students won't be missing anything.

At Norwalk Community College (NCC), the class on programming mobile devices uses this book. It has been taught online the last two times it has been offered, and it uses the entire book with the following changes. First, students are asked to install the software at the beginning of the class, so Appendix A is covered first. This method leads to far fewer headaches later in the term. Second, the Detective Work features and Programming Exercises in Chapter 6 are optional because for many students, particularly those at community colleges, requiring students to have a Mac is too much of a financial burden. NCC does have Mac labs with the development tools installed available for students, but asking students to come to campus defeats the purpose of an online class! When the class is taught on campus, it meets for 5 hours per week: 3 hours lecture and 2 hours supervised lab time. It takes place in the Mac labs for the iOS chapter and in the PC labs for all other chapters.

Instructor Resources

The following teaching tools are available on the Instructor Resources CD or through *login.cengage.com* to instructors who have adopted this book:

Instructor's Manual. The electronic Instructor's Manual follows the book chapter by chapter to assist in planning and organizing an effective, engaging course. The manual includes learning objectives, chapter overviews, lecture notes, teaching tips, ideas for classroom activities, and additional resources. A sample course syllabus is also available.

ExamView®. This book is accompanied by ExamView, a powerful testing software package that allows instructors to create and administer printed, computer (LAN-based), and Internet exams. ExamView includes hundreds of questions corresponding to the topics covered in this book, enabling students to generate detailed study guides that include page references for further review. These computer-based and Internet testing components allow students to take exams at their computers and save instructors time by grading each exam automatically. Test banks are also available in Blackboard, WebCT, and Angel formats.

PowerPoint Presentations. This book comes with PowerPoint slides for each chapter. They're included as a teaching aid for classroom presentations, to make available to students on the network for chapter review, or to be printed for classroom distribution. Instructors can add their own slides for additional topics or customize the slides with access to all the figure files from the book.

Solution files. Solution files for all end-of-section exercises are provided.

Source code. The source code for this book's programs is provided for students. In addition to being on the Instructor Resources CD and *login.cengage.com*, it's available for students through *www.cengagebrain.com*.

Acknowledgements

Programming with Mobile Applications: Android, iOS, and Windows Phone 7 is the product of a wonderful team of professionals working toward a single goal: providing students with pertinent, engaging material to further their knowledge and careers. Thank you to the folks at Cengage—specifically Acquisitions Editor Brandi Shailer; Senior Product Manager Alyssa Pratt; Content Project Manager Heather Hopkins; Associate Product Manager Stephanie Lorenz; Karen Annett, the copyeditor; Suzanne Huizenga, the proofreader; and Serge Palladino, Susan Whalen, and Susan Pedicini, the MQA testers. I need to say a special thanks to Lisa Lord, the development editor, for her insights, her professionalism, and especially her humor. Quite frankly, this book would never have been finished without her.

Thank you to the reviewers of this book: Tyler Dockery, Wake Tech Community College; Robert Dollinger, University of Wisconsin Stevens Point; Jim McKeown, Dakota State University; Barbara Myers, Dakota State University; Roseann Rovetto, Horry-Georgetown Technical College; and Mark Segall, Metropolitan State College of Denver. It's because of their insights and experience that *Programming with Mobile Applications* is a book that can actually be used in the classroom.

Thank you to Paul Gruhn, Professor of Computer Science at Asnuntuck Community College for convincing me that students other than my own would benefit from this book.

Finally, thank you to my beautiful wife, Kelli Duffy, for her patience and understanding while the lonely writing process took over our lives. I can't think of anyone with whom I'd rather spend the rest of my life.

1

The Computer of the Future Is in Your Hand

In this chapter, you learn to:

- ◎ Define programming terms
- ◎ Describe the three major smartphone platforms
- ◎ Choose a target platform
- ◎ Describe available development tools
- ◎ Define what a smartphone is
- ◎ Summarize the smartphone's history
- ◎ Explain current device capabilities

Smartphones are the personal computers of the future. These powerful, connected devices give users access to the full power of the Internet to communicate with each other in a variety of ways, locate themselves anywhere on the globe, and record their experiences in pictures, video, and sound. No longer do users need to carry several devices to accomplish these tasks and more. A single smartphone can handle them all.

For these reasons, sales of smartphones are skyrocketing. In the second quarter of 2011 alone, more than 110 million smartphones were sold. That's up 74% year-over-year (FierceMobileContent.com, *www.fiercemobilecontent.com/story/npd-android-dominates-52-us-smartphone-sales-q2/2011-08-23*). In the next 10 years, Mark Andreessen, co-founder of Netscape, estimates that more than 5 billion people worldwide will own smartphones (The Wall Street Journal Online, *http://online.wsj.com/article/SB10001424053111903480904576512250915629460.html*). Gartner Research Group (*www.gartner.com/technology/about.jsp*) estimates that more than two-thirds of smartphone owners use Google Android, Apple iOS, or Microsoft Windows Phone 7 as their operating systems (FierceMobileContent.com, *www.fiercemobilecontent.com/story/gartner-android-ends-q2-434-worldwide-market-share/2011-08-11*). These figures indicate that these three platforms are increasing their market share while others are fading away. It appears that, at least for the foreseeable future, there will be three viable platforms.

Given the potentially explosive growth of smartphones, you'd expect that the job market for smartphone app development would be hot, too—and you'd be right. The number of jobs posted on Freelancer.com for smartphone developers jumped 12% from the first quarter of 2011 to the second quarter. Job offers for both Android and iOS developers spiked 20%.

This chapter covers what you need to know to start developing smartphone apps on the three major platforms. It describes these platforms and some devices available for each platform and helps you decide which platform to target. The chapter also gives you an overview of available tools for each platform.

What You Need to Know

Although it doesn't matter what programming language you've studied, you do need to be familiar with the following basic concepts:

- A **literal** is a piece of data stored in memory, such as a name, an address, or a phone number. It's immutable, meaning it can't be changed.

- A **variable** is a named pointer to data in your program that can change.

- An **array** is a collection of data, usually of the same type. You can access each member of a collection by its index (place in the collection). In Java, Objective-C, and C#, arrays have a fixed, declared length, and all array members are of the same data type.

- A **string** is a collection of character data. Strings are immutable in Java, Objective-C, and C#, the programming languages used in this book.

- **Methods** and **functions** are blocks of program code that run when they're called. They're the verbs of a program and represent what a program does.

- **Parameters** are data values passed to other parts of a program, usually methods and functions.

- **Properties** are data associated with the objects of a program and can be compared with adjectives. They describe what an object is and does.

- **Loops** are mechanisms for repeating a set of programming instructions until some condition is met.

- **Conditional statements** are tests in a program that evaluate to true or false.

 Object-oriented principles are discussed in Chapter 3.

In addition, you should know that a platform generally provides a **software development kit (SDK)** and an **integrated development environment (IDE)** to build apps. An SDK, which is the underlying engine of the IDE, includes all the platform's libraries an app needs to access. It's more basic than an IDE because it doesn't usually have graphical tools. The SDKs used in this book, however, include extensive documentation to help developers build apps. You should also be familiar with at least one IDE, such as NetBeans, Eclipse, Visual Studio, Xcode, and so forth, and be able to follow the standard development process in any IDE: write, compile, run, and debug.

Mobile Device Programming

Mobile devices have evolved dramatically over the past decade. They have grown from cellphones that could just make calls to full-fledged computers capable of doing nearly everything a desktop computer can. With them, users can find information on a variety of levels, ranging from social networks to corporate data and e-mail. Coupled with the evolution of high-speed data networks, mobile devices are essential in an increasingly connected world.

In addition, mobile devices have become multifunctional. They represent the **device convergence** that began at the start of the 21st century. No longer do users need to carry a phone, music player, and digital camera. Today's mobile devices can perform all these tasks and more with ease. Most mobile devices are also "location-aware," meaning they use the global positioning system (GPS) to determine where they are in the world. As a developer, you have access to all these features when you create applications.

As of this writing, three major consumer operating systems (OSs) are available on mobile devices: Apple iOS on the iPhone, iPad, and iPod Touch; Google Android on Android devices ranging from smartphones to tablets; and Microsoft Windows Phone 7 on a variety of WinPhone devices. Arguments can be made for the primacy of each platform. In terms of model units sold, iPhone probably reigns supreme. Apple sold more than 19 million units in the second quarter of 2011. In terms of OS units sold, Android is probably at the top. More than 47 million Android OS units were sold in the same period. Windows Phone 7 is so new that its market share is small, but this can be exciting in terms of development simply because the potential market is so large (FierceMobileContent.com, *www.fiercemobilecontent.com/ story/gartner-android-ends-q2-434-worldwide-market-share/2011-08-11*). For example, Microsoft and Nokia recently announced a joint venture: All Nokia smartphones sold in the United States will run Windows Phone 7.

Potentially profitable apps can be developed in all three platforms, and each one has an online **marketplace** with many potential customers, where you can sell your apps for a fairly small fee. This book dedicates chapters to each platform, which should help you decide which one you want to use.

How Do You Choose a Platform?

When choosing a platform for your apps, ask yourself these four questions:

- *Who will use your apps?* As with any application you develop, identifying the target audience helps determine on which platform you should build apps. Are you trying to reach a large market? Android and iPhone are the obvious choices. Are most of your users running Windows on a desktop, or are you targeting an organization that uses a specific device? Maybe Windows Phone 7 is your best bet. In short, you must identify who will use your app before you build it.

- *Is there a future for the platform?* This question requires more thought. In the short term, all the platforms discussed in this book have a future. In the long term, however, their prospects might look different. If you're trying to build a career developing mobile apps, you need to look at market share trends to help you determine which platform will have staying power. If you're creating apps for your personal use, you just need to know which phone you'll be using when your contract expires.

- *What are your app's technical requirements?* Each platform has its advantages and disadvantages. Are you considering a multitasking app? Need a lot of screen real estate or proprietary application programming interfaces (APIs)? What's most important is knowing which platforms support your technical needs. If your app is appealing enough, users will change to your platform of choice.

- *What are the platform's development tools?* The available tools and your ability to use them influence how you develop apps. Is the platform vendor the only choice for writing your app? Are third-party tools available? What programming language is used to develop for the platform, and are you familiar with it? In short, if you can't work with the available tools, your app won't get written.

Of course, there are more questions—not the least of which is whether you can make money developing apps on a platform. Find out what the platform's revenue-sharing model is and whether its marketplace has enough activity to warrant targeting it. Which vendors offer phones for your platform? Which carriers offer these phones? All these questions help you determine which platform you'll choose.

Programming Languages and Development Tools

Each platform in the mobile device landscape uses its own programming language and tools for development. Sometimes the provider designates the tool, and sometimes the tool has emerged as part of the platform. In this book, you use the preferred tool for development on each platform but learn about other available tools, too. Whenever possible, you can choose the tool you like to write your apps. The preferred tool, however, is an IDE, which includes tools for writing and compiling code, running your program in a simulator or on a device, debugging code, and, finally, deploying your app. Table 1-1 lists each platform's programming language and preferred tool.

Table 1-1   Platform languages and tools

Platform	Programming language	Preferred tool
Google Android	Java	Google App Inventor, IBM Eclipse with plug-ins
Apple iOS	Objective-C	Apple Xcode, Interface Builder
Microsoft Windows Phone 7	C#	Visual Studio 2010 for Windows Phone

Web Applications

All smartphones include a surprisingly capable Web browser. Writing Web applications opens up the possibility of creating a single app that's accessed over the Web via the browser. If you have expertise in creating Web applications, this method might be your best bet to create apps for multiple platforms, using one set of files. The languages of choice for Web apps are Hypertext Markup Language (HTML), Cascading Style Sheets (CSS), and JavaScript. Knowing these languages can make creating Web apps easier.

Web apps are discussed in Chapter 8. For more information on PhoneGap, refer to Chapter 9.

PhoneGap is a free, open-source tool that enables you to create Web apps and deploy them to a variety of platforms, including, as of this writing, Android and iOS. The PhoneGap team is working to include Windows Phone 7, too. With PhoneGap, you can migrate a Web app directly to a device, store your files there, and access them as though they were on the Web. You also have access to device capabilities, such as the accelerometer, location services, and the camera. The result is a Web app that's indistinguishable from any other app on the device.

5

What Is a Smartphone?

You can think of a **smartphone** as a contemporary cellphone combined with a handheld computer you can use to develop apps that run on the underlying platform. A **native app** is one that's compiled for a specific platform's architecture. That's both a boon and a bane. On the one hand, you can create apps that are small, fast, and look like other apps on the device, but you need different versions of the same app to support multiple platforms.

Historically, **Java Micro Edition (ME)** was intended to address the concerns of multiple small-device platforms. It was developers' first attempt to facilitate creating apps for multiple devices. The thinking was that if all devices supported Java ME, developers could create apps targeting Java ME and deploy them on many devices. The premise of Java in any environment is to enable developers to create a single app by using the Java development stack and then deploy it on a virtual machine available on almost any platform. A **virtual machine** is a collection of resources that enables programs to run applications on a host OS. The Java slogan "Write once, run anywhere" reflects the capability to write apps that can run on multiple platforms, including those for smartphones.

Unfortunately, because of Java ME's "least common denominator" approach, it wasn't suited for the touch screens and sophisticated graphics of smartphones. Although developers could build apps in Java and run them on most phones, these apps just didn't look right on smartphones. Further, the Java ME platform was built to target phones with dial pads and physical buttons, and it didn't translate well on touch screens, even in the first smartphones. The Java platform has been updated to address the capabilities of touch screens, but it might be too little too late. The smartphone market has moved on.

History of the Smartphone

IBM and BellSouth introduced the first smartphone in 1994 as a joint effort: the IBM Simon (see Figure 1-1). In addition to mobile phone capabilities, the Simon included a calendar, an address book, a world clock, a calculator, a note pad, e-mail, and games. It also sported a touch screen rather than physical buttons and offered 1 MB each of RAM and system memory. Memory could be expanded via an external memory card slot.

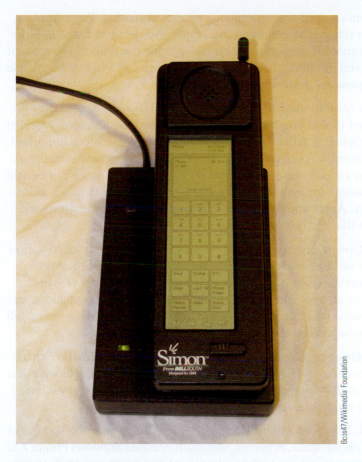

Bcos47/Wikimedia Foundation

Figure 1-1 The IBM Simon

In the next decade or so, hybrid devices were released that melded a mobile phone with a personal digital assistant (PDA). With these devices, most of which ran Palm OS or Windows CE Pocket PC, users could browse the Web wirelessly, organize personal information, and sync with a PC. On most devices, a stylus was used to select items onscreen. Third-party apps were available by downloading them on the device or syncing with a PC.

The smartphone took off in 2007. Nokia released the N95, which included many of the features now considered standard on a smartphone: GPS capabilities, a 5 megapixel (MP) camera with autofocus and flash, and Wi-Fi connectivity. The first iPhone from Apple came out the same year. Developers couldn't create and deploy apps on iPhones; Apple supplied all apps and included mobile versions of desktop apps, such as Mail, Safari, and iTunes. In essence, the original iPhone was an iPod Touch that could make phone calls. The iPhone shared Apple's **iOS** operating system with the iPod Touch, opening the door for developers to create apps for both devices.

In 2008, two major developments helped the smartphone market skyrocket. First, Apple released the second-generation iPhone. More important, Apple also debuted the App Store with its accompanying SDK. It enabled developers to create apps for the iPhone and made it possible for users to download and install them without connecting to a PC. In essence, Apple made the smartphone an independent device.

The iPhone turned out to be a revolutionary device. With the iPod Touch, Apple had changed the way people listened to and purchased music. Apple used the knowledge gained from designing the iPod Touch's user interface and applied it to the iPhone. More important, Apple learned that the way content was delivered to a device was as important as making a device that works. The only way to load music on an iPod is via iTunes. The same can be said of apps on the iPhone: Apple maintains a closed, controlled system from both users' and developers' perspectives. In fact, Apple approves every app available at the App Store and reserves the right to reject any that are deemed undesirable.

The second development was Google's release of the Android OS. **Android** is an open-source platform that makes all system services available to developers. Google hoped to entice developers by allowing third-party apps to have access to the entire underlying OS. In Android, everything is treated as an app, and nothing is off limits. Google also included an open-source SDK and mobile versions of its apps, such as Gmail, Calendar, Maps, and a full WebKit-based Web browser (now offered as Chrome on the desktop).

Handset makers on multiple platforms adopted Android, which increased its market share quickly; there were options other than the iPhone available at a variety of prices. Google also launched the Android Market in 2008, which gave developers and users a way to exchange apps without a PC connection, much like Apple's App Store.

During this inflationary period, Microsoft did little to keep pace. After seeing the success of Apple and Google in the smartphone space, however, Microsoft released **Windows Phone 7** in late 2010. Compared with previous Windows Mobile releases, it has a new user interface, new development tools, and the Marketplace, which is similar to the App Store and the Android Market. Of course, Microsoft is betting that tight integration with Windows and Office will entice users to choose Windows Phone 7. Microsoft has also made the development tools free to help get existing Windows developers to write apps for Windows Phone 7.

Device Capabilities

When discussing the capabilities of any computing device, you generally look at processing power, memory, display, and peripherals. Because smartphones represent device convergence, you should also look for additional features, such as camera specifications, GPS capabilities, battery life, size, network speeds, synchronization, and voice features. Table 1-2 lists capabilities of the leading handsets for each platform covered in this book.

The information listed in Table 1-2 is current as of this writing.

Table 1-2   Comparing devices for each platform

	Google Nexus S 4G	iPhone 4	HTC Trophy
OS	Android 2.3	iOS 4	Windows Phone 7
Processor	1 GHz Hummingbird	1 GHz ARM Cortex-A8	1 GHz Snapdragon
Memory (RAM)	512 MB	512 MB	576 MB
Memory (internal)	16 GB	16 or 32 GB	16 GB
Memory (external)	MicroSD	N/A	MicroSD
Display	Super AMOLED (16 million colors, 480 × 800)	TFT Retina Display (16 million colors, 640 × 960)	TFT (16 million colors, 480 × 800)
Camera	5.0 MP	5.0 MP	5.0 MP
GPS	Yes	Yes	Yes
Talk time	6.7 hours	14 hours	6.8 hours
Standby time	17 days	12.5 days	15 days
Network speed	4G (WiMAX)/3G	3G	3G
Synchronization	USB 2.0	USB 2.0 (iTunes)	USB 2.0 (My Phone)
Voice-enabled	Yes	Yes	Yes
Browser	WebKit	Safari Mobile	Internet Explorer 8 Mobile
Release date	First quarter 2010	Second quarter 2011	Second quarter 2011

With the exception of the Nexus S access to 4G speeds, these phones are nearly identical. The iPhone and Windows Phone 7 models will almost certainly reach 4G speeds, if they haven't already by the time you read this.

Most current Android devices aren't as powerful as the Nexus S. Android is an evolving system, and handsets have been available for a while from multiple vendors at various prices. That's usually considered a plus for Android—that it's open and accessible to developers, and multiple vendors can use and enhance it. The problem is that there will always be Android devices running older versions of the OS.

Most people don't trade in their phones often enough to stay current. They wait for the next upgrade, which can be up to two years away, before they start thinking about buying their next phone. Even then, most users don't choose the latest model because they can save money staying "a model back." The result is that when you create Android apps, you need to decide which Android version your app will support. You need to weigh using the newest, hottest technologies against the number of devices that can run them.

Software updates for Android are device and carrier dependent, so carriers and handset makers decide if and when an Android device will get an official update. For the most part, these updates are downloaded to the device wirelessly. Most upgrades are incremental, not version increases. For example, if a device is shipped with Android 1.5, its next update is Android 1.5.1. It might, at some point, be upgraded to 1.6. Chances are, however, that it won't ever be updated to Android 2.0 or higher.

Updates are different for iOS and Windows Phone 7 but for different reasons. Apple is a closed system, so users must use iTunes to sync their devices. When Apple rolls out an update to iOS, it's done through iTunes, and most users install it—a result of a single vendor controlling both hardware and software. Windows Phone 7, on the other hand, will probably follow the same path as Android. For now, however, because it's so new, you know that Windows Phone 7 apps are running on fairly new hardware that's capable of doing what iOS and current Android devices can do. This knowledge makes development much easier.

From a programming perspective, you need to keep in mind that the device you target has limited capabilities compared with desktop PCs. The amount of RAM and processor speeds are far lower, for example. Today's PCs have far more RAM and processors at least twice as fast as in the latest smartphone. Further, your app must be able to run on the phone in a shared space. So if your app needs more memory than what's available (or, with Windows Phone 7, if users navigate away from your app), all three platforms can stop your app and remove it from memory. As you develop your apps, remember that lean and mean is the way to go!

Chapter Summary

- Three major platforms are available on today's smartphones: Apple iOS, Google Android, and Microsoft Windows Phone 7.

- Each platform has its own software development kit (SDK), which is a collection of libraries, tools, and documentation that programmers use for building apps. An integrated development environment (IDE) is a programming tool that wraps SDK features into a user-friendly environment. IDEs enable programmers to write, compile, run, and debug code and ultimately deploy apps.

- Each platform discussed in this book includes a marketplace for developers to sell their apps.

- Device convergence is the concept that users no longer need separate devices to perform multiple tasks. For example, today's smartphones include a camera and a music player. Users don't need to carry phones in addition to dedicated devices.

- A native app is one that's compiled for a specific platform's architecture.

- Web applications are written in Hypertext Markup Language (HTML), Cascading Style Sheets (CSS), and JavaScript.

- Android, iOS, and Windows Phone 7 include a capable Web browser that can run Web applications.

- PhoneGap is a cross-platform tool used to create native apps for Android and iOS by packaging Web applications.

- A smartphone is a handheld computer integrated with a cellphone that can run apps that are native to the underlying OS.

- The premise of Java in any environment, including Java ME, is to enable developers to create a single app with the Java development stack and then deploy it on a virtual machine available on almost any platform.

- A virtual machine is a collection of resources that enables programs to run applications on a host OS.

- IBM and BellSouth introduced the first smartphone—the IBM Simon—in 1994.

- In 2007, Apple released the first iPhone, and in 2008, an SDK for developing third-party apps. It also opened the App Store for third-party developers to sell apps to iPhone users.

- Google released the Android OS and SDK in 2008 and opened the Android Market. Android is an open-source OS adopted by multiple handset makers and deployed by multiple service carriers.

- Microsoft released Windows Phone 7 in 2010.

- Android software updates are released by handset makers and service carriers and delivered to devices wirelessly. When Apple rolls out an update to iOS, it does it through iTunes.

Key Terms

Android—Google's open-source OS for smartphones and similar devices. It includes a free SDK that integrates with various IDEs for creating native apps, which are written in Java.

arrays—Collections of data, usually of the same type. Array members are accessed by index (place in the collection).

conditional statements—Tests in a program that evaluate to true or false.

device convergence—The concept that users no longer need separate devices to perform multiple tasks.

functions—Blocks of code in a program that run when called; can be thought of as the verbs in a program and represent what a program does.

integrated development environment (IDE)—A collection of tools programmers use for writing, compiling, running, and debugging code and deploying apps; usually has graphical tools and includes extensive documentation to help developers build apps.

iOS—Apple's OS for mobile devices.

Java Micro Edition (ME)—This platform, intended to address the concerns of multiple small-device platforms, uses Java as its programming language.

literal—A piece of immutable data stored in memory.

loops—Programming mechanisms for repeating a set of programming instructions until some end condition is met.

marketplace—An online location hosted by platform providers where programmers can sell apps.

methods—*See* functions.

native app—An application compiled for a specific platform's architecture.

parameters—Data values passed to other parts of a program, usually methods and functions. *See also* functions.

properties—Data associated with the objects of a program. They can be thought of as adjectives, describing what an object is and does.

smartphone—A handheld computer integrated with a cellphone; it runs native apps. *See also* native app.

software development kit (SDK)—A collection of platform libraries, tools, and documentation that developers use for building applications.

strings—Collections of character data. Strings are immutable in Java, Objective-C, and C#.

variable—A named pointer to data in a program that can change.

virtual machine—A collection of resources used to run applications on a host OS.

Windows Phone 7—The Microsoft platform for developing smartphone apps. Its IDE is Visual Studio 2010, and Windows Phone 7 apps are written in the C# programming language.

Review Questions

1. Which of the following is *not* an example of device convergence?

   a. Carrying a camera, phone, and music player

   b. Taking a picture with your phone

   c. Listening to music on your phone

   d. Using your phone as a GPS device

2. A software development kit usually includes which of the following? (Choose all that apply.)

   a. Libraries used for development

   b. Tools for testing code

   c. Documentation about the libraries

   d. A free smartphone

3. An integrated development environment usually makes it easier to work with an SDK. True or False?

4. You can pass parameters to which of the following?

   a. Loops

   b. Functions

   c. Properties

   d. Conditions

5. Suppose these values are used in your program: x=10 and y=15. What will the results of the following code be?

   ```
   if(y > x){
      System.out.println(y);
   }else{
      System.out.println(x);
   }
   ```

   a. 15 is displayed onscreen.

   c. 1015 is displayed onscreen.

   b. 5 is displayed onscreen.

   d. 25 is displayed onscreen.

6. If a < b evaluates to false, which is always true?

   a. a > b

   c. a <= b

   b. a = b

   d. a >= b

7. Suppose an array contains the following elements: {1,2,3,4}. What's the value of the element at index 2?

   a. 2

   c. 1

   b. 4

   d. 3

8. Suppose an array contains the following elements: {1,2,3,4}. What kind of loop is best for accessing all array elements in sequential order?

   a. A for loop

   b. A while loop

   c. A do while loop

   d. There's no way to access the elements sequentially.

9.   In the following expression, which part is the literal?

     myName = "Tom Duffy";

     a.   myName   c.   "Tom Duffy"
     b.   =   d.   There's no literal.

10. Which of the following does *not* describe a smartphone?

     a.   It's a handheld device.
     b.   It runs native apps.
     c.   It requires a virtual machine to run apps.
     d.   It integrates a cellphone.

11. Which of the following is Java's premise?

     a.   One language, one platform   c.   Java, Java everywhere!
     b.   Write once, run anywhere   d.   None of the above

12. Which of the following describes a virtual machine? (Choose all that apply.)

     a.   A collection of resources
     b.   Allows nonnative applications to run
     c.   Another type of SDK
     d.   Runs on a host OS

13. Who introduced the first smartphone?

     a.   Microsoft   c.   IBM and BellSouth
     b.   Apple   d.   Google

14. Which of the following did Google release in 2008?

     a.   The Android platform
     b.   A new version of iTunes
     c.   A new programming language for creating Android apps
     d.   Both b and c

15. Which of the following is true of the Android platform?

     a.   It's open source.
     b.   It's licensed to a single handset maker.
     c.   It's licensed to a single service carrier.
     d.   None of the above

16. Android software updates:

    a. Are usually delivered wirelessly

    b. Are offered by handset makers and service carriers

    c. Both a and b

    d. None of the above

17. Which of the following is true of iOS software updates?

    a. Most users ignore updates.

    b. Most users install updates.

    c. Users can get updates from multiple sources.

    d. All of the above

Up for Discussion

1. Do an Internet search for current market trends in the smartphone market. Discuss platform trends separately and in relation to each other. If you want to target a single platform, which one would you choose? Why?

2. Find at least three job postings that include developing applications for all three major platforms: Android, iOS, and Windows Phone 7. Compare the postings in salary, duties, and length of employment. Are there any job market trends you should consider when choosing a platform?

3. Discuss the relationship between a software development kit (SDK) and an integrated development environment (IDE). Give examples of each. How do SDKs and IDEs work together to make developers' lives easier?

4. Research smartphones introduced between the IBM Simon and Nokia N95. What features did these devices share? What differentiated them?

Programming Exercises

1. Write a program in your language of choice that displays the numbers 1 through 10 onscreen.

2. Write a program in your language of choice that uses a loop to display the first 10 positive, even integers onscreen.

3. Write a program in your language of choice that reverses the order of the array {1,2,3,4}.

4. Workers at Sam's Discount earn $15 per hour. If they work more than 35 hours in a week, they earn time and a half for any hours over 35. Write a program in your language of choice that calculates weekly pay for a given number of hours. Display the results onscreen.

5. Rewrite the code for Programming Exercise 4 so that it includes a method or function that does the calculation. The method should take the number of hours worked as a parameter. Display the results onscreen.

CHAPTER 2

Developing for Small Devices

In this chapter, you learn to:

- ◎ Describe the architecture of each platform
- ◎ Summarize the similarities and differences between platforms
- ◎ Explain the life cycle of an app on each platform
- ◎ Compare life cycle features in each platform

This chapter explains how the three major platforms are structured and how your apps interact with and run on each one. These platforms have much in common, but they also have differentiating characteristics, especially from a developer's viewpoint. In addition, they have well-defined processes that govern the events determining an app's life cycle. Life cycle events provide a mechanism for you to handle how users interact with your app. The similarities and differences discussed in this chapter help you begin making decisions about which platforms you'll support. You also learn how apps are started and terminated in each platform.

Platform Architecture

Each platform consists of an **application layer**, a **core libraries layer**, an **operating system layer**, and a **hardware layer** (see Figure 2-1):

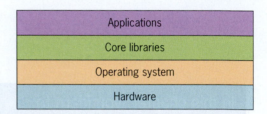

Figure 2-1   General platform architecture

- *Application*—This layer, where apps run, sits on top of the platform stack and is the layer users interact with.

- *Core libraries*—This layer provides device functionality that developers use to create apps.

- *Operating system*—This layer is responsible for translating programming instructions into machine language the device understands.

- *Hardware*—This layer is the physical device, including the screen, buttons, switches, and so on. The result is a stack of resources that apps can access.

The extent to which core library functions are made available depends on the platform, but for the most part, apps have access to all the device's functionality. Granting access to as much device functionality as possible makes perfect sense; the goal is to get users to purchase products. For example, Microsoft realized that most users don't care what the OS is; they care about applications that make PCs useful. On the desktop, Microsoft has been the undisputed leader in helping developers produce applications for Windows. It offers extensive online resources on how to create applications and makes them available to everyone. Microsoft knows that applications drive the sales of Windows.

A great example is the killer Windows application: Microsoft Office. Office is tied to Windows from both a sales and a developer's perspective. Of course, Office has access to all the functionality of Windows, so it works better in Windows than other office applications do. The result is that sales of Office lead to more sales of Windows. Office has become the standard, especially in the corporate world, so it should be no surprise that Windows holds the market share it does. There's even a version of Office for the Mac, and even though Apple offers a competing product—iWork—most Mac users still use Microsoft Office. Simply put, exchanging documents in anything other than Office is difficult because of the sheer number of Office users. Pure genius!

Interestingly, Apple has duplicated Microsoft's strategy in smartphone apps. Apple realized early that apps make the difference, which is clear in any recent Apple advertising. Remember "There's an app for that" or "If you don't have an iPhone, you don't have iBooks"?

Each platform vies for developers in its own way. Although these platforms are nearly identical conceptually, there are subtle differences, discussed in the following sections, that developers must understand if they want to create great apps.

The Android Platform

As Figure 2-2 shows, apps you write operate at the same level as core apps on the device—phone, contacts, browser, and so forth. Other platforms see these core apps as different from third-party apps and give core apps preference. The Android platform is built on the premise that *all* functionality at the application layer is the same. In essence, phone capabilities, for example, are just another app.

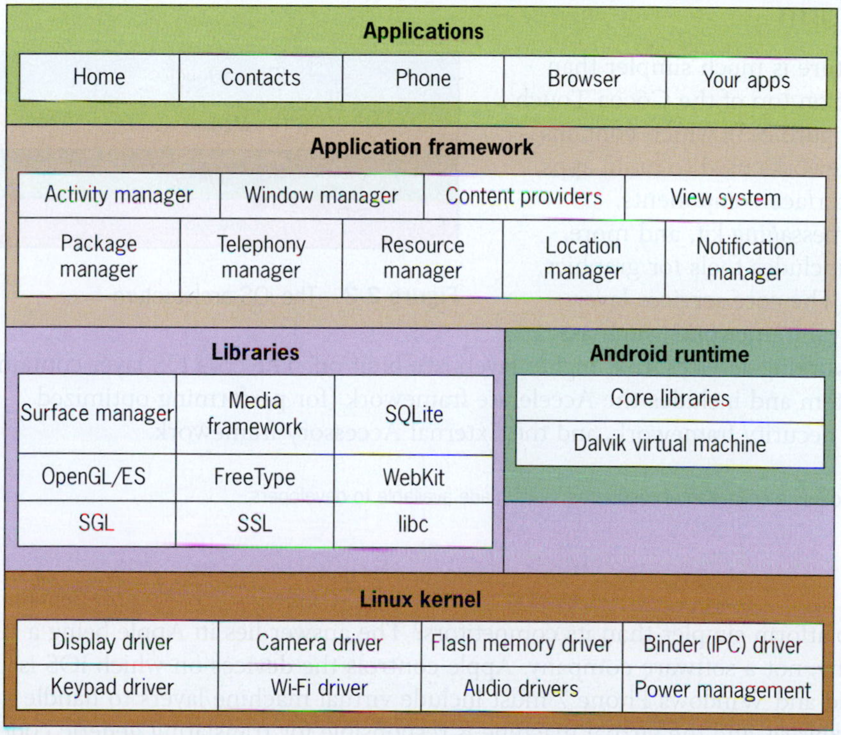

Applications				
Home	Contacts	Phone	Browser	Your apps

Application framework				
Activity manager	Window manager	Content providers		View system
Package manager	Telephony manager	Resource manager	Location manager	Notification manager

Libraries			Android runtime	
Surface manager	Media framework	SQLite	Core libraries	
OpenGL/ES	FreeType	WebKit	Dalvik virtual machine	
SGL	SSL	libc		

Linux kernel			
Display driver	Camera driver	Flash memory driver	Binder (IPC) driver
Keypad driver	Wi-Fi driver	Audio drivers	Power management

Figure 2-2 The Android architecture

As you've learned, Android apps are written in Java. All Java programs are compiled into bytecode and then run in a virtual machine that's on the host OS. Technically speaking, Java programs aren't native to the OS, so the Android platform includes the **Dalvik virtual machine** for running Android apps written in Java on Android devices.

Using Java as the programming language has benefits. Many developers already use this language, so they don't need to learn a new one to create Android apps. In addition, these developers are familiar with the tools used to create Java programs, so they don't need to learn new IDEs, either.

Typically, Android apps use components in the application framework and library layers to provide new functionality. They're compiled into bytecode suitable for a virtual machine to run. The virtual machine is responsible for converting bytecode into instructions that run in the Linux OS, which then translates the instructions into machine language the device understands.

All Android devices use the Linux OS.

The iOS Platform

The iOS architecture is much simpler than Android. Apps sit on top of the Cocoa Touch layer (shown in Figure 2-3), which contains many of the frameworks used to build apps, including user interface components, the map kit, the messaging kit, and more. The media layer includes tools for graphics, audio, and video. The core services layer contains lower-level frameworks, such as

Figure 2-3 The iOS architecture

location and networking services, that higher layers are built on. The core OS layer contains the operating system and includes the Accelerate framework (for performing optimized calculations), the Security framework, and the External Accessory framework.

A framework is a collection of resources that's made available to developers.

Why is the iOS platform simpler than its competitors? The answer lies in Apple being a hardware company, not a software company. Apple controls the devices on which iOS is deployed. Android and Windows Phone 7 must include virtual machine layers to handle differences in hardware, and the virtual machine is responsible for translating generic code into device-specific instructions. This abstraction isn't necessary in iOS because the hardware is the same on all iOS devices. No virtual machine is necessary.

When creating your own apps, you have access to all layers in the iOS platform. However, when you're creating iOS apps, writing code that makes use of layers higher in the stack is better than accessing lower layers directly. Using the higher layers insulates you from the complexity of lower layers and protects you from any future changes Apple might make at

20

the lower layers. That way, should Apple decide to change the lower layers that access hardware directly in a new device, for example, you can be confident your app will still function as intended. In other words, using the higher layers makes your app forward-compatible with future devices.

The Windows Phone 7 Platform

The Windows Phone 7 platform, shown in Figure 2-4, is much like Android. Your app sits on top of available frameworks. For example, you use the Silverlight framework when you want to build an application based on Windows Forms and Controls or use the XNA framework for developing 2D and 3D games. Use HTML/JavaScript to build apps that can be deployed in a WebView control. You can combine frameworks as you see fit to meet your needs.

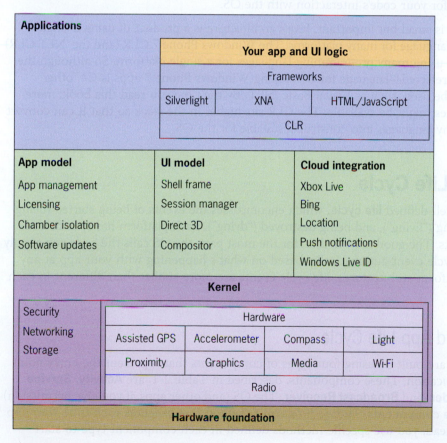

Figure 2-4   The Windows Phone 7 architecture

Originally, XNA was an abbreviation for "Xbox New Architecture." When the new Xbox was released (the Xbox 360), the meaning changed to stand for "XNA is Not an Acronym."

A WebView control is a browser window you can embed in an app. You can use Web languages, such as HTML and JavaScript, to create content that can be viewed in a WebView control. A WebView control is an instance of Internet Explorer Mobile, the Web browser available in Windows Phone 7.

The Windows Phone 7 platform also contains a virtual machine: the **Common Language Runtime (CLR)**. It converts compiled resources into machine-readable code. The difference between the CLR and the Dalvik virtual machine is where they sit in the platform stack. The CLR is an interface between your code and core libraries. The Dalvik virtual machine is an interface for your code's interaction with the OS.

The difference is small but important. Java's architecture is a product of using a single programming language for many platforms. The Windows Phone 7 CLR (and the .NET CLR) is a product of using many programming languages for a single platform. So although the default—and preferred—language for developing Windows Phone 7 apps is C#, other languages can be used, such as Visual Basic .NET. By the time you read this book, more language choices might be available. The CLR sits higher in the stack so that it can convert code from many languages into constructs suitable for the OS.

The App Life Cycle

Apps have a well-defined **life cycle**, which encompasses the events of being started (being "born"), running ("living"), and being destroyed ("dying"). Each platform has specific code for these events. The good news is that, for the most part, the OS calls the code you supply for each life cycle event automatically, based on what's happening with your app at any time. Like platform architectures, life cycle events are more similar than different in each platform.

The Android App Life Cycle

Android apps are built by using four types of components that represent the entry point into your application. These components, described in Table 2-1, are **Activity**, **Service**, **Content Provider**, and **Broadcast Receiver**. The OS (and other apps, if you give permission) can start these components. There's no `main()` method that executes each time your app is started. Instead, you use specific methods defined in each component type to start your app.

Table 2-1 Android components

Component	Functionality
Activity	Represents a single screen with a user interface
Service	Runs in the background to perform long-running operations
Content Provider	Manages a shared set of application data
Broadcast Receiver	Responds to systemwide broadcasts

Activities are the app components that users interact with and what users generally think of as an app. Typically, a user action starts them: tapping an icon on the home screen, for example. Table 2-2 lists the methods defining an activity's life cycle, and Figure 2-5 shows the Activity component's life cycle.

Table 2-2 Life cycle methods in the Activity component

Method	Description
onCreate()	Called when an activity is first created. This method is where any initialization should be done.
onRestart()	Called after an activity has stopped and been restarted.
onStart()	Called just before an activity becomes visible to the user.
onResume()	Called just before an activity becomes available to the user. At this point, the activity is in the foreground and able to accept input.
onPause()	Called just before the OS is about to start another activity. This method is where you should save any data. After onPause() executes, the activity is moved to the background.
onStop()	Called when an activity is no longer visible to the user.
onDestroy()	Called just before an activity is destroyed. It's the last call the activity receives.

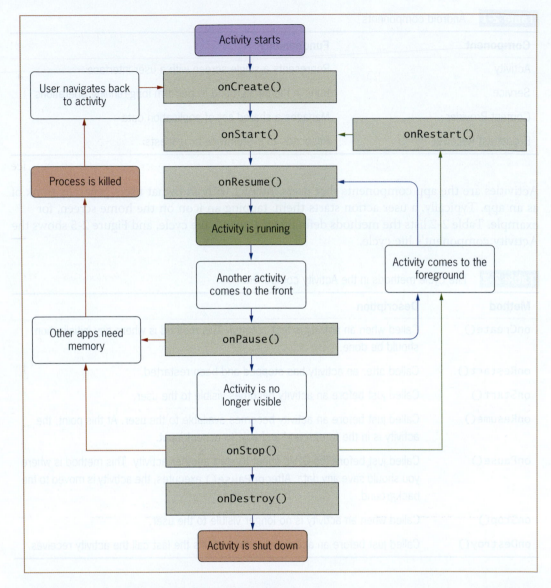

Figure 2-5   Life cycle events in the Activity component

You can write code in any of the life cycle event handlers. Practically speaking, you usually use the onCreate() method. For activities that interact with data, you should use onPause() and/or onDestroy(). Placing code in these methods enables you to save changes to data before your app moves from the foreground. Most code in an activity responds to user events generated by onscreen objects. In the Contacts app, for example, users navigate through lists to get data by tapping on entries in these lists.

Services differ from Activity components by having no user interface. They generally take two forms: started and bound. A started service might handle network operations or file I/O, for example. It might be started by an app for a specific purpose and then run until the task is finished. Because started services can run even when the app that started them terminates, started services should always stop themselves.

A bound service might supply background music for other apps, for example. Binding to a service allows your app to interact with the service. Your app can query the service, get results, and process them as needed, depending on the service. If your service supports binding, it must provide functionality in the onBind() method. Multiple apps could bind to the service, and when there are no longer any apps bound, the service stops.

Services include the life cycle methods listed in Table 2-3, and Figure 2-6 shows the Service component's life cycle.

Table 2-3   Life cycle methods in the Service component

Method	Description
onCreate()	The OS calls this method to create the service. If the service is already running, the method isn't called. Any initialization is performed in this method.
onStartCommand()	The OS calls this method when another component starts a service by calling startService(). The service runs indefinitely, so you must make sure you stop it eventually. This method is optional. With a bound service, this method isn't needed.
onBind()	The OS calls this method when a component wants to bind with the service. The method returns an IBinder object, an interface that clients use to communicate with the service. You must provide this method, but the method can return a null object if you don't want to allow binding.
onDestroy()	The OS calls this method when the service is no longer bound to any component or is being destroyed. Use it to clean up any resources.

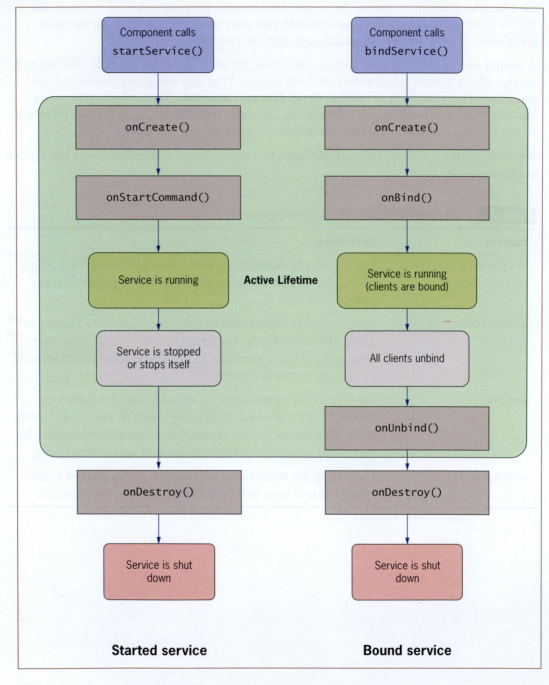

Figure 2-6 Life cycle events in the Service component

Content Providers store and retrieve data, so they don't really have life cycle events. They're the only way to share data between apps because there's no central repository that all Android packages can access. Android includes these components for many common data types, such as audio, video, and contact information, and your app can query them for the data they contain. You can create Content Providers for any data your app needs to make available to other apps.

Broadcast Receivers respond to systemwide broadcasts, such as the battery running low or a text message arriving. They have a limited life cycle: They're valid only within the scope of the `onReceive()` method. When the broadcast they're waiting for occurs, the OS calls `onReceive()`. When this method returns, the receiver is killed.

The iOS App Life Cycle

The iOS app life cycle is simpler than Android's because an iOS app has a *single* entry point. As with any C program, the `main()` function in an app is the entry point and triggers starting the app. In an iOS app, the `main()` function exists merely to call the app's `UIApplicationMain()` function and hand control to the UIKit framework, which is responsible for running an app.

The `UIApplicationMain()` function is the heart of an app: It creates and loads the application object, the application delegate, and the user interface. The **application delegate** is where you write code to interact with both the OS and the user. It's also where life cycle events occur. Table 2-4 lists the application delegate's life cycle methods.

 You learn more about these objects in Chapters 3 and 6.

Table 2-4   iOS life cycle methods

Method	Description
`application:didFinishLaunchingWithOptions:`	Called by `UIApplicationMain()` to initialize the app, including data structures, the main window, and any views.
`applicationDidBecomeActive:`	Called when an app enters the foreground.
`applicationWillResignActive:`	Called when an app is interrupted by a system event.

(continues)

Table 2-4	iOS life cycle methods (*continued*)	
Method	**Description**
applicationDidEnterBackground:	Called when an app moves to the background.
applicationWillEnterForeground:	Called when an app is restarted from the background.
applicationWillTerminate:	Called when an app is to be terminated. It allows approximately 5 seconds to do any resource cleanup.

iOS apps are a mixture of C and Objective-C. In C methods, parentheses are used to specify passing arguments, separated by commas, to functions. In Objective-C methods, arguments are separated with colons, and no parentheses are used. So when you see parentheses, you're looking at a C language function. When you see colons, that's Objective-C.

Figure 2-7 is a simplified diagram of an iOS app's life cycle. It shows when code is called by the OS at defined times during the process. As in every GUI application, an event loop is executed, where events are initiated by the user or the OS, and code is called to handle the events involved in the app's functioning.

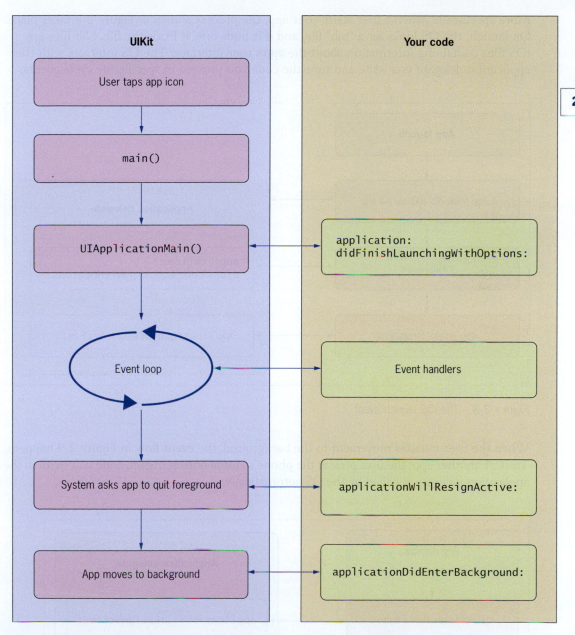

Figure 2-7 The iOS app life cycle

More specifically, when a user starts your app, the process shown in Figure 2-8 takes place. On launch, the OS looks for a "nib" file, and if it finds one, it loads the file. Nib files are iOS files containing information about the app's user interface. The OS interacts with the application delegate you write and runs the code you provide in specific life cycle events.

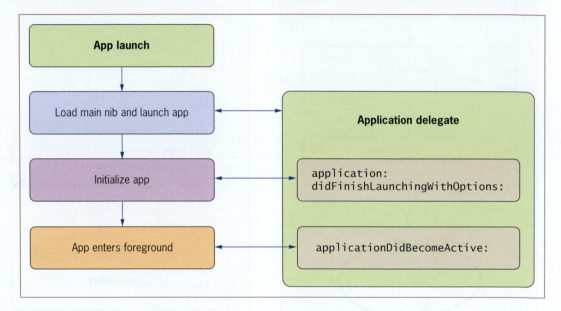

Figure 2-8   The iOS launch event

When the user initiates movement to the background, the event flow in Figure 2-9 happens. To start another app, the user presses the phone's Home button. Again, code you write in the application delegate is called by the OS automatically.

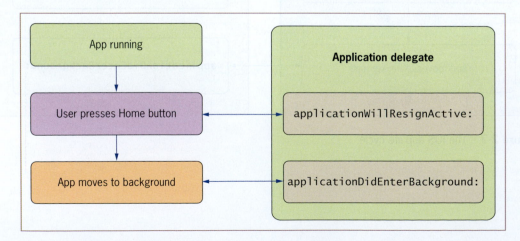

Figure 2-9   User-initiated app movement to the background

If your app is interrupted by a system event (see Figure 2-10), the user must decide whether to ignore it. If the interruption is ignored, the app resumes foreground execution. If not, the app enters the background. In either case, code you provide in the application delegate is called automatically.

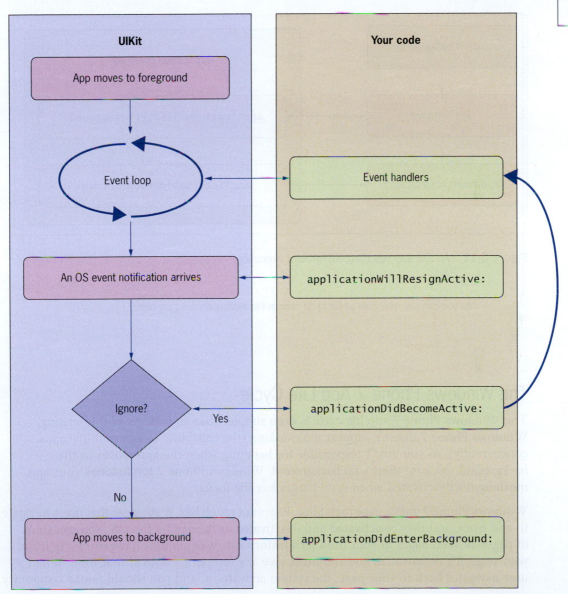

Figure 2-10   OS-initiated app movement to the background

When your app resumes foreground execution, the events in Figure 2-11 are fired. Note that the same events fire in different circumstances. So although there are a number of ways for your app to come to the foreground, the code you write in `applicationDidBecomeActive:` is always called.

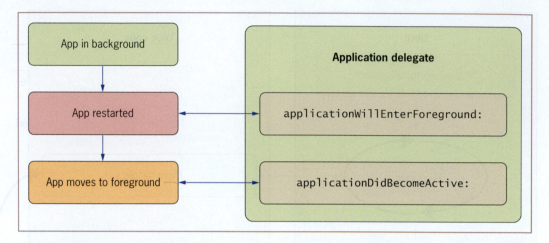

Figure 2-11   An iOS app resuming foreground execution

As you can see, you write all life cycle code in the application delegate object.

The Windows Phone 7 App Life Cycle

The Windows Phone 7 app life cycle is even simpler than in iOS. As of this writing, Windows Phone 7 doesn't support multitasking (the capability to run multiple apps concurrently), so you aren't responsible for handling when the app moves to the background. Because there's no background, Windows Phone 7 **tombstones** your app, meaning it's deactivated when it no longer has the focus.

Windows Phone 7 uses a page metaphor. Pages act much like Web pages that users navigate to and from, and they're activated and deactivated as needed by the OS. You can think of pages as Web pages in your browser's history list. When a user navigates away from your page, it's deactivated, and you must save any temporary data at that time. When a user navigates back to your page, the system activates it, and you should reload temporary data then. As long as the page exists in the list of active pages, it's tombstoned. If a user navigates back past your app's first page, effectively removing it from the active list, the app is closed, and the user must start a new instance. Windows Phone 7 supports the life cycle methods listed in Table 2-5, and Figure 2-12 illustrates the Windows Phone 7 app life cycle.

Table 2-5   Windows Phone 7 life cycle methods

Method	Description
Application_Launching()	Called by the system to start the app. Global variables and other data are initialized in this method.
InitializeComponent()	Called by a Windows page. Resources for the page are initialized in this method.
Application_Deactivated()	Called when the user loads another app and stored data for your app.
NavigatedFrom()	Indicates that the user has moved off the current page to another page in your app or to another app.
Application_Activated()	Called when a user returns to a deactivated (tombstoned) app.
NavigatedTo()	Called when a user navigates to a page in your app.
Application_Closing()	Called when the user navigates back past your app's first page so that data can be saved in this method. If the app is restarted, it's considered a new instance.

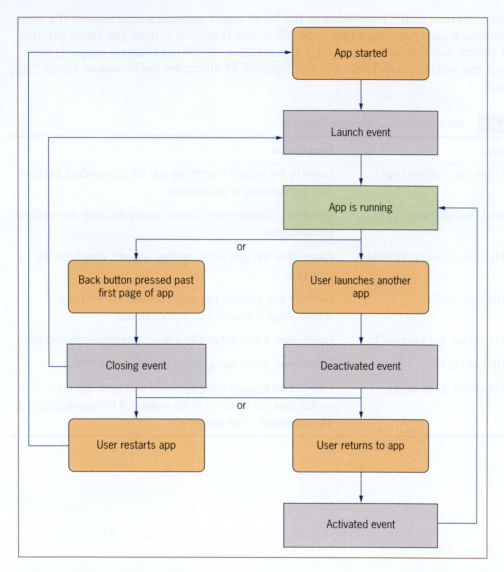

Figure 2-12   The Windows Phone 7 app life cycle

Comparing Life Cycles

From a user's perspective, an app's life cycle is nearly identical in any platform. The user starts an app, interacts with it in some fashion, and then moves on to something else, whether it's another app, an incoming call, or a text message. The user might or might not return to the app.

From a programmer's perspective, the life cycle model doesn't matter, either. The programmer is interested only in entry points to load and save data needed for the app to function. Careful attention to life cycle management leads to faster and better apps and, more important, a better user experience. Table 2-6 summarizes the differences in life cycle events in the three platforms.

Table 2-6   Comparing platform life cycle events

Event	Android	iOS	Windows Phone 7
Start	onCreate()	application: DidFinishLaunchingWithOptions:	Application_Launching(), InitializeComponent()
Running	onStart(), onResume()	applicationDidBecomeActive:	
Deactivated	onStop(), onPause()	applicationWillResignActive:, applicationDidEnterBackground:	Application_Deactivated(), NavigatedFrom()
Activated	onResume()	applicationWillEnterForeground:	Application_Activated(), NavigatedTo()
Closing	onDestroy()	applicationWillTerminate:	Application_Closing()

Chapter Summary

- Each platform architecture consists of an application layer, a core libraries layer, an operating system layer, and a hardware layer.

- Microsoft helps developers create applications for Windows to increase sales of the OS. Apple has duplicated Microsoft's strategy in smartphone apps.

- Android apps are written in Java. Java programs are compiled into bytecode and then run in a virtual machine on the host OS. The Android platform includes the Dalvik virtual machine for running Android apps written in Java. All Android devices use the Linux OS.

- The iOS architecture is simpler than Android and Windows Phone 7 because no specialized virtual machines are necessary. This abstraction isn't necessary because the hardware is the same on all iOS devices.

- The Windows Phone 7 platform is similar to the Android platform, as it has a specialized virtual machine for running apps: the Common Language Runtime (CLR).

- Smartphone apps have a well-defined life cycle, which encompasses the events of being started (being "born"), running ("living"), and being destroyed ("dying"). Each platform has specific code for these events.

- Android apps are built with four types of components that can be started by the OS: Activity, Service, Content Provider, and Broadcast Receiver. There's no main() method to start Android apps.

- iOS apps have a single entry point, the main() function. All life cycle events in an iOS app occur in the application delegate object.

- Both iOS and Android support multitasking. Apps remain in memory even when they're not in the foreground. Windows Phone 7, however, doesn't support multitasking. Apps not in the foreground are tombstoned (deactivated).

- Windows Phone 7 uses a page metaphor that's much like the history list stored in a desktop Web browser.

- All three platforms have events you can use to handle life cycle events in your apps.

Key Terms

Activity—An Android component that represents a single screen with a user interface.

application delegate—In iOS, this object is where you write code to interact with the OS and the user; it's also where life cycle events occur.

application layer—The highest level in a platform architecture; includes third-party apps that interact with core libraries to provide functionality. *See also* core libraries layer.

Broadcast Receiver—An Android component that responds to systemwide broadcasts.

Common Language Runtime (CLR)—The virtual machine used in Windows Phone 7.

Content Provider—An Android component that manages a shared set of application data.

core libraries layer—A platform architecture level that represents functions the platform makes available for apps.

Dalvik virtual machine—A specialized Java virtual machine designed to run on Android.

hardware layer—A platform architecture level that represents physical components, such as memory, the screen, and so forth.

life cycle—The series of events from an app's launch to its destruction.

operating system layer—A platform architecture level that represents the platform's interface between programs and the device's underlying hardware.

Service—An Android component that runs in the background to perform long-running operations.

tombstones—A term used in Windows Phone 7 to describe deactivating an app.

Review Questions

1. Which of the following is true of all Java programs? (Choose all that apply.)
    a. They're compiled into bytecode.   c. They're Windows-only programs.
    b. They run on a virtual machine.   d. They run only in a Web browser.

2. The Dalvik virtual machine is specialized for which platform?

    a. iOS   c. Windows Phone 7

    b. Android   d. None of the above

3. The iOS architecture is simpler than Android and Windows Phone 7 because:

    a. iOS devices offer fewer functions than other devices do.

    b. iOS devices are less complex than other devices.

    c. All iOS devices use the same hardware.

    d. All of the above

4. The Common Language Runtime (CLR) is the virtual machine for which platform?

    a. Windows Phone 7   c. iOS

    b. Android   d. None of the above

5. Which Android component does *not* have a life cycle model?

    a. Activity   c. Content Provider

    b. Service   d. Broadcast Receiver

6. All Android apps contain a `main()` method. True or False?

7. All iOS apps have a single entry point: the `main()` function. True or False?

8. In iOS apps, you write code for life cycle events in which of the following?

    a. `main()` function   c. Application delegate

    b. `UIApplicationMain()` function   d. None of the above

9. Which platform does *not* support multitasking?

    a. Android

    b. iOS

    c. Windows Phone 7

    d. All three platforms support multitasking.

10. "Tombstoning" means a Windows Phone 7 app has been:

    a. Launched   c. Activated

    b. Deactivated   d. Closed

11.   Which platform offers life cycle events for handling state transitions in apps?

a.   Android

b.   iOS

c.   Windows Phone 7

d.   All three platforms offer life cycle events.

 Up for Discussion

1.   Based on what you know about the three platform architectures discussed in this chapter, which one would you choose to develop apps? Explain your answer.

2.   Discuss the pros and cons of tombstoning versus multitasking. Why do you think Microsoft chose tombstoning?

Research Projects

1.   Prepare a table comparing the three major platforms in terms of market share, number of devices available, and number of apps available. Make sure to cite your sources.

2.   Describe the similarities and differences of the Dalvik virtual machine and the .NET CLR in more detail. Which one is better? Explain your answer.

3.   Choose a platform and prepare a sales pitch directed at a fictitious company looking to standardize on a platform for its employees. Your pitch should include some visual aids as well as documentation comparing the platform you chose with the others. (*Hint*: You might start with the data you gathered in Research Project 1.)

CHAPTER 3

Best Practices for Small Device Programming

In this chapter, you learn to:

◎ Describe best practices for smartphone development

◎ Explain object-oriented programming techniques, including encapsulation, inheritance, and polymorphism

◎ Use design patterns

◎ Optimize your code for smartphones

Best practices are accepted ways of doing things that result in favorable outcomes. It doesn't matter what the context is; usually, there's some accepted standard way to achieve results. Sometimes the practice is formalized. More often, best practices are informal techniques that over time have proved to achieve results. Eating a balanced diet is an example of a formal best practice because it's backed by scientific data. Eating chicken soup when you have a cold is an informal best practice. There's no real data to support it, but it seems to work!

When discussing best practices, software development is no different from any other context. In almost every software development effort, a best practice for achieving your goal exists. In other words, someone has probably come up with an efficient solution for the problem you're facing.

Developing software for small devices is really no different from developing software in general. Other than considering constrained resources, the best practices established for software development generally apply to developing software for smartphones. Specifically, you use object-oriented techniques in certain design patterns to create apps for smartphones.

It's important to keep in mind that best practices for software development are informal. You can choose to use them or not. If you don't use best practices, the software police won't come knocking on your door, asking why you didn't use a particular technique or process. Your results, though, might not be as efficient as they could be had you followed the best practices.

 Best practices aren't just about efficiency. They should be followed to make your code more robust, more scalable, more maintainable, and more secure, among many other possible improvements.

Object-Oriented Programming

Because all the languages discussed in this book are object oriented, it makes sense to introduce the concepts of **object-oriented programming (OOP)**. This discussion is by no means extensive. Entire books can be (and have been) written on the topic of OOP. Instead, this chapter covers the basics so that you can use the best practices inherent in OOP to build apps.

Java, Objective-C, and C# are derivatives of the C programming language. C is a **procedural language**, meaning programs run as a series of commands, one after the other. Sometimes code is grouped into functions and subroutines, but for the most part, execution is linear.

In addition, in C programs it's common for all functions and code to have access to the program's data. That is, the data in a C program is global—it can be accessed and modified at any point. That's usually fine for small and even medium-sized programs. In large programs, however, allowing data to be modified from anywhere is dangerous because potential bugs can have wide-ranging effects.

Unlike procedural programs, OOP programs are data centered. You design the objects in your OOP program to hold data and then determine how that data is accessed inside the object. This close control of data access results in fewer bugs and more code reuse.

Object-oriented programs are built by creating objects that interact with each other. They can contain multiple objects of different types, many objects of the same type, or any combination. Each object possesses its own data, and data access for each type of object is the same. You grant access to data by writing special methods stored in the object.

The fundamental construct of OOP is the **class**, which can be thought of as a template for creating objects. Figure 3-1 shows a Unified Modeling Language (UML) diagram for a class used to create `Rectangle` objects.

Rectangle
double length double width
double getArea() double getPerimeter()

Figure 3-1 A UML diagram for a `Rectangle` class

In UML class diagrams, the class name is placed at the top, and sections are created for data members and member methods. Figure 3-1 is used to define the `Rectangle` class and specify that each `Rectangle` object created has the data members `length` and `width`. These data members have been defined as the `double` data type (that is, double-precision numbers, or decimal numbers).

In addition, each `Rectangle` object knows how to calculate its own area and perimeter, using the member methods shown in the UML diagram: `getArea()` and `getPerimeter()`. These methods return values that are also defined as `doubles`.

What's the difference between a method and a function? Structurally, functions, methods, and subroutines are similar, in that they group functionality into blocks of code that can be run with a single call. The difference is that a method is called by an object on its own data. Functions and subroutines are usually supplied with data and work with only that data. Methods can also be supplied with data, but they manipulate an object's internal data, too.

Because Java is the only cross-platform language discussed in this book, most of the generic examples are written in Java. Java runs on Windows, Mac, and Linux. You don't need a Mac or Windows PC to use Java, as you do with Objective-C for iOS development and C# for Windows Phone 7 development.

A `Rectangle` class written in Java might look something like this:

```
public class Rectangle{
  double length;
  double width;

  public double getArea(){
    return length * width;
  }

  public double getPerimeter(){
    return 2 * (length+width);
  }

}
```

From a coding perspective, a variable's scope can be loosely defined as the block of code in which the variable is declared. In the `Rectangle` class, the member variables, `length` and `width`, have a scope in the entire class, so they can be accessed from anywhere in the class definition. Variables whose scope is the entire class are called **instance variables**. This means each Rectangle object (or instance) has its own length and width values.

Don't confuse instance variables with class, or shared, variables. Class variables are shared among all instances of an object, and the static keyword is usually associated with them. Class variables are outside the scope of this book.

Remember that classes are templates for objects. To make use of the Rectangle class, you need to write a test program that creates Rectangle objects. The process of creating objects from classes is called **instantiation**: You create an instance of the object from the class (the template). You can create as many instances as you want, based on available memory. Each instance is identical in structure but contains its own data. Here's an example of a test program written in Java that creates Rectangle objects:

```java
public class MakeRectangles{
  public static void main(String[] args){

// Create the first Rectangle
    Rectangle rect1 = new Rectangle();

// Set values for data members
    rect1.length = 4.0;
    rect1.width = 2.0;

// Display data onscreen
    System.out.println("Rectangle 1:\nlength: " + rect1.length +↵
"\nwidth: " + rect1.width + "\nArea: " + rect1.getArea() + "\nPerimeter: "↵
+ rect1.getPerimeter());

// Create a second Rectangle object
    Rectangle rect2 = new Rectangle();

// Set values for data members
    rect2.length = 8.0;
    rect2.width = 6.0;

// Display data onscreen
    System.out.println("Rectangle 2:\nlength: " + rect2.length +↵
"\nwidth: " + rect2.width + "\nArea: " + rect2.getArea() + "\nPerimeter: "↵
+ rect2.getPerimeter());
  }
}
```

In Java programming, as in C, the entry point for a program is the main() method. Inside the main() method, two Rectangle objects are instantiated: rect1 and rect2. Instantiation takes place in the lines containing the new operator, as shown in this example:

```java
Rectangle rect1 = new Rectangle();
```

The new operator sets aside enough memory to hold the object's data members. In this case, each Rectangle object holds length and width data members. Note that rect1 and rect2 have different values for length and width, but both are still Rectangle objects. After values for `length` and `width` are set, information on area and perimeter is displayed onscreen, as shown in the following output:

```
Rectangle 1:
length: 4.0
width: 2.0
Area: 8.0
Perimeter: 12.0
Rectangle 2:
length: 8.0
width: 6.0
Area: 48.0
Perimeter: 28.0
```

Each `Rectangle` object works only with its own data. In other words, no matter how many `Rectangle` objects you create, each has its own length and width, and each returns its own area and perimeter.

Encapsulation

Technically speaking, the code in the previous section is object oriented. `Rectangle` objects are defined in a class named `Rectangle`, each `Rectangle` has its own data, and each `Rectangle` returns its own area and perimeter. The test program creates a couple of `Rectangle` objects and displays the data contained in each object.

So what's the problem? There are a few issues with the current `Rectangle` class. The first is that the program can set the data values in any `Rectangle` object directly by manipulating the `length` and `width` instance variables. That doesn't sound like a big deal, but what would happen if, for example, the program asked a user for input? Suppose the user inputs a negative number accidentally? Obviously, rectangles can't have negative values for length or width.

A best-practice solution is for the `Rectangle` class to provide a mechanism for setting instance variables that includes error checking. This mechanism should make instance variables private and supply public methods for accessing and setting data values and for handling any errors. These kinds of methods are called **accessor methods** (or, more commonly, getters and setters). Test programs then use these getters and setters to access the object's data.

Another issue with the current `Rectangle` class is that all `Rectangle` objects are created the same: Setting data for each `Rectangle` object happens one line at a time. Although this process isn't too tedious because there are only two instance variables, for more complex objects, it could be tedious and error prone. In addition, because `Rectangle` objects are defined by `length` and `width` variables, wouldn't it make more sense to create them by supplying these values at creation time? Methods that supply data at creation time and initialize objects are called **constructors**, and they are an important feature in object-oriented programming.

Finally, at least for this brief discussion, the test program is responsible for displaying data onscreen. Wouldn't it be better if each `Rectangle` object knew how to display its own data onscreen? In fact, wouldn't it be best if each `Rectangle` object knew how to do everything a `Rectangle` object should know how to do? That way, each `Rectangle` object can perform all the tasks any `Rectangle` should know how to handle.

The object-oriented concept of encapsulation solves these problems. In object-oriented terms, **encapsulation** is a combination of bundling data and behavior into discrete units and protecting them from outside programs. The discrete unit in Java, Objective-C, and C# is the class. The idea is to design classes so that the data is protected, and programs can make use of the data and behaviors defined in the class. Outside programs shouldn't need to know how, for example, a `Rectangle` object displays its data onscreen. Rather, they should be able to tell each `Rectangle` object to display its own data onscreen. Further, outside programs shouldn't be concerned with how output is produced. In short, each `Rectangle` object should exist inside its own capsule—hence the term "encapsulation."

Following is an example of a reworked `Rectangle` class that makes use of encapsulation:

```java
public class Rectangle{
// Instance variables
  private double length;
  private double width;

// Getters and setters for length and width
  public double getLength(){
    return length;
  }

  public void setLength(double length){
    this.length = checkData(length);
  }

  public double getWidth(){
    return width;
  }

  public void setWidth(double width){
    this.width = checkData(width);
  }

// Constructor
  public Rectangle(double length, double width){
    this.length = checkData(length);
    this.width = checkData(width);
  }

// Error-checking method
public double checkData(double val){
// If value is negative, make it positive
    if(val < 0)
      val = val * -1;
    return val;
  }
  public double getArea(){
    return length * width;
  }
  public double getPerimeter(){
    return 2 * (length + width);
```

```
    }
    public String getData(){
        return "Length: " + this.length + "\nWidth: " + this.width +
    "\nArea: " + this.getArea() + "\nPerimeter: " + this.getPerimeter();
    }
}
```

Encapsulation means putting everything an object needs to know about itself into the class definition. Notice that the instance variables are now declared as private, which protects them from being accessed directly by outside programs. Outside programs are forced to use the public accessor methods, which make sure valid data is entered. Also, note that the constructor now takes two arguments: a length and a width. This makes more sense than the previous code, as you wouldn't try to create a rectangle without a length and a width.

Don't confuse the `checkData()` method used in the preceding example with true exception handling. This method was used to keep the code as clean as possible while illustrating encapsulation. A true validation routine throws an error when it gets negative input. Instead, use a true exception-handling routine. The `checkData()` method assumes that a negative value is entered by accident, but this isn't a safe assumption. Exception handling is, for the most part, outside the scope of this book.

Finally, take note of the `this` keyword. In Java, you use `this` to point to the current instance of an object. So when a `Rectangle` object is instantiated, adding `this` means the data for this particular `Rectangle` is being manipulated. Other `Rectangle` objects aren't affected.

All object-oriented languages use a metaphor to refer to the current object. Java and C# use the `this` keyword, and Objective-C uses `self`.

Now that the `Rectangle` class is encapsulated, take a look at a test program that makes use of the new `Rectangle` class:

```
public class MakeRectangles{
    public static void main(String[] args){
// TO DO: code application logic here
        Rectangle rect1 = new Rectangle(-4.0, 2.0);
        Rectangle rect2 = new Rectangle(8.0, 6.0);
        System.out.println("Rectangle 1:\n" + rect1.getData());
        System.out.println("Rectangle 2:\n" + rect2.getData());
    }
}
```

This code is much simpler. Because the `Rectangle` class is now handling its own data and behavior, the program just needs to create `Rectangle` objects and let them do all the work. Most object-oriented programs work this way. Typically, the main program creates the objects needed for the program to work. The objects then interact to perform tasks.

The new `Rectangle` class hides its data and makes an **application programming interface (API)** public. An API is simply public data and behaviors made available to outside programs. Now that the new `Rectangle` class is encapsulated, it can be reused in any situation where a

Rectangle is called for. Through encapsulation, any program using a Rectangle object needn't worry about how the API is implemented. Instead, it can make use of the API. After the Rectangle class has been coded, creating it again each time it's used isn't necessary. Code reuse is one of the major benefits of object-oriented programming.

Note that a negative length value (parameter) is included for the first Rectangle, which allows testing the error-checking method by examining the program's output:

```
Rectangle 1:
Length: 4.0
Width: 2.0
Area: 8.0
Perimeter: 12.0
Rectangle 2:
Length: 8.0
Width: 6.0
Area: 48.0
Perimeter: 28.0
```

The sign of the first length value changes to positive, so the area and perimeter information still makes sense.

Inheritance

Inheritance, specifically class inheritance, is usually considered a prerequisite for any OOP language. It gives a class you're writing automatic access to information in other classes above it in a hierarchy. In object-oriented languages, all classes are part of a strict hierarchy that's defined by referring to a particular class's position in the inheritance tree. So when you write a class, you have to define only how your class differs from another class.

In a class inheritance tree, each class has a **superclass** (the class above it in the hierarchy) and can have one or more **subclasses** (classes below it in the hierarchy). Subclasses inherit behavior from superclasses above them in the hierarchy. Therefore, the farther up the hierarchy a class is, the more abstract it is, and the farther down the hierarchy a class is, the more concrete it is. In short, classes farther down the hierarchy generally gain information that distinguishes them from the superclass.

For example, Figure 3-2 shows an inheritance tree for the Vehicle class. The top level, Vehicle, is the most abstract and contains information common to all vehicles. It's the superclass to the UnpoweredVehicle and PoweredVehicle classes, which distinguish whether a certain vehicle is motorized. They're subclasses of Vehicle and superclasses of the third level, which contains the most concrete or specific objects. These objects have inherited all the information above them in the tree.

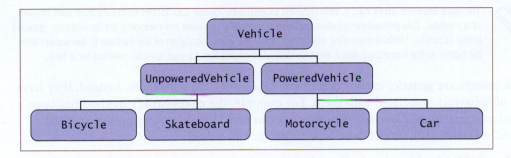

Figure 3-2 An inheritance tree for the `Vehicle` class

C#, Java, and Objective-C use a **single inheritance model**, meaning a class can have only one parent class (superclass). This model helps prevent some problems seen in multiple inheritance languages, such as method name clashing in C++. When an object inherits from multiple superclasses, these superclasses can contain methods with the same name. This can cause problems in the subclass as to which method should be called.

Figure 3-3 shows a UML diagram for a class representing `Circle` objects. As you can see, `Circle`s have much in common with `Rectangle`s, especially when you look at the methods, because both circles and rectangles are geometric shapes.

Circle
double radius
double getArea() double getPerimeter() String getData() double checkData()

Figure 3-3 A `Circle` class

However, instead of jumping into creating a `Circle` class by copying code from the `Rectangle` class, it makes more sense to create a superclass named `Shape` and factor out the behavior common to all geometric shapes. Then both `Rectangle` and `Circle` can inherit from `Shape`.

When defining a `Shape` class, ask yourself what a shape is and what each shape should know how to do. Mathematically speaking, a geometric shape is a two-dimensional entity. Every geometric shape has an area and a perimeter, and both are positive numbers. In a program, each geometric shape should know how to calculate its own area and perimeter, ensure that its data is valid, and be able to display its own data. Following is a class that defines `Shape` objects:

```
public abstract class Shape{
  public abstract double getArea();
  public abstract double getPerimeter();
  public abstract String getData();
  public double checkData(double val){
// If value is negative, make it positive
    if(val < 0)
      val = val * -1;
    return val;
  }
}
```

The Java keyword `abstract`, when applied to methods, forces subclasses to create their own version of a method. This procedure is called **method overriding** because the method's implementation appears in the subclass. Method overriding effectively hides any implementation of the method in the superclass (or higher in the hierarchy), which ensures that each object has its own specific method for a task.

Shape objects are generic, so they don't have data associated with them. Instead, they have a set of behaviors associated with them. For example, the `checkData()` method has been moved into the `Shape` class, so every subclass can check its data by using this method. A `Circle` class that inherits from `Shape` might look like this:

```java
public class Circle extends Shape{
  private double radius;
  public double getRadius(){
    return radius;
  }
  public void setRadius(double radius){
    this.radius = checkData(radius);
  }
  public Circle(double radius){
    super();
    setRadius(radius);
  }
  public double getArea(){
    return Math.PI * radius * radius;
  }
  public double getPerimeter(){
    return 2 * Math.PI * radius;
  }
  public String getData(){
    return "Radius: " + radius + "\nArea: " + getArea() + "\nPerimeter:
" + getPerimeter();
  }
}
```

Java uses the `extends` keyword to indicate inheritance. C# and Objective-C use the colon character (`:`).

The `checkData()` method is used in the `setRadius()` method, but it isn't defined in the `Circle` class. Because `Circle` inherits from `Shape`, it inherits all the behaviors defined in `Shape`. Java, C#, and Objective-C use **dynamic method invocation** to call methods, which means a program looks in the current class first for a method. If it doesn't find the method, it looks in the superclass. If it doesn't find it in the superclass, it looks in the superclass's superclass, and so on up the hierarchy. If the method isn't found, an exception is thrown. In this case, a program looks in the `Circle` class first for the `checkData()` method. It isn't there, so the program looks in the `Shape` class next, finds the method, and runs the code there.

Also, notice that the constructor first makes what looks like a method call that isn't defined anywhere, not even in `Shape`. Java, C#, and Objective-C include the keyword `super`, which refs to the superclass. In Java and C#, you use the `super()` method to do any initialization defined in the superclass. In Objective-C, you accomplish the same thing by sending the `init` message to the `super` object. The concept is the same: You call the superclass constructor so that any inherited data members are initialized.

Following is a `Rectangle` class that inherits from `Shape`. It follows the same format as the `Circle` class:

```
public class Rectangle extends Shape{
  private double length;
  private double width;
  public double getLength(){
    return length;
  }
  public void setLength(double length){
    this.length = checkData(length);
  }
  public double getWidth(){
    return width;
  }
  public void setWidth(double width){
    this.width = checkData(width);
  }
  public Rectangle(double length, double width){
    super();
    setLength(length);
    setWidth(width);
  }
  public double getArea(){
    return length * width;
  }
  public double getPerimeter(){
    return 2 * (length + width);
  }
  public String getData(){
    return "Length: " + this.length + "\nWidth: " + this.width +
  "\nArea: " + this.getArea() + "\nPerimeter: " + this.getPerimeter();
  }
}
```

The following program, `MakeShapes.java`, instantiates a `Rectangle` and a `Circle` and displays their data:

```
public class MakeShapes{
  public static void main(String[] args){
    Rectangle rect = new Rectangle(6.0, 8.0);
    Circle circle = new Circle(2.0);
    System.out.println("Rectangle:\n" + rect.getData());
    System.out.println("Circle:\n" + circle.getData());
  }
}
```

As you can see in the following program output, all is still well:

```
Rectangle:
Length: 6.0
Width: 8.0
Area: 48.0
Perimeter: 28.0
Circle:
Radius: 2.0
Area: 12.566370614359172
Perimeter: 12.566370614359172
```

Polymorphism

Polymorphism literally means "many shapes." In object-oriented languages, it describes an object's capability to be treated as more than one type. For example, you can create methods that act on Shape objects and substitute Circles or Rectangles because they're subclasses of Shape. Being able to use a subclass when a superclass is called for is called **polymorphism**. C#, Java, and Objective-C support this feature.

The MakeShapes.java program from the preceding section has been rewritten to use polymorphism:

```java
public class MakeShapes{
  public static void main(String[] args){
    Rectangle rect = new Rectangle(6.0, 8.0);
    Circle circle = new Circle(2.0);
// Pass the Circle and Rectangle objects to getData()
    System.out.println("Rectangle:\n" + getData(rect));
    System.out.println("Circle:\n" + getData(circle));
  }
// This method expects a Shape object
// You can pass rectangles and circles because they
//    inherit from the Shape class and are shapes
  public static String getData(Shape s){
    return s.getData();
  }
}
```

The interesting part is the getData() method, which takes a Shape as an argument. This method doesn't do much except tell the Shape object to call its own getData() method and return the value. The main() method creates a Rectangle and a Circle object. It then displays each object's data onscreen by passing it to the getData() method. This process works because each object is a Shape as well as a Rectangle or a Circle. The method is polymorphic because Rectangle and Circle objects are treated as instances of the Shape class instead of instances of the Rectangle or Circle class.

The dynamic method invocation model works here, too, but in reverse. Each Shape is guaranteed to have a getData() method, but the program first looks in the current object for the method. In each case, the method is found and executed.

Polymorphism isn't limited to the inheritance tree. Both C# and Java support another type of polymorphism by using interfaces. Interfaces are declared in class files and contain collections of methods. In fact, when programmers say "class," they really mean "class or interface." Classes are said to implement interfaces, and in C# and Java, implementing an interface means all methods declared in the interface exist in the class implementing the interface. There's no limit on the number of interfaces a class can implement.

Although Objective-C uses protocols rather than interfaces, Objective-C protocols were the model for Java interfaces (which were the model for C# interfaces). Objective-C classes are said to "conform to a protocol" instead of implementing an interface, but the term means the same thing: All methods in the protocol exist in the class conforming to the protocol. For this discussion, implementing an interface is equivalent to conforming to a protocol.

 Objective-C actually contains two types of protocols: formal and informal. Conforming to a formal protocol means implementing all methods defined in the protocol and is the same as implementing an interface in C# and Java. Informal protocols aren't bound by this requirement.

Interfaces provide templates of behavior that classes are expected to provide. They represent what an object of a particular type can do and pass methods to be implemented, not instance variables. They form their own hierarchy separate from the class hierarchy and are said to provide multiple inheritance.

The single inheritance model of C#, Java, and Objective-C can be too restrictive. Suppose you have a good implementation of the `Jewelry` class and an interface, `JewelLike`, that represents what `Jewelry` objects are expected to be able to do. You'd like to create a class for `Necklace` to be a `Jewelry` object, but you'd also like it to be a `PreciousMetal` object that can be melted down, and so on.

A possible solution is for `Necklace` to extend `Jewelry` and implement the `JewelLike` and `PreciousMetal` interfaces. This solution would ensure that `Necklaces` can behave like a `Jewelry` as well as a `PreciousMetal` object. The code might look something like this:

```
public interface JewelLike{
  void shine();
  void wear();
  // Other methods
}
public class Jewelry implements JewelLike{
  private double value;
  private int carats;
  public void shine(){
    // required for JewelLike interface
  }
  public void wear(){
    // required for JewelLike interface
  }
  // more data and methods specific to Jewelry
}
public interface PreciousMetal{
  void melt();
```

```
    // other methods unique to PreciousMetal objects
}
public class Necklace extends Jewelry implements PreciousMetal{
    public void melt(){
        // melt method required for PreciousMetal interface
    }
    // other PreciousMetal methods as defined in interface
    // shine() and wear() defined in superclass
    // override shine() and wear() methods as needed
    // other members unique to Necklace
}
```

Necklace objects can now be passed to any method that requires these types of objects:
Necklace, Jewelry, JewelLike, and PreciousMetal. The multiple inheritance interface
structure enables classes scattered throughout a hierarchy to use the same set of methods.
Although these classes share a common superclass somewhere, it's unlikely that *all* the
classes below this common superclass need to use a certain group of methods. So putting all
the methods a subset of classes might need in a single location (presumably a class at or near
the top of the hierarchy) isn't an ideal solution. Instead, create as many interfaces as you like
and use them where needed.

Design Patterns

Design patterns are best practices for structuring an application, not for writing the
application's code. Two design patterns are widely used when writing smartphone apps:
Model-View-Controller and Delegate.

Model-View-Controller

The **Model-View-Controller (MVC)** design pattern represents a structure in which each
program task is in a different tier, as shown in Figure 3-4. The Model tier manages the
application's data. The View tier renders the model into a usable form, usually as a user
interface. The Controller tier mediates requests between the Model and View tiers and
provides the application's logic. The MVC design pattern allows a loose coupling between an
application's data and how the data is viewed.

Figure 3-4   The Model-View-Controller model

Loose coupling is itself a design pattern, with an emphasis on reducing (loosening) dependencies between program tiers. It promotes designing the logic tier independently of the data and how it's viewed. See *www.soaprinciples.com/service_loose_coupling.php* for more information.

The MVC design pattern is prevalent in two familiar places. The first is graphical user interface (GUI) event-driven programs. In these programs, a user might initiate an action by, for example, clicking a button. The button exists in the View tier. When it's clicked, an event handler is triggered to perform an action (usually manipulating data). The action, event handler, and access to data reside in the Controller tier. The Model tier might be a data store, a database, an XML file, and so forth.

The second familiar example is Web applications, specifically e-commerce apps. When you browse through an online catalog, for instance, you make a request to a controller to display items stored in the model. You might be shopping from your desktop or your smartphone, and each shows different views of the data. The controller is responsible for servicing the request for data and returning the data to the correct view. How the data is viewed is irrelevant to both the model and controller.

The following short example of the MVC design pattern is a small GUI application written in JavaScript and HTML to run in a Web browser; it uses circles as the data in the model. (To keep this example simple, Java isn't used. Java GUI programming can get complex quickly.) The view is the HTML file, which asks the user to input the radius for a circle. The controller, written in JavaScript, gets the radius, checks its validity, instantiates a `Circle` object, and displays its data in the view. The controller must know details of the view and model, but the model and view have no knowledge of each other. Here's the JavaScript code for the model:

```
function Circle(r){
  this.radius = r;
  this.getArea = getA;
  this.getPerimeter = getP;
  this.getData = getD;
}
function getA(){
  return this.radius * this.radius * Math.PI;
}
function getP(){
  return 2 * this.radius * Math.PI;
}
function getD(){
  return 'Area: ' + this.getArea() + '<br />Perimeter: ' +↵
 this.getPerimeter();
}
```

The `Circle()` function, which is the constructor, expects a value to be assigned to a radius. It then creates function pointers for `getArea()`, `getPerimeter()`, and `getData()`. So, for example, each time a `Circle` object calls its `getArea()` method, the code in `getA()` is called. The same is true for `getPerimeter()` and `getData()`.

The controller is also a JavaScript file that gets the radius data from the view and performs the calculations. Here's the code for the controller:

```
function calculate(){
  var r = parseFloat(document.getElementById('radius').value);
// Check for nonnumeric data
  if(isNaN(r)){
    document.getElementById('data').innerHTML = "Please enter↵
 numbers only";
    return;
  }
// Check for negative data
  if(r<=0){
    document.getElementById('data').innerHTML = "Negative numbers↵
 don't make sense";
    return;
  }
// Data is good
  var myCircle = new Circle(r);
  document.getElementById('data').innerHTML = myCircle.getData();
}
```

The entire controller is stored in a single function called `calculate()`. Users click the Calculate button in the view, which calls the `calculate()` function to get the radius and convert it to a number. Next, the data is validated. If nonnumeric or negative data is entered, an error message is displayed and the function returns. If the data is valid, a `Circle` object is created and its data is displayed.

The view is a simple HTML page that displays instructions, a text field where the user can type the radius, and a button to trigger the calculation. The results of calculations are displayed under the text field and button. The HTML file contains the following code:

```
<html>
  <head>
    <title>Circles</title>
    <script src="circle.js"></script>
    <script src="controller.js"></script>
  </head>
  <body>
    <h3>Program Calculates Area and Perimeter of Circles</h3>
    <p>Enter the radius: <input type="text" id="radius" value="" />
    <input type="button" value="Calculate" onClick="calculate()" /></p>
    <p id="data"></p>
  </body>
</html>
```

Figure 3-5 shows what the application looks like when it loads.

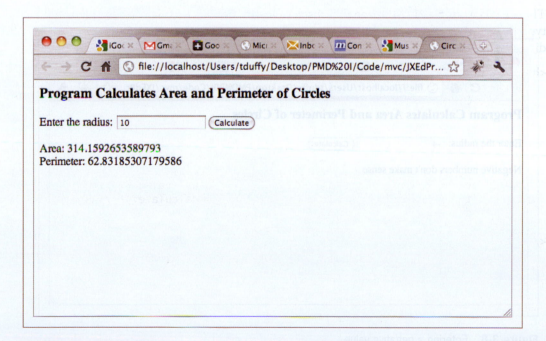

Figure 3-5   The Circle GUI when it loads

Figure 3-6 shows what happens when the user enters data and clicks the Calculate button.

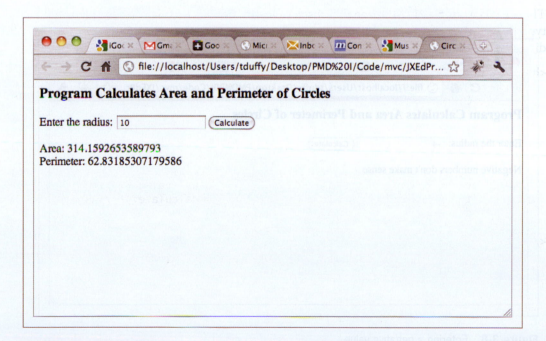

Figure 3-6   Valid input

Figure 3-7 shows what happens when the user enters nonnumeric data, and Figure 3-8 shows what happens if the user enters a negative value.

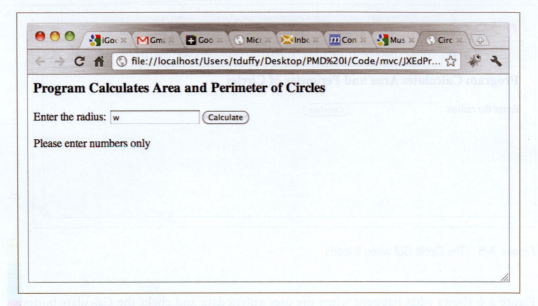

Figure 3-7   Entering nonnumeric data

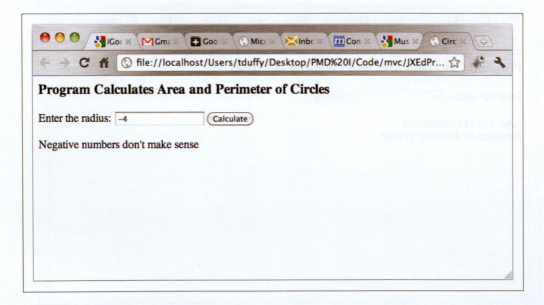

Figure 3-8   Entering a negative value

Delegates

The **Delegate design pattern** is a mechanism whereby an object hands off some of its work to another object, called a delegate. The delegate works on behalf of the other, presumably more complex, object. Delegates typically hold a reference to the more complex object so that they can send information back to it, and the complex object can act on the information.

In many situations, the Delegate design pattern enables you to avoid the shortcomings of subclassing. Instead of adding behavior to a subclass and forcing the subclass to assume its position in the inheritance hierarchy, a delegate can be written that performs the work and adds its own behavior. The delegate isn't required to reside in the hierarchy beneath a more complex object.

For example, say you have a `Cylinder` class. You can think of a cylinder as a circle with a height. In this case, a cylinder is a circle and, therefore, should be a subclass of `Circle`. Another way to think of a cylinder is as a three-dimensional object with a circle as its base. In this case, it uses a `Circle` object as a delegate to perform parts of the calculations that make sense for a cylinder. A UML diagram for this class might look something like Figure 3-9.

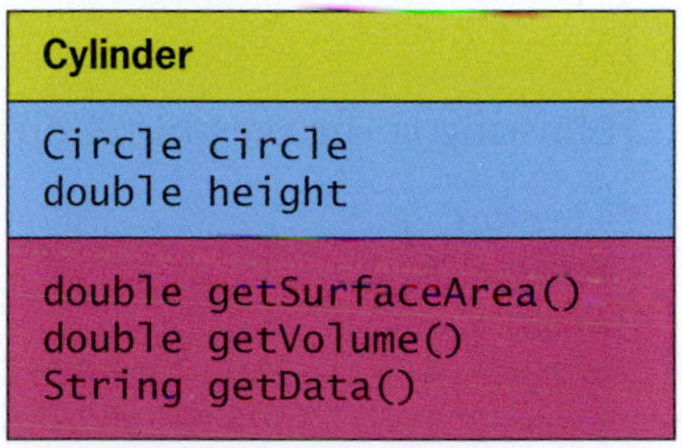

In the following example, the `Cylinder` class, written in Java, uses a `Circle` object as a delegate:

Figure 3-9 A `Cylinder` class

```java
public class Cylinder{
  private Circle circle;
  private double height;

  public Circle getCircle(){
      return circle;
  }
  public void setCircle(Circle circle){
      this.circle = circle;
  }
  public double getHeight(){
      return height;
  }
  public void setHeight(double height){
      this.height = circle.checkData(height);
  }
  public Cylinder(double radius, double height){
      circle = new Circle(radius);
      setHeight(height);
  }
  public double getSurfaceArea(){
    return (2*circle.getArea()) + (circle.getPerimeter() * height);
  }
  public double getVolume(){
    return circle.getArea() * height;
```

```
  }
  public String getData(){
    return "Radius: " + circle.getRadius() + "\nHeight: " + getHeight()
 + "\nSurface Area: " + getSurfaceArea() + "\nVolume: " + getVolume();
  }
}
```

The Cylinder class uses the Circle instance variable to check that only positive values are entered and to calculate the perimeter and area of the cylinder's base. The surface area is calculated by adding twice the base's area and the lateral area—or the base's perimeter multiplied by the height. The volume is calculated by multiplying the base's area by the cylinder's height. Here's a program for testing Cylinder objects:

```
public class MakeCylinders{
  public static void main(String[] args){
    Cylinder cyl1 = new Cylinder(4.0, 2.0);
// Check negative data handler
    Cylinder cyl2 = new Cylinder(-4.0, -2.0);
    System.out.println("Cylinder 1:\n" + cyl1.getData());
    System.out.println("Cylinder 2:\n" + cyl2.getData());
  }
}
```

Following is the program's output:

```
Cylinder 1:
Radius: 4.0
Height: 2.0
Surface Area: 150.79644737231007
Volume: 100.53096491487338
Cylinder 2:
Radius: 4.0
Height: 2.0
Surface Area: 150.79644737231007
Volume: 100.53096491487338
```

Using the Delegate design pattern in this fashion is often called **object composition**, which represents a "has a" relationship instead of the "is a" relationship in inheritance. The Cylinder class in the preceding example has a Circle as its base and delegates some calculations in the class to the Circle, so the Circle works on behalf of the Cylinder.

Optimization

In programming, **optimization** is the process of making programs run faster or on less memory. Recent exponential growth in desktop processor speeds and decreasing costs for physical memory have resulted in somewhat lazy practices by many developers. The truth is that most desktop programs are fast enough on today's processors. In addition, most desktop computers now have enough physical memory that programs will never run out of space. So although optimization isn't strictly necessary for desktop applications, learning optimization techniques and when to use them is certainly beneficial, regardless of the application type.

Smartphones, however, represent a step back to when memory was expensive, so how code made use of memory mattered. This section describes some techniques for optimizing code to make it run faster on less memory. Most of these techniques apply to any application, not just to smartphone apps.

 The optimizations discussed in this section are suggestions for improving program performance. Keep in mind that some introduce complexity into your code, so decide whether using these optimizations improves performance enough to warrant the added complexity.

Strings, Buffers, and Operations

In C#, Java, and Objective-C, String objects are immutable, meaning that after strings are created, they can't be changed. Take a look at the following Java code:

```
String aString = "this is a string";
aString = aString + " too";
```

The preceding code is fine from the compiler's perspective, so it will compile and run without error. However, the line specifying that the variable aString contains "this is a string too" is inefficient. Because strings are immutable, changing a String object's contents results in creating a new, temporary String object to hold the new value, destroying the first object, and re-creating the object with the value stored in the temporary object. The temporary object is also destroyed.

When you know your program will work with strings of values that change, you should use string buffers instead of String objects. **String buffers** are objects that hold character data but are mutable, meaning their content can change. Table 3-1 describes the mutable string buffers built into C#, Java, and Objective-C.

Table 3-1 Strings and mutable String objects

Language	String object	String buffer
C#	String	StringBuilder
Java	String	StringBuffer, StringBuilder
Objective-C	NSString	NSMutableString

The mutable string buffers in all the programming languages covered in this book come with built-in methods for tasks such as appending, inserting, removing, and replacing character data. In addition, each string buffer can make its string data available, so they're just as convenient as String objects. NSMutableString in Objective-C is actually a subclass of NSString, so it can be used wherever an NSString is called for.

The following is a better way to write the preceding code:

```
StringBuffer buffer = new StringBuffer("this is a string");
buffer.append(" too");
String aString = buffer.toString();
```

Each mutable string buffer has a capacity associated with it that expands to contain new data as needed. Making an educated guess about the buffer's maximum size and initializing the buffer to this size at creation time can increase optimization of the program further. If you know you need to hold the contents of a 20 MB text file, for example, initializing a 20 MB buffer is far more efficient than letting the program expand the buffer incrementally.

In general, buffers double in size when their capacity is exceeded. The default size of the Java StringBuffer and C# StringBuilder objects is 16 characters. When this size is exceeded, the buffer's contents are copied to a buffer of 32 characters, and the original buffer is discarded. When the buffer's size exceeds 32 characters, the contents are copied into a 64-character buffer. This process repeats until the capacity is no longer exceeded. The default size of an Objective-C NSMutableString object depends on how it's initialized: with the contents of a String object or a designated capacity.

Initializing the buffer to its maximum size can optimize the previous code further. Note that the buffer's initial capacity is 16. When you initialize a StringBuffer object with a String, the buffer's capacity is the same size as the string. The string supplied in the following code happens to have 16 characters. When the call to append() is made, the buffer exceeds its capacity, and its content is copied into a 32-character buffer. To minimize the extra object creation, the following code is a better solution:

```
StringBuffer buffer = new StringBuffer(20);
buffer.append("this is a string");
buffer.append(" too");
String aString = buffer.toString();
```

The lesson is that if your program works with many strings whose value changes, a more efficient solution is using mutable string buffers.

Loops and Conditional Statements

There are tried-and-true optimization techniques for loops and conditional statements that apply to any programming situation, including smartphone apps. Loops slow programs down, especially when they're designed inefficiently. It's a simple math equation: Executing inefficient algorithms repeatedly results in exponential inefficiency. You must take care to design loops to be as efficient as possible.

The first optimization technique involves loop selection. C#, Java, and Objective-C have three types of loops: for, while, and do. Selecting the right loop for your algorithm is important. In general, you should use a for loop when you know how many times the loop should iterate.

The `while` and `do` loops are similar, except for placement of the termination rule—the statement that determines whether the loop should end. Both are used when you aren't sure how many times the loop will execute. The difference is that the `while` loop places the termination rule at the beginning of the loop and evaluates it before the first iteration, and the `do` loop places the termination rule at the end of the loop and evaluates it after the first iteration. So use the `do` loop when you want to guarantee that the code in the loop executes at least once; otherwise, use the `while` loop.

The `do` loop evaluates the condition one time less than the `while` loop does, which could make a huge difference in efficiency if the loop is accessed millions of times.

The second optimization technique involves making the loop condition as efficient as possible. To do this, avoid having any calculations take place in the loop because they must be performed during each iteration through the loop. The same advice applies to method calls. Placing method calls in a conditional statement means the call stack for the method must be built up and then torn down for each iteration. Suppose you're populating a collection of data by using a `for` loop. You might use the following code:

```
ArrayList a = new ArrayList(5);
  for(int b=0;b<a.size();b++){
    a.add(new Integer(b));
  }
```

The `for` loop calculates the array's size in every repetition of the loop, but the size never changes. A better solution is calculating the array's size ahead of time and using this data in the loop declaration, as shown:

```
ArrayList c = new ArrayList(5);
  int cLen = c.size();
  for(int d=0;d<cLen;d++){
    c.add(new Integer(d));
  }
```

Another optimization technique involves moving invariants out of the loop. A **loop invariant** is a quantity that doesn't change inside the loop. For example, say you have an algorithm that performs calculations on two arrays. Typically, you use nested `for` loops (loops inside loops) to iterate through each pair of data entries, as in this example:

```
int[] yAxis = {1,2,3,4,5};
  int[] xAxis = {5,4,3,2,1};
  for(int i=0;i<yAxis.length;i++){
    for(int j=0;j<xAxis.length;j++){
      int k = yAxis[i]*yAxis.length + xAxis[j]*xAxis.length;
      System.out.println(k);
    }
  }
```

An optimized loop structure might look like the following:

```
int yLen = yAxis.length;
int xLen = xAxis.length;
for(int m=0;m<yLen;m++){
  int temp = yAxis[m]*yLen;
  for(int n=0;n<xLen;n++){
    System.out.println(temp + xAxis[n]*xLen);
  }
}
```

Each array's length is precalculated and moved out of the loop declaration. Also, the calculation involving the y values is moved out of the inner loop because it's invariant for the inner loop; its value changes in the outer loop, not the inner loop. Finally, the interim variable that holds the result of the calculation is eliminated. In this example, not much is gained by these optimizations. However, apply these techniques to an image-processing app that must handle millions of pixels, one at a time, and you can see that they would clearly result in performance improvements.

Fortunately, C#, Java, and Objective-C include optimized logical operators: && (and operation) and || (or operation). These operators perform only the calculations needed to continue running the program. Say you write the following code:

```
if(x && y){
// Do something
}
```

The body of the conditional statement takes place only if both x and y evaluate to true. However, if x evaluates to false, y isn't calculated, as the entire condition can't evaluate to true. The same can be said for the or operator:

```
if(x || y){
// Do something
}
```

In this case, the body of the conditional statement takes place if either x or y evaluates to true. If x evaluates to true, there's no need to calculate y, so it's ignored.

The only real optimization you can make in conditions is done by ordering clauses carefully. This reordering varies from program to program, but it can be very productive. Suppose you have an if/else if statement, in which the condition in the top-level if statement rarely evaluates to true, and an else block containing another condition. It's far more likely the else block will be evaluated, so it makes more sense to move it to the primary condition clause. Take a look at the following example:

```
if(rareCondition)
  executeRareBlock();
else if(commonCondition)
  executeCommonBlock();
```

In this example, the `rareCondition` expression is always evaluated. A simple optimization, reversing the conditional expressions, results in more efficient code. In this case, the `rareCondition` isn't usually computed:

```
if(commonCondition)
  executeCommonBlock();
else if(rareCondition)
  executeRareBlock();
```

Memory Management

Memory management is a thorny problem, regardless of the programming language. For the most part, C#, Java, and Objective-C have built-in memory management. Java and C# have built-in memory allocation and automatic garbage collection (cleanup of unused objects). Objective-C 2.0 includes a switch to turn on automatic garbage collection. However, it's not available in iOS, so it's useless for smartphone apps.

All three programming languages use a reference count mechanism as a way to keep track of the objects (and, therefore, the memory) used in an application. Each process that makes use of an object increases the reference count by 1. As the object falls out of scope or is released, the reference count is decreased by 1. When the reference count reaches 0, the object is tagged for garbage collection. In Objective-C, the object is destroyed at a defined time, such as the end of a user-initiated event. In C# and Java, the object is destroyed the next time the garbage collector runs.

A **memory leak** occurs when the program no longer needs an object, but its reference count is greater than 0. In other words, an object exists in a program that can't be accessed by the running code. The object is never destroyed, and the memory it uses isn't recovered. If a lot of these objects are created and never reclaimed, your program's memory use will grow exponentially over time, resulting in slower performance and, at worst, program and system crashes.

Automatic garbage collection is unavailable for iOS apps, so you're responsible for the reference count of every object. There are three rules for memory management in Objective-C:

- If the `new`, `alloc`, or `copy` methods are used to create an object, its reference count is 1. You're responsible for sending a release message to an object when you have finished using it.

- If another mechanism is used to get a reference to an object, assume it has a reference count of 1 and has been auto-released. If you know the object will be used for an extended period, retain it and eventually release it yourself.

- If you retain an object, you must eventually release it.

At some point, automatic garbage collection might become available in iOS. Until then, here are some optimization tips you can use regardless of the programming language:

- Create objects only when needed. Unnecessary object creation is the most common mistake made by programmers new to OOP.

- Create the fewest number of objects possible. Limiting the number of objects can improve memory management substantially.

- Close everything you open, including files, streams, and connections.

- Be careful with collections of objects. Pointers to members of a collection increase the reference count for the entire collection.

- Restrict the scope of objects when possible. The smaller the scope, the more likely the reference count will eventually reach 0.

Chapter Summary

- Best practices are accepted ways of doing things that result in favorable outcomes. Best practices established for software development generally apply to software development for smartphones, too.

- Programs written in procedural languages run as a series of commands, one after the other.

- Object-oriented programs are data centered. You design objects in an OOP program to hold data and then determine how that data is accessed inside the object.

- The fundamental construct of object-oriented programming is the class. Classes can be thought of as the templates for creating objects.

- Variables whose scope is the entire class are called instance variables. The process of creating objects from classes is called instantiation.

- A method is a block of code called by an object on its own data.

- Accessor methods or, more commonly, getters and setters, get and set private data. Methods that supply data at creation time and initialize objects are called constructors.

- Encapsulation bundles data and behavior into discrete units and protects them from outside programs.

- All object-oriented languages use a metaphor to refer to the current object. Java and C# use the `this` keyword. Objective-C uses `self`.

- An application programming interface (API) is simply a collection of the public data and behaviors made available to outside programs.

- Inheritance gives a class you're writing automatic access to information in other classes above it in a hierarchy. In object-oriented languages, all classes are part of a strict hierarchy that's defined by referring to a particular class's position in the inheritance tree. When you write a class, you have to define only how your class differs from another class.

- A superclass sits above a class in a class hierarchy, and a subclass sits below a class in a class hierarchy. Generally, class hierarchies are more abstract at the top and more concrete at the bottom.

- C#, Java, and Objective-C use a single inheritance model.

- Method overriding means a method's implementation appears in the subclass.

- Java, C#, and Objective-C use dynamic method invocation to call methods; in this process, the OS looks locally first for code to run, and then looks up the class hierarchy if code isn't found.

- Polymorphism is an object's capability to be treated as more than one type. The capability to substitute subclasses when a superclass is called for is a clear benefit of polymorphism.

- Design patterns are best practices for structuring an application.

- The Model-View-Controller (MVC) design pattern represents a structure in which each program task exists in a different tier or bundle. The Model tier manages an application's data; the View tier renders the model into a usable form, usually as a user interface; and the Controller tier mediates requests between the Model and View tiers and provides the application's logic.

- The Delegate design pattern is a mechanism whereby an object hands off some of its work to another object, called a delegate.

- Object composition is the process of building objects with other objects. It represents a "has a" relationship rather than the "is a" relationship denoted by inheritance.

- Optimization is the process of making programs run faster or on less memory.

- In C#, Java, and Objective-C, `String` objects are immutable, meaning they can't be changed, and string buffers are objects that hold character data but are mutable. Making an educated guess about a buffer's maximum size and initializing the buffer to this size when it's created are more efficient than letting the system increase the buffer size as needed.

- C#, Java, and Objective-C include three types of loops: `for`, `while`, and `do`.

- A loop invariant is a quantity that doesn't change inside the loop. Move loop invariants outside loops to increase speed.

- C#, Java, and Objective-C include optimized logical operators, which ensure that only necessary calculations take place.

- Garbage collection is the OS process for removing objects from memory that are no longer used.

- C#, Java, and Objective-C use a reference count mechanism to determine whether objects should go through garbage collection. A memory leak occurs when the program no longer needs an object, but its reference count is greater than 0.

65

Key Terms

accessor methods—Methods for making instance variables private and providing mechanisms for accessing and setting data values and handling errors; often called "getters" and "setters."

application programming interface (API)—A collection of public data and behaviors made available to outside programs.

best practices—Accepted ways of doing things that result in favorable outcomes.

class—A template for creating objects; classes are the fundamental constructs of object-oriented programming. *See also* object-oriented programming (OOP).

constructors—Methods that supply data at creation time and initialize objects.

Delegate design pattern—A mechanism whereby an object hands off some of its work to another object, called a delegate. *See also* design patterns.

design patterns—Best practices for structuring an application.

dynamic method invocation—The process by which the system first looks locally for code to execute then looks up the class hierarchy if code is not found.

encapsulation—The process of bundling data and behavior into discrete units and protecting them from outside programs.

inheritance—A prerequisite for any OOP language that makes it possible for classes lower down a hierarchy to have automatic access to classes higher up the hierarchy.

instance variables—Data members whose scope is the entire class.

instantiation—The process of creating objects from classes.

loop invariant—A quantity that doesn't change inside a loop.

memory leak—When an object exists in a program that can't be accessed by the running code, a memory leak occurs when the program no longer needs an object but its reference count is greater than 0. Memory leaks result in slower programs and possibly system crashes.

method overriding—A programming technique used to make a method's implementation appear in the subclass.

Model-View-Controller (MVC)—A design pattern that represents a structure in which each program task is in a different tier. *See also* design patterns.

object composition—An aspect of the Delegate design pattern that represents a "has a" relationship rather than the "is a" relationship denoted by inheritance. Objects that make use of object composition contain other objects that perform some task. *See also* Delegate design pattern.

object-oriented programming (OOP)—A programming model in which programs are built by creating objects that interact with each other. Each object possesses its own data, and access to data is granted by writing methods stored in the object.

optimization—Techniques for making programs run faster or on less memory.

polymorphism—An object's capability to be treated as more than one type. It can be achieved through inheritance or the interface/protocol mechanism of C#, Java, and Objective-C.

procedural language—A programming language that executes instructions as a series of commands, one after the other.

single inheritance model—A model in which a class can have only one superclass. C#, Java, and Objective-C use this model.

string buffers—Objects that hold character data but are mutable.

subclass—A class below another class in an inheritance tree. It's defined by adding functionality to an existing superclass. *See also* inheritance.

superclass—A class above another class in an inheritance tree. It contains information common to all subclasses beneath it in the hierarchy. *See also* inheritance.

Review Questions

1. Your program compiles only if you follow best practices. True or False?

2. In procedural programming languages, code runs linearly. True or False?

3. Object-oriented programs follow the loose coupling principle to facilitate accessing data stored in objects. True or False?

4. Which of the following is *not* an object-oriented language?
   a. Java
   b. C
   c. C#
   d. Objective-C

5. Classes can be thought of as templates for which of the following?
   a. Creating objects
   b. Creating variables
   c. Assigning memory locations to variables
   d. Both a and b

6. Data members whose scope is the entire class are called which of the following?
   a. Objects
   b. Functions
   c. Instance variables
   d. None of the above

7. Which of the following is the process of creating an object from a class?

    a. Instantiation
    c. Event handling

    b. Optimization
    d. None of the above

8. Constructor methods do which of the following? (Choose all that apply.)

    a. Make instance variables private
    c. Handle errors

    b. Supply data at creation time
    d. Initialize objects

9. By bundling data and behaviors into discrete units, encapsulation ensures which of the following?

    a. Consistency of objects

    b. Treating objects as different types

    c. Protection from access by outside programs

    d. Inheritance of variables

10. Which of the following statements about superclasses is true? (Choose all that apply.)

    a. They're ignored by subclasses.

    b. They provide methods and data to subclasses.

    c. They're more abstract than subclasses.

    d. They're more concrete than subclasses.

11. Which of the following statements about subclasses is true?

    a. They provide more information than superclasses.

    b. They're more abstract than superclasses.

    c. They're situated above superclasses in a class hierarchy.

    d. They work on behalf of more complex objects.

12. Which of the following programming languages supports multiple inheritance?

    a. C#
    c. Java

    b. C++
    d. Objective-C

13. Polymorphism is:

    a. An optimization technique

    b. An object's capability to be treated as a different type

    c. Bundling data and behavior

    d. Another word for inheritance

14. The Model-View-Controller design pattern is used to do which of the following?

    a. Provide protection from outside programs
    b. Separate application data from its visual representation
    c. Implement a single inheritance model
    d. Use an object on behalf of another object

15. Which of the components in the MVC design pattern must have information about the other two for the pattern to work?

    a. Model   c. Controller
    b. View   d. All of the above

16. Which of the following is a feature of the Delegate design pattern? (Choose all that apply.)

    a. It allows one object to work on behalf of another.
    b. It forces you to write a subclass.
    c. It hides data in a superclass.
    d. It enables you to avoid the shortcomings of subclassing.

17. String buffers are mutable, meaning their content can change. True or False?

18. A loop invariant is:

    a. A calculation inside a loop that changes for each iteration
    b. A calculation inside a loop that doesn't change for each iteration
    c. An object that changes over the course of the loop
    d. None of the above

19. When an object's reference count reaches 0, which of the following happens to the object?

    a. It's tagged for garbage collection.
    b. It's removed from memory immediately.
    c. It's stored in memory permanently.
    d. It might explode and shower you with computer components.

20. Memory optimizations include which of the following techniques? (Choose all that apply.)

    a. Limiting the number of objects created
    b. Restricting the scope of objects
    c. Creating objects only when needed
    d. Adding memory chips to your system

Up for Discussion

1. Discuss the relationship between a class and an object.

2. Do an Internet search for multiple inheritance in programming languages. What are the pros and cons of multiple inheritance? Why do you think the developers of C#, Java, and Objective-C chose a single inheritance model? Explain your answer.

3. How does object-oriented programming promote code reuse?

4. C#, Java, and Objective-C include optimized logical operators. Why is this feature important? If logical operators weren't optimized, how would you structure conditional statements to best optimize them?

5. Both C# and Java have automatic garbage collection, but it's not available in Objective-C when developing iOS apps. The developer is responsible for managing memory. Which model works better? Explain your answer.

Programming Exercises

1. Using the programming language of your choice, create a class for `Triangle` objects. This `Triangle` class should inherit from a `Shape` class and implement its own `getArea()` and `getPerimeter()` methods. Include a constructor that expects three `double` values for a triangle's sides. Create a program to test your `Triangle` class, and include a method that takes a `Shape` object as a parameter. Pass a `Triangle` object to this method to display the data. *Hint*: To find a triangle's area, use the following formula (given three sides):

    ```
    public double getArea(){
    double s = (side1 + side2 + side3)/2;
    return Math.sqrt(s * (s-side1) * (s-side2) * (s-side3));
    }
    ```

2. Use the MVC design pattern to create a GUI program for `Triangle` objects. You should include a form for users to enter values for a triangle's three sides and a button that, when clicked, displays data from the `Triangle` object created from the input. Use your `Triangle` class from Programming Exercise 1 as the model.

3. Write a program that displays the multiplication table for the first 10 integers. Then write a program that displays the squares for the first 10 integers. Finally,

write a program that displays the sum of the squares of each integer in the multiplication table. Make sure to include some optimizations you learned about in this chapter.

The first program's output should be similar to the following:

```
     1   2   3   4   5 ...
1    1   2   3   4   5 ...
2    2   4   6   8  10 ...
```

The second program's output should look something like this:

```
1    1
2    4
3    9
4   16 ...
```

The final program's output should resemble the following:

```
     1   2    3    4    5 ...
1    2   5   10   17   26 ...
2    5   8   13   20   29 ...
```

CHAPTER 4

Google Android: App Inventor

In this chapter, you learn to:

- ◎ Describe the Android architecture
- ◎ Use Google App Inventor to create Android apps
- ◎ Use the App Inventor app designer
- ◎ Use the App Inventor Blocks Editor
- ◎ Use non-visible components
- ◎ Incorporate messaging, locations, and media into an app
- ◎ Deploy an app created with App Inventor

This chapter explains how to work with Google's Web-based IDE: App Inventor. App Inventor makes it possible for anyone to create Android apps. In general, you design the way the app looks, and then you snap together blocks of code that provide functionality for your app. App Inventor includes user interface components and code blocks for just about anything you can think of for an app. It's simple but powerful and includes access to features such as the GPS sensors, all the telephony features, and even the underlying file system for storing data.

 At the time of publication, Google is planning to turn over App Inventor to MIT Research Labs. By the time you read this chapter, the URL in Appendix A pointing to App Inventor might no longer work. Because App Inventor's new location is unknown at this time, look for updated information at www.cengagebrain.com. Search by ISBN for this book, select Access Now, and choose Updates in the left navigation bar. Steps and screens might differ slightly from what's shown in this chapter.

Review of the Android Architecture

As you learned in Chapter 2, the Android architecture consists of these five components:

- *Linux kernel*—This component is the OS; it's the communication layer between the hardware and the software.

- *Android runtime components*—This component includes the Dalvik virtual machine (a specialized virtual machine for low-memory appliances) and the core libraries, described next.

- *Core libraries*—Developers have access to all the core libraries Android supplies, such as SQLite, FreeType, and the Scalable Graphics Library (SGL). Access to these core libraries is what makes Android stand out from its peers.

- *Application framework*—You use this component to write applications that make use of the core libraries and any libraries you create. It includes a Content Provider, a Resource Manager, an Activity Manager, a Notification Manager, and more. It also includes many views you can access, including a wide variety of user interface components.

- *Applications*—The uppermost component is the application layer. It includes built-in apps, such as a Web browser and e-mail, as well as any apps you write. It's the layer that's directly available to users.

Android is open-source software, meaning you can download the code and modify it, and your modifications don't need to be open source. All the software is available free.

Your First App: Hello App Inventor

App Inventor is a Web-based IDE for creating Android apps and includes a user interface designer and a code block editor. It's not a traditional IDE because instead of writing code, you assemble prefabricated blocks of code. Although this method sounds like building a program with puzzle pieces, App Inventor gives you access to powerful Android libraries you can use when creating apps.

For more information on App Inventor, see *www.appinventorbeta.com/about/moreinfo/*.

Don't be fooled into thinking App Inventor can be used only to develop lightweight apps because you don't have to write code to use it. Although it's easy to use, it has some powerful features. You have access to data storage, location services via GPS, telephony and messaging capabilities, and more features built into Android. In short, you'll be able to create full-strength apps that rival apps written by professional, well-seasoned programmers.

See the "App Inventor" section in the appendix for instructions on installing the extra software you need to run App Inventor and use the Android emulator. The **emulator** is where you test apps if you don't have an Android phone. Even if you have an Android device, however, testing as you go in the emulator is faster than waiting for compiled apps to load on your device. When you get close to finishing your app, testing it on as many devices as possible is a good idea.

Because App Inventor is a Web application, you just need a working Java installation. Java runs on almost every platform that can access the Web, and you can use App Inventor on all these platforms. Just fire up your browser and get busy!

When you create apps with App Inventor, you use the designer to select components to use for your app and the code block editor to specify how these components work together. App Inventor stores your projects "in the cloud" (on Google's servers) and can even organize them for you for easy access.

Designing a User Interface

Your first App Inventor app is the traditional "Hello, World" program you've seen in practically every programming book. In this section, you learn how to design a user interface, work with code blocks, and run apps in the emulator. After creating the app, you'll be well on your way to discovering all the things you can do with App Inventor.

HOW-TO 4-1

Before starting, make sure you've followed the instructions in the appendix to install the software you need to use App Inventor.

1. Start your Web browser, if necessary, and go to **www.appinventorbeta. com**. Click **My Projects** to go to the Projects page. (*Note:* You might need to sign in before being able to access the Projects page. See Appendix A for more information on signing in.)

(*continues*)

(*continued*)

2. Click **New**. In the dialog box that opens, type **HelloAppInventor** for the project name (see Figure 4-1), and then click **OK**. The project opens in the App Inventor workspace, shown in Figure 4-2.

You can name your project whatever you like, but following the Java naming conventions can help eliminate confusion down the road. Nothing is worse than trying to remember what name you gave to a project. The best advice is to pick a naming scheme and stick to it.

For more information on the Java naming conventions, see *www.oracle.com/technetwork/java/codeconventions-135099.html#367*.

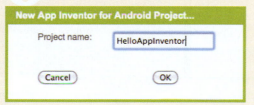

Figure 4-1   The New App Inventor for Android Project dialog box

(*continues*)

(continued)

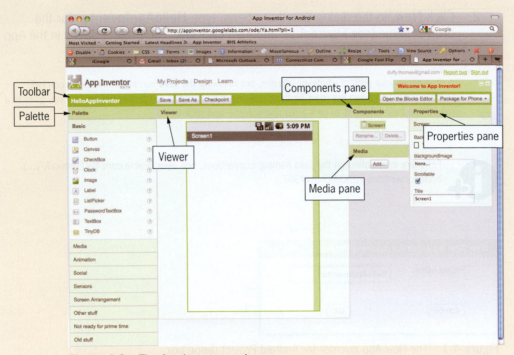

Figure 4-2 The App Inventor workspace

The App Inventor Design view looks like what you see in most IDEs. On the left is the Palette, which lists components available for use in your app. It expands and collapses to display the group of components you have selected. The groups are easy to figure out, but expanding each one to see what's available is a good idea.

The Viewer in the middle represents an Android phone's screen, and it's where you drag components from the Palette. After you drop a component in this area, it becomes the active component. To activate another component, click it in the Viewer.

The right side of the window is dedicated to objects in your project. You can use the Components pane on the right to view your app hierarchically or select components to make them active. You use the Properties pane to set properties for the currently selected component. This feature is "smart," as it displays available properties for a selected component automatically. The Media pane is where you upload custom audio or video you need for your app, such as MP3 files.

(continues)

(continued)

3. In the Properties pane, click to select the text in the **Title** property, and type **Hello App Inventor** in the text box (see Figure 4-3). This text is what's displayed in your app's title bar.

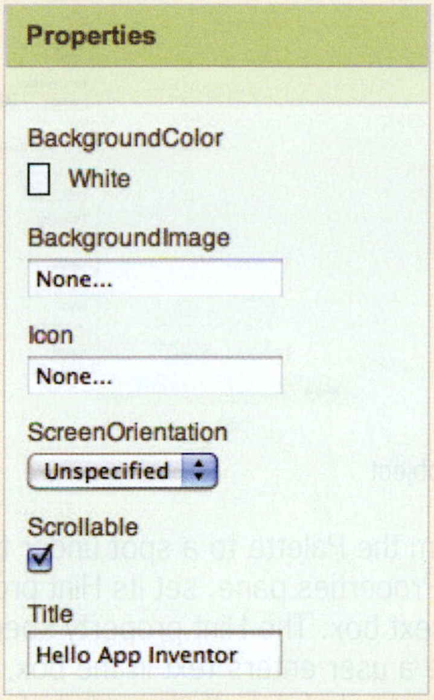

Properties

BackgroundColor
☐ White

BackgroundImage
None...

Icon
None...

ScreenOrientation
Unspecified ▲▼

Scrollable
☑

Title
Hello App Inventor

Figure 4-3 Setting the screen title in the Properties pane

4. In the Palette, click to expand the **Basic** group, if necessary. Drag a **Label** component to the top-left corner of the Viewer. In the Properties pane, type **Enter Your Name** in the Text text box (see Figure 4-4).

(continues)

(*continued*)

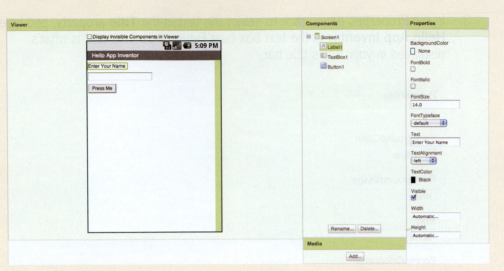

Figure 4-4 Setting the Text property for a Label object

5. Next, drag a **TextBox** component from the Palette to a spot under the Label component in the design area. In the Properties pane, set its Hint property by typing **Enter Your Name** in the Hint text box. The Hint property specifies the grayed-out text that's displayed before a user enters text in the box. It gives users a hint (hence the name!) about the kind of data that needs to be entered (see Figure 4-5).

(*continues*)

(continued)

Notice that the Text property for the TextBox component is empty. This makes sense, as you don't want users to have to delete text before entering data. You could write code to have some text displayed and then removed, but the Hint property does it for you. No extra work necessary!

6. Next, drag a **Button** component to the Viewer under the TextBox component. In the Properties pane, set its Text property by typing **Press Me** in the Text text box. When you have finished, your app should look like Figure 4-6.

Figure 4-5 Setting the Hint property for a TextBox component

(continues)

(continued)

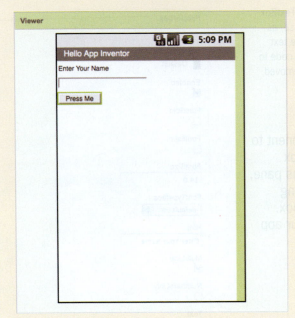

Figure 4-6   The HelloAppInventor user interface

Working with Blocks

The Blocks Editor is where you wire together your app's functionality. **Blocks** are graphical representations of code snippets, much like puzzle pieces, that snap together to form your program's logic. The Blocks Editor includes code blocks for a slew of programming activities and for objects you create in the user interface.

The Blocks Editor is a Java Web Start program stored on Google's servers. **Java Web Start** is a technology that enables developers to deploy apps without the installation headaches usually associated with desktop applications. The downside is that the entire application must be downloaded before it can be started. The Blocks Editor, like all Java Web Start applications, is contained in a Java Native Launch Protocol (JNLP) file.

 For more information on Java Web Start, visit *http://download.oracle.com/javase/6/docs/technotes/guides/javaws/*.

This tool is the ultimate example of encapsulation because it hides everything from outside programs and provides a strict API, meaning you can use only what's supplied. The good news is that because everything is hidden, you can assume that if you use the API correctly, your app should work just fine.

HOW-TO 4-2

1. Back in the App Inventor main window, click the **Open the Blocks Editor** button at the top right. After the Blocks Editor tool and its JNLP file are downloaded, the Blocks Editor starts automatically. Figure 4-7 shows the main window. Note that the Blocks Editor runs in its own window.

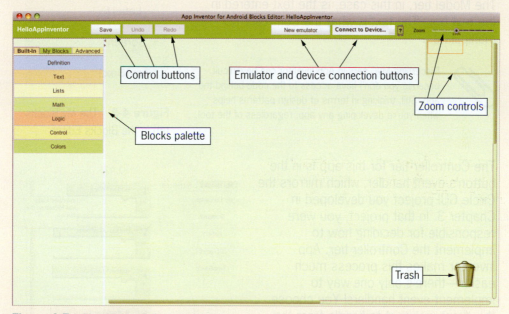

Figure 4-7   The Blocks Editor workspace

 If the Blocks Editor doesn't start automatically, you might need to start it manually by double-clicking the JNLP file you downloaded.

There are three sets of blocks: the Built-In blocks supplied by App Inventor, a set called My Blocks, which includes objects you've created in the App Inventor Design view, and a set named Advanced containing mechanisms for setting global properties of certain components. Each time you click an object, a group of available code blocks for the object is displayed. Some blocks are methods, some blocks are properties, and some built-in objects are graphical representations of code items, such as loops, conditional statements, and logical operators.

2. Click the **My Blocks** tab, which lists all the objects you created in the Design view as well as a My Definitions object, where you can create your own variables outside the Design view (see Figure 4-8).

(continues)

(*continued*)

82

In this simple app, the user is expected to enter his or her name in the text box and then click the button, which displays a message. In terms of architecture, this simple app uses the MVC design pattern. You've already designed the View tier. The Model tier, in this case, is the text entered in the text box. The text is what the Controller tier manipulates.

 Discerning MVC tiers in App Inventor can be difficult because you don't have access to the code behind the app. Still, thinking in terms of design patterns helps when you're developing any app, regardless of the tool.

Figure 4-8   The My Blocks tab in the Blocks Editor

The Controller tier for this app is in the button's event handler, which mirrors the Circle GUI project you developed in Chapter 3. In that project, you were responsible for deciding how to implement the Controller tier. App Inventor makes this process much easier—there's only one way to implement event handlers! You choose the event you want to handle from the available blocks and fill in the pieces to implement the handler.

3. Click the **Button1** object in the My Blocks tab. When you do that, a list of all blocks associated with the button in your user interface is shown (see Figure 4-9).

4. Click the **Button1.Click** block to add the Click event block to the workspace. The Click event block can be dragged. For now, because it's the only event you need for this app, you can leave it in the top-left corner of the workspace (see Figure 4-10).

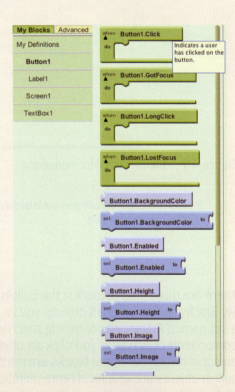

Figure 4-9   Displaying available blocks for the Button1 object

(*continues*)

(continued)

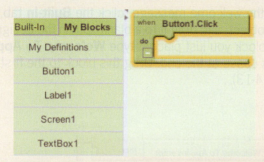

Figure 4-10   Adding the button's Click event to the workspace

5. When the user clicks **Button1**, the text from the TextBox component should be displayed as part of a welcome message in the Label component. To do this, you need to set the Text property of Label1 to a message that includes the value the user enters in the TextBox1 component. Click **Label1** in the My Blocks tab, and then drag the **set Label1.Text** block so that it fits inside the Button1.Click block, as shown in Figure 4-11.

 The set Label1.Text block fits perfectly into the Button1.Click block. One benefit of using App Inventor is that it accepts only blocks that fit together. So although your program might have some logic errors (that is, it doesn't behave the way you expect), compile-time errors don't really exist. If you try to use blocks that don't fit, the IDE simply rejects them.

Figure 4-11   Adding the set Label1. Text block to the button's Click event

Next, you need to get the name a user enters in the TextBox component and include it in the welcome message displayed in the Label component. To do this, the welcome message consisting of the string literal "Welcome to App Inventor" is combined (concatenated) with the text entered in the TextBox component. In App Inventor, concatenating strings in this way is called a **join**.

6. To use the join block, click the **Built-In** tab, and then click the **Text** object. Drag a **join** block to the Label1 object's Text block, as shown in Figure 4-12.

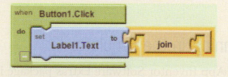

Figure 4-12   Adding a join block

(continues)

(continued)

7. To add a string literal for the welcome message, click the **Built-In** tab, if necessary, click the **Text** object, and drag it to a blank spot in the design area. Click the text of the Text block you just placed, type **Welcome To App Inventor**, and add a blank space at the end. Drag this block to the first slot in the join block (see Figure 4-13).

Figure 4-13   Adding a string literal as text to a join block

8. Next, you need to add the user's name that's entered in the TextBox component to the right side of the join block. Click the **My Blocks** tab, and then click the **TextBox1** object. Click the **TextBox1.Text** block, and drag it to the slot on the right of the join block (see Figure 4-14).

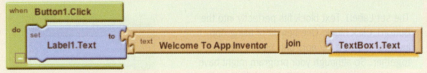

Figure 4-14   Adding text from the TextBlock object to the join block

  Don't be alarmed by the lack of the word "get" in the TextBox1.Text block. Although it seems you have direct access to the instance variable stored in the TextBox object holding the Text property, the block is just a graphical representation. Under the hood, App Inventor creates code that uses the getter method to access the text.

Running in the Emulator

The App Inventor Software Extras package includes a full-fledged emulator that you can use to test apps if you don't have an Android device.

HOW-TO 4-3

Running apps in the emulator is straightforward. Just follow these steps:

1. In the Blocks Editor window, click the **New emulator** button at the top. A Help window is displayed (see Figure 4-15), and the emulator starts in its own window.

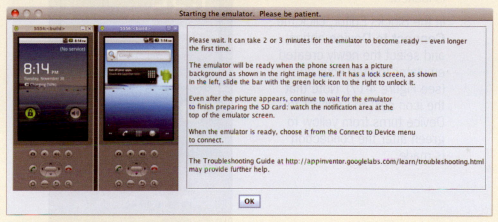

Figure 4-15 Starting the emulator

(*continues*)

(continued)

2. After the emulator has started, you might need to unlock it. To do this, slide the **green lock** icon to the right. The emulator shown in Figure 4-16 is locked.

3. In the Blocks Editor, click the **Connect to Device** option, and select the newly created emulator to start your app (see Figure 4-17). Note that the icon next to Connect to Device turns from yellow to green after the connection is made.

Figure 4-16   The locked emulator

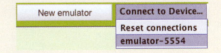

Figure 4-17   Connecting to the new emulator

(continues)

(*continued*)

4. After the emulator is running and the connection to the device has been made, your app should load. Type your name in the text box, and click the **Press Me** button. You should see the welcome message displayed (see Figure 4-18).

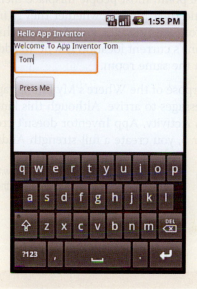

Figure 4-18 The HelloAppInventor app running in the emulator

 When an app runs in the emulator, you click the button with the mouse. When an app is running on a device, you press the button with your finger. The Android SDK and App Inventor refer to this event as a "click" event, which is a holdover from desktop development.

 ## Detective Work

1. Modify the app so that it displays "Welcome To App Inventor, *Username*!" (with *Username* replaced by the name the user enters).

2. Ensure that the message is displayed correctly when no name is entered. (*Hint*: You don't want a comma displayed if no name is entered.)

3. Modify the app so that the user's name is displayed in the title at the top of the screen after the button is pressed.

Advanced Android Apps: Where's My Phone?

At some point, most people misplace their phones. Where's My Phone? is an app that helps users find their phones, whether they're in the house or anywhere in the world. The app listens for text messages, and if one matching a specified phrase is received, a reply containing the phone's current location is sent. In addition, a sound is played, in case the phone happens to be in the same room.

The purpose of the Where's My Phone? app is to run in the background waiting for specified text messages to arrive. Although this kind of app is better suited to be an Android Service than an Activity, App Inventor doesn't create Services, so an Activity will have to do. In Chapter 5, you create a full-strength Android Service version of this app.

Now that you've had a chance to work with App Inventor, the steps in this section aren't as detailed. When new features are introduced, however, they're explained, as with the previous project.

HOW-TO 4-4

1. Start a new project in App Inventor. Name it **WheresMyPhone**, and then click **OK**. Set the screen title to **Where's My Phone?**, as you did in the HelloAppInventor project.

    This app has no user interface, but it includes what App Inventor calls **non-visible components**. These components aren't visible in the user interface; they simply supply data to visible components. If you're thinking these components are in the Model tier, you're on the right track!

2. In the Palette, click **Sensors**, and drag a **LocationSensor** object to the Viewer (see Figure 4-19). The LocationSensor object has no user interface; it just supplies location data for the app.

(continues)

(continued)

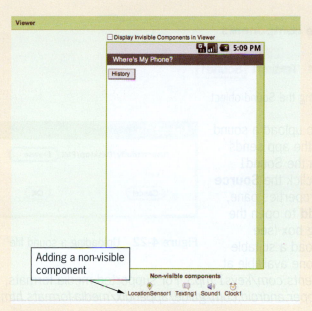

Adding a non-visible component

Figure 4-19   Adding the LocationSensor object

3. Next, in the Palette, click **Social**, and drag a **Texting** object to the Viewer (see Figure 4-20). Note that the Texting object is a non-visible component, too.

Figure 4-20   Adding the Texting object

 One benefit of developing Android apps is that you have access to all the services available on the phone. So instead of having to write your own messaging mechanism, for example, you can simply access the existing messaging function already on the phone.

4. In the Palette, click **Media**, and drag a **Sound** object to the Viewer, as shown in Figure 4-21.

(continues)

(continued)

90

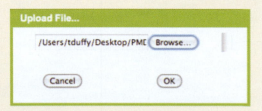

Non-visible components

LocationSensor1   Texting1   Sound1

Figure 4-21   Adding the Sound object

5. Next, you need to upload a sound file to play when the app sends the location. With the Sound1 object selected, click the **Source** text box in the Properties pane, and then click **Add** to open the Upload File dialog box (see Figure 4-22). Upload a suitable file, such as the one available at

Upload File...

/Users/tduffy/Desktop/PME [Browse...]

[Cancel]   [OK]

Figure 4-22   Uploading a sound file

www.bright-moments.com/keys1.mp3. For supported media formats, see *http://developer.android.com/guide/appendix/media-formats.html*.

You've finished the app's design. Right now, it's just a blank screen with the title at the top. You might think that for the app to function correctly, users would have to keep this blank screen visible. Fortunately, Android is a multitasking platform, so users can start the Where's My Phone? app and then press the Home button. Where's My Phone? then runs in the background, waiting for incoming text messages (added in the next steps).

Because the App Inventor version of Where's My Phone? is an Android Activity, it must be started at least once and continue running for it to work. Where's My Phone? is better suited to be an Android Service, as you see in Chapter 5.

The general idea behind Where's My Phone? is for the app to listen for text messages containing a specific phrase. When a text message containing the specified phrase is received, the app replies to the message with the device's GPS coordinates and plays the sound file associated with the Sound object.

6. Open the Blocks Editor so that you can add functionality to the app. In the My Blocks tab, click **Texting1** and then **Texting1.MessageReceived**. MessageReceived is the event you want to handle (see Figure 4-23).

(continues)

(continued)

Figure 4-23   Adding the Texting1.MessageReceived block

Note that the number and messageText blocks are created for you. They're the arguments supplied by the text message's sender. You use messageText to determine whether a request has been made for the phone's location and use number to send the response. You can access these blocks by clicking My Definitions in the My Blocks tab.

7.   Where's My Phone? responds to messages containing a specified phrase. Because you don't want to respond to every incoming text message, you need to set up a condition to determine whether the message contains the specified phrase. In the Built-In tab, click **Control**, and drag an **if** block to the MessageReceived block, as shown in Figure 4-24.

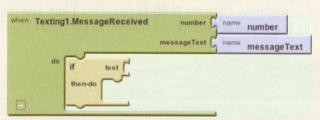

Figure 4-24   Adding an if block to the MessageReceived block

8.   To complete the condition statement, you need a comparison operator. In the Built-In tab, click **Math**, and drag an = block (the equals logical operator for comparisons) to the "test" part of the if block (see Figure 4-25).

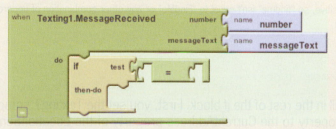

Figure 4-25   Adding an = block to the if block

(continues)

(continued)

9. Next, you create a comparison to see whether the incoming message contains the phrase you specify. To do this, you compare the messageText object with the specified phrase to see whether they match. Click the **My Blocks** tab, and then click **My Definitions**. Drag the **messageText** value to the left of the = block (see Figure 4-26).

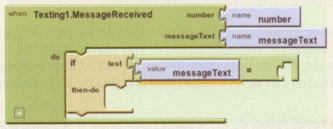

Figure 4-26   Adding the messageText value to the condition test

10. Next, you need to supply the phrase for your comparison. Choose one that isn't normally sent in a text message but makes sense. In Figure 4-27, "findme" is used as the comparison, so a text message containing only the phrase "findme" triggers a response. Click the **Built-In** tab, click **Text**, and click a **text** component. Set its text equal to **findme**, and drag it to the right of the = block.

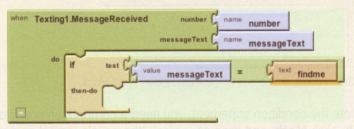

Figure 4-27   Adding a comparison phrase to the condition

Java is case sensitive, so "findme" isn't equal to "FindMe" or any other combination of uppercase and lowercase letters.

11. It's time to fill in the rest of the if block. First, you set the Texting1 component's Message property to the CurrentAddress property of the LocationSensor1 object. To do this, click the **Texting1** object in the My Blocks tab, and then

(continues)

(continued)

drag the **set Texting1.Message** block to the workspace. Next, click the **LocationSensor1** object, and then drag its **CurrentAddress** block into the opening of the Texting1.Message block. Finally, drag the combination into the interior of the if then-do block.

12. Next, you set the PhoneNumber property of the Texting1 component to the sender's number. To do this, click the **Texting1** component in the My Blocks tab, and drag its **set Texting1.Phone Number** block to the workspace. Then click the **MyDefinitions** component in the My Blocks tab, and drag the **number** block into the opening of the PhoneNumber block. Snap the combination into the if then-do block beneath the Texting1.Message block.

13. Next, call the SendMessage method on the Texting1 component. To do this, drag the **SendMessage** block of the Texting1 component into the if then-do block. The SendMessage block is a method call that takes no arguments. That's why there aren't any places on the block to add data. Instead, you set the properties of the Texting1 object, and then these properties are used when the message is sent.

14. To play the sound stored in the Sound1 object when a message containing the special phrase is received, you must call the Play method on the Sound object. To do this, drag the **Sound1.Play** block of the Sound1 object to the bottom of the if then-do block. Try to make your project look like Figure 4-28.

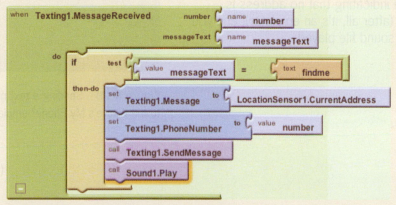

Figure 4-28   Completing the body of the condition

15. Start the emulator, if you haven't already. Unlock the phone, if necessary, and then click the **Connect to Device** button in the Blocks Editor. Connect to the current emulator to start the app.

(continues)

(continued)

To test the app, you need to send the emulator a text message. To do this, you start another instance of the emulator (with the New emulator button) in the Blocks Editor. The numbers to use for text messages are the ports displayed at the top of the emulator window. The default port for the emulator is 5554, so you can send a text message from the new emulator to 5554, and the first emulator (which is running Where's My Phone?) will receive it.

16. Click the **New emulator** button, and unlock the phone. Click the **Launcher** icon (grid of dots in the lower-middle screen), click the **Messaging** icon, and then click **New message**. Type **findme** (see Figure 4-29), and send this message to the first emulator's port number (5554, by default). (*Hint:* If the emulator changes the lowercase "f" to an uppercase "F" automatically, move back to the "F" with the arrow key and delete it, and then retype the "f.")

As shown in Figure 4-30, you get a return message indicating that no address is available (after all, it's an emulator), and you hear the sound file played.

Figure 4-29 Sending a text message to the Where's My Phone? emulator

(continues)

(*continued*)

Figure 4-30   Message received and response sent

Packaging and Deploying Applications

App Inventor makes packaging and deploying apps easy. Packaging an app is the process of gathering all the resources an app needs to run on a device. Deploying an app is synonymous with installing an app on a device. If you have an Android device, you can connect it to your computer and communicate with it via the Blocks Editor. Instead of sending the app to the emulator, you send it directly to your phone. Your device then installs the app automatically and adds it to the apps list.

If you don't have an Android device, you aren't out of luck. In the App Inventor Design view, click the Package for Phone drop-down button, and select one of the three options for packaging an app (see Figure 4-31): Show Barcode, Download to this Computer, and Download to Connected Phone.

The barcode mechanism (which is just a machine-readable URL pointing to an app) is useful for apps stored in the cloud. App Inventor can create a unique barcode for your app. When users scan it, Android downloads and installs the app automatically.

When you select the Download to this Computer option, an **Android Package (.apk)** file is created. You can install `.apk` files directly on Android devices via a USB drive or Bluetooth. In addition, you can store an `.apk` file on a Web server and navigate to it by using the Android Web browser. Essentially, you transfer an `.apk` file to a device, and the device takes care of installing the app.

Figure 4-31   App Inventor app packaging options

 As of this writing, App Inventor apps aren't allowed on the Android Market, but this restriction will most likely be lifted in the future. For now, however, users must select Settings, Applications from the menu, and then click the Unknown sources check box, which enables them to install apps from any source. App Inventor selects this option automatically in the emulator.

Detective Work

1. Add a display mechanism to keep track of who has sent findme text messages, as shown in Figure 4-32. (*Hint*: The mechanism isn't a button; it's a ListPicker component.)

2. Display the date and time of each findme message, as shown in Figure 4-33. (*Hint*: A list is used.)

Figure 4-32   Triggering a display mechanism

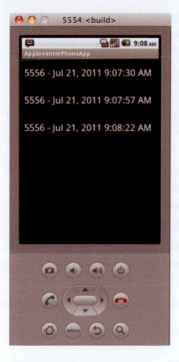

Figure 4-33 Keeping track of findme messages

Chapter Summary

- App Inventor is Google's Web-based IDE for creating Android apps. It gives you access to data storage, location services via GPS, telephony and messaging capabilities, and more features built into the Android OS.

- The Android emulator is where you test your code if you don't have an Android phone. It's a software-based phone that makes most of the Android OS available for testing.

- When creating apps with App Inventor, you select and place user interface components for your app and use the Blocks Editor to specify how the components work together.

- App Inventor stores your projects in the cloud on Google's servers.

- The App Inventor workspace is divided into several sections. The Palette expands and collapses to display the group of app components you want to work with. The Viewer represents an Android phone's screen and is where you drop components. The

Components pane gives you a hierarchical view of your app and can also be used to select components. You use the Properties pane to set properties for the currently selected component and the Media pane to upload custom audio or video for your app.

- Blocks are graphical representations of code snippets that snap together to form your program's logic.

- The Blocks Editor is a Java Web Start program stored on Google's servers. Java Web Start enables you to deploy apps without the installation headaches associated with desktop applications.

- The Blocks Editor supplies sets of code blocks you can use to develop apps: the Built-In blocks provided by App Inventor, a group called My Blocks that represents the objects created in the App Inventor Design view, and an Advanced block that provides mechanisms for setting global properties of certain components.

- App Inventor can make it hard to discern tiers in the MVC design pattern because you don't have access to the code behind the app. However, one benefit of using App Inventor is that it accepts only blocks that work together.

- In App Inventor, the process of concatenating strings is called a join. You can add a string literal by typing a value in a text block.

- App Inventor doesn't create Android Services.

- Non-visible components have no user interface; they simply supply data.

- You have three choices for packaging and deploying an app: Show Barcode, Download to this Computer, and Download to Connected Phone. App Inventor can create a unique barcode for your app that users scan so that Android downloads and installs the app automatically. An Android Package (.apk) file is a deployment bundle for installing Android apps.

- As of this writing, App Inventor apps aren't allowed on the Android Market; however, users can select the option to allow unknown sources so that they can install apps from any source.

Key Terms

Android Package (.apk)—A file used as a deployment bundle for installing Android apps.

App Inventor—Google's Web-based IDE for creating Android apps. It includes a user interface designer and a code block editor.

blocks—Graphical representations of code snippets that snap together to form an app's logic.

emulator—A program for testing code that can be used if an Android phone isn't available. The emulator is a software-based phone that makes almost the entire Android OS available for testing.

Java Web Start—A technology that enables developers to deploy full-strength applications without the installation problems of typical desktop applications.

join—The process of concatenating strings in App Inventor.

non-visible components—Objects that have no user interface and are used to access Android system services, such as location and messaging services.

Review Questions

1. App Inventor is considered a traditional IDE. True or False?

2. Which of the following is *not* included with App Inventor?
   a. Viewer
   b. Code Editor
   c. Blocks Editor
   d. Emulator

3. Which part of the Design view can you use to see available components?
   a. Palette
   b. Properties pane
   c. Media pane
   d. Design area

4. Where can you upload graphics and sounds for an app? (Choose all that apply.)
   a. Media pane
   b. Properties pane
   c. Palette
   d. All of the above

5. App Inventor's Blocks Editor is an example of encapsulation. True or False?

6. Which of the following is a benefit of using App Inventor?
   a. It allows you to customize the code that's generated.
   b. You can "force" blocks together.
   c. Projects are stored on your hard drive.
   d. It accepts only blocks that fit together.

7. Which of the following is a Blocks Editor group? (Choose all that apply.)
   a. Built-In
   b. My Blocks
   c. Advanced
   d. Social

8. The process of concatenating strings in the Blocks Editor is called which of the following?
   a. Join
   b. Combination
   c. Stitch
   d. Meld

9. Non-visible components belong in which tier of the MVC design pattern?

    a. Controller

    b. View

    c. Model

    d. They don't fit into this design pattern.

10. Which of the following is *not* a packaging option in App Inventor?

    a. Show Barcode   c. Download to Connected Phone

    b. Download to this Computer   d. Publish to Market

Up for Discussion

1. Why do you think Google adopted the Java Web Start technology for the App Inventor Blocks Editor? Explain your answer.

2. As of this writing, App Inventor apps aren't allowed on the Android Market. Name at least three reasons for not allowing these apps. Do you agree with the policy? Explain your answer.

3. Why do you think Android services can't be built in App Inventor? Explain your answer.

4. Which of the deployment options for App Inventor apps is the most convenient? Which is the least convenient? Why?

5. Discuss the pros and cons of open-source software, and relate the open-source model to free versus paid apps.

Programming Exercises

1. Create an App Inventor app that calculates and displays a circle's area and circumference. Ask users to supply a radius for the circle.

2. Create an App Inventor app that calculates and displays a rectangle's area and perimeter. Ask users to supply the length and width for the rectangle.

3. Create an App Inventor app that converts temperatures from degrees Fahrenheit to degrees Celsius. Ask users for the temperature in degrees Fahrenheit, and use the following formula for the conversion:

    $C = 5/9(F - 32)$

4. Create an App Inventor app that converts temperatures from degrees Celsius to degrees Fahrenheit. Ask users for the temperature in degrees Celsius, and then use the following formula for the conversion:

    $F = 9/5 * C + 32$

5. Create an App Inventor app that combines Programming Exercises 3 and 4. It should allow users to choose to convert the temperature from Celsius to Fahrenheit and vice versa.

6. Create an App Inventor app that sends SMS text messages. Ask users to enter data that specifies the number to send the message to and the body of the message.

7. Create an App Inventor app that displays a device's GPS coordinates. Update the location every 15 minutes.

CHAPTER 5

Google Android: Motorola MOTODEV Studio

In this chapter, you learn to:

- ◎ Distinguish between Eclipse and MOTODEV Studio
- ◎ Use MOTODEV Studio to create Android apps
- ◎ Create Android Services and Broadcast Receivers
- ◎ Create a standard "Hello World" app that displays an alert message
- ◎ Handle click and touch events
- ◎ Write a basic game program that draws onscreen
- ◎ Use the Java `Timer` and `TimerTask` classes
- ◎ Create context menus
- ◎ Store and retrieve app data
- ◎ Play sounds in code
- ◎ Use the Location API
- ◎ Send and receive text (SMS) messages

In Chapter 4, you learned how to build Android apps with Google's cloud-based IDE, App Inventor. In this chapter, you learn how to write Android apps with Motorola's MOTODEV Studio. Why a second tool? With App Inventor, you can create only Android Activities, and you're stuck with code blocks (powerful as they are) supplied by App Inventor. If you want to create an app to do something that's not available in the Blocks Editor, you're out of luck.

App Inventor was invented for nonprogrammers. Because you aren't one of these folks, you can learn how to write your own code for Android apps. MOTODEV Studio is based on IBM's Eclipse IDE, the preferred tool for writing Android code. It incorporates the Google SDK and many Android-specific tools. If you want to develop more sophisticated Android apps, this chapter is for you.

Eclipse and MOTODEV Studio

Motorola's **MOTODEV Studio** is an IDE for developing Android apps. It's being used in this book for a few reasons:

- It uses the latest version of the Eclipse IDE.

- It integrates the Android SDK.

- It allows you to choose the Android version, including the latest version, your app supports.

- A single installation includes everything you need.

 Make sure you follow the installation instructions in the "MOTODEV Studio" section of Appendix A before starting this chapter's exercises.

Studio includes Android-specific tools to help make developing Android apps as easy as possible. (It also includes some extensions to target Motorola handsets, although you aren't using any in this chapter.) As mentioned, it's based on Eclipse, which is an open-source platform with powerful plug-ins.

At its core, Eclipse is a robust application framework. It includes mechanisms for developers to work with files and network resources. The idea is that developers can use Eclipse to develop their own apps and not have to worry about the things most apps must do. Instead, developers can focus on what makes their apps different from others by creating plug-ins, which are bundles of functionality that add to Eclipse's capabilities.

The Java development tools that ship with Eclipse consist of the Java Development Environment (JDE) plug-in that runs on the IDE. The JDE supplies tools that enable Eclipse to perform many tasks associated with Java development: editing Java files, compiling Java files, debugging Java files, and so forth. MOTODEV Studio is also a plug-in that includes many features from the Java Development Environment (JDE) plug-in in addition to those targeted at Android development.

Eclipse has its own vocabulary to define available objects. A **workspace** is a set of files on disk to help organize your development projects. This term is based on the metaphor of a **workbench**, which is simply an arrangement of windows in the Eclipse IDE. These windows are called perspectives and views. A **perspective** is an editor for working with specific file types. A **view** is a window that displays some aspect of the project. When you start Studio, you see the default workbench for Android development.

This chapter doesn't delve into details of the Eclipse development, as entire books on this subject are available. MOTODEV Studio includes the Eclipse Help system, however, which is quite good. You can access it through the Help menu.

Android App Development

A central feature of the Android OS is that your app can make use of other apps as long as permission is given. To make this happen, the OS needs a way of activating different objects, including objects you create and those that Android provides. You learned in Chapter 2 that Android can activate four types of components: Activities, Services, Broadcast Receivers, and Content Providers. The following paragraphs give you a quick review of these components.

Activities are visual components that the user sees when running your app. Your app can contain a single activity or multiple activities. Usually, one activity is marked as the first activity, and it activates the next activity based on user input or your program design. Activities inherit from the `Activity` class that the Android SDK makes available.

Services can be thought of as activities with no user interface. All services inherit from the `Service` class. The classic example of a service is a background music player that runs while the user interacts with your app's activities.

Broadcast Receivers, which inherit from the `BroadcastReceiver` class, wait for events outside your app to happen. Many are activated via code to let users know a text message has been received or the battery is low, for example. An app can have as many broadcast receivers as needed to receive messages. These components don't have a user interface, but they can start an activity that does.

Content Providers make specific parts of your app available to other apps. These parts might be stored in the file system or in a database. Content providers inherit from the `ContentProvider` class. The built-in Contacts app, for example, makes a content provider available so that other apps, including those you write, can have access to the user's contacts list.

The Anatomy of a Java Class

All Java classes have the same basic structure; most begin with a package declaration, as follows:

```
package com.packageName;
```

Packages are nothing more than the combination of a unique identifier and folder information. They allow Java developers to keep their code separate from code developed by others. The convention is to use the URL of a company Web site because it's guaranteed to be unique. The package declaration must be the first uncommented line of code.

Next is the import section. You must import any classes that aren't included in the package—that is, classes declared in other packages. Import statements are placed outside the class declaration (usually before it), and if you have more than one import statement, their order doesn't matter. These statements have the following syntax:

```
import com.packageName.ClassName;
```

If you want to use multiple classes in the same package, you can import the entire package by using the * wildcard, as shown:

```
import com.packageName.*;
```

Using this wildcard might seem to be a problem, given that packages can include hundreds of classes, which could make your program unnecessarily large. The Java compiler is smart enough, however, to include only the classes you actually use in your program, so you're safe using a wildcard in this manner.

The class declaration is where you name your class, declare its superclass (if any), and declare which interfaces it implements. The convention is to capitalize class names. The class definition is placed inside the class declaration's curly braces.

```
public class ClassName extends Superclass implements Interface1, ↵
  Interface2{
    // class definition
}
```

The class definition is where you declare variables and methods. For the most part, the order in which you declare them doesn't matter. The scope of a variable or method is loosely defined by the block in which it's declared. Instance variables are variables declared inside the class declaration but outside any method. They're in scope for the life of any object instantiated from the class. The convention is to include instance variables at the beginning or end of the class definition in a group. Although you can include instance variables anywhere in the class definition, scattering them throughout your code makes it much harder to read and debug.

Methods are declared inside the class definition and include curly braces, too. The code you write between braces runs whenever the method is called. Any variables you declare in a method go out of scope when the method is finished and aren't available outside the method.

Constructors are special kinds of methods declared in the class definition. They don't include return types because by definition, they return instances of the class. They always have the same name as the class, as in this example:

```
public ClassName(){
    // any object initialization
}
```

A full Java class might look something like this:

```
package com.packageName;
import com.packageName.ClassName1;
import com.packageName.ClassName2;
public class ClassName extends Superclass implements Interface1, ↵
```

```
Interface2{
  private int instanceVariable;
  public void setInstanceVariable1(int instanceVariable){
    this.instanceVariable = instanceVariable;
  }
  public int getInstanceVariable(){
    return instanceVariable;
  }
  public ClassName(int instanceVariable){
    this.instanceVariable = instanceVariable;
  }
  public void someMethod(){
    int aMethodVar = someMethodReturnValue();
    doSomething(aMethodVar);
  public int someMethodReturnValue(){
    // must return an int
    return 0;
  }
  public void doSomething(int val){
    // do something here
  }
  }
}
```

All class information must be stored in a file with the same name as the class and with a `.java` extension. So the preceding code, for example, would be stored in `ClassName.java`.

Your First Android App: Hello Android!

Your first app written in MOTODEV Studio is identical to the one you created with App Inventor. It consists of a text box for user input, a display label, and a button that triggers an event when the user touches it. Along the way, you use different perspectives and views to work with the files that make your app work.

 If you haven't installed or set up MOTODEV Studio, refer to the "MOTODEV Studio" section of Appendix A for installation steps and instructions on setting up Studio.

 HOW-TO 5-1

1. Start Studio. To create a new project, click **File**, point to **New**, and click **Android Project Using Studio for Android**. In the New Android Project dialog box (see Figure 5-1), type **HelloAndroid** in the Project name and Application name text boxes. Leave the default settings shown in the figure for the rest of the project's properties, and then click **Finish**.

(continues)

(*continued*)

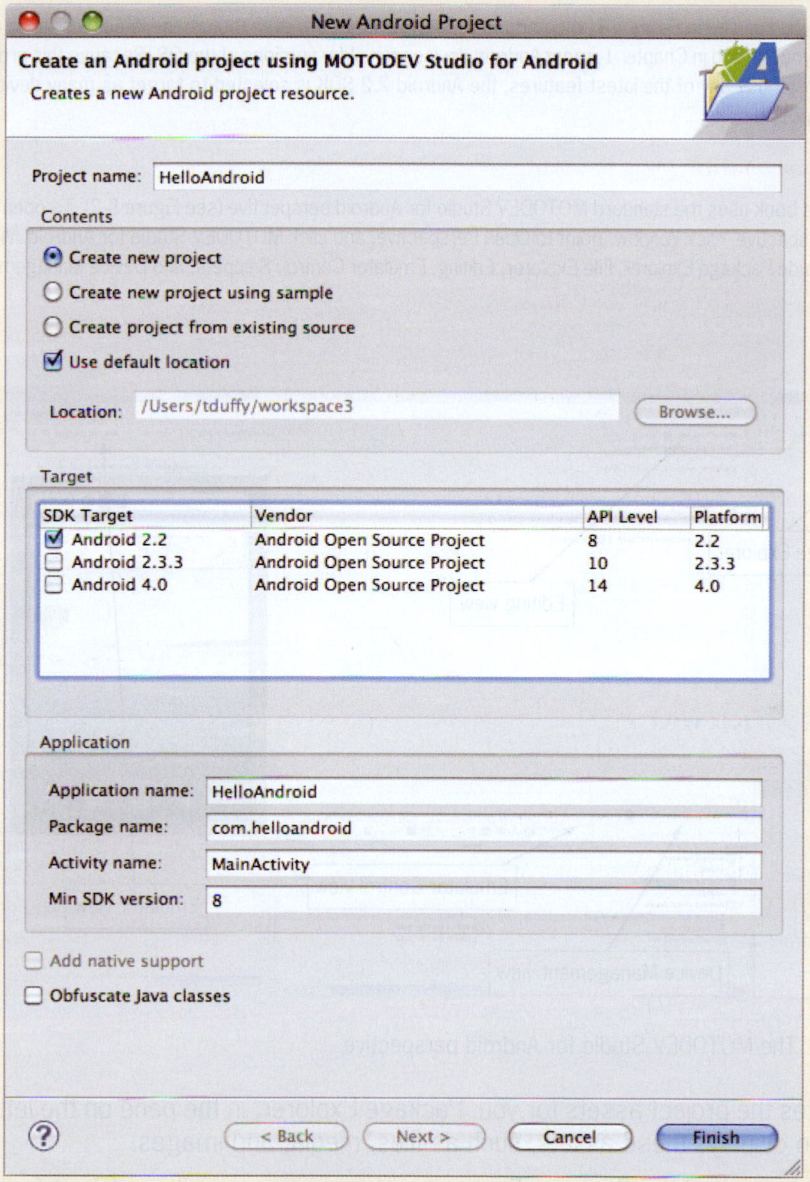

Figure 5-1 Creating a new Android project

(*continues*)

(continued)

 As you can see in Figure 5-1, the Android 2.2 SDK is targeted, even though the latest version is 4.0. As you learned in Chapter 1, most Android devices run older versions of the OS. Because this project doesn't use any of the latest features, the Android 2.2 SDK is selected to target as many devices as possible.

 This book uses the standard MOTODEV Studio for Android perspective (see Figure 5-2). To open this perspective, click Window, point to Open Perspective, and click MOTODEV Studio for Android. Views include Package Explorer, File Explorer, Editing, Emulator Control, Snippets, and Device Management.

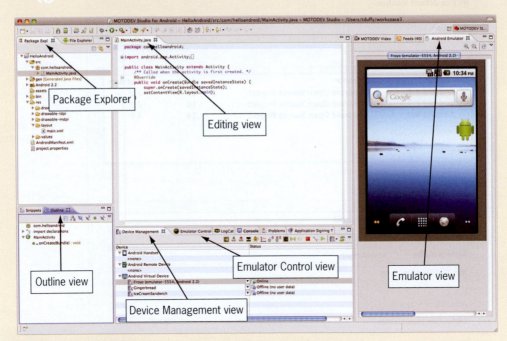

Figure 5-2   The MOTODEV Studio for Android perspective

Studio creates the project assets for you. Package Explorer, in the pane on the left, is where Studio displays these assets, such as files, media, and images.

2.   Click to expand the Package Explorer nodes **src**, **gen**, and **res** (short for source, generated, and resource), as shown in Figure 5-3, so that you can see the `MainActivity.java`, `R.java`, and `main.xml` files.

(continues)

(continued)

Extensible Markup Language (XML) is a tag-based language designed to store information. Developers can use it to define the structure of the information they want to store and include the structure with the information.

XML is outside the scope of this book. For more information, start with the XML tutorial at *www.w3schools.com/xml/*.

3. As you've probably guessed, `main.xml` in the layout folder defines your UI. Double-click the **main.xml** file to open it. The code in this file is specific to Android apps and includes properties for each component as well as the app's structure. Click the **main.xml** tab at the lower left of the Editing view to view the code (see Figure 5-4).

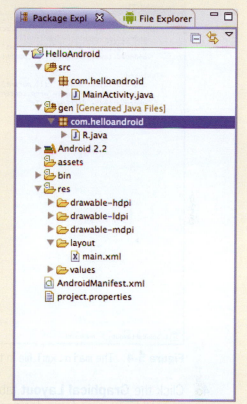

Figure 5-3 Expanding nodes in Package Explorer

(continues)

(continued)

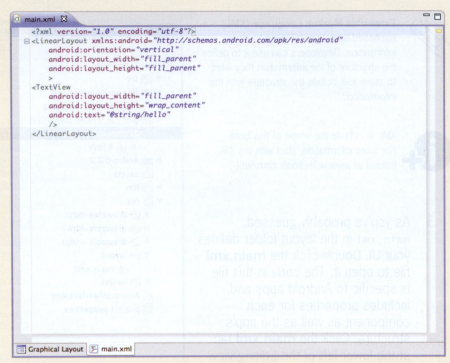

Figure 5-4   The `main.xml` file in the Editing view

4. Click the **Graphical Layout** tab (see Figure 5-5). You use this view to design your UI by using a form designer and component palette, much like what you used in App Inventor.

(continues)

(continued)

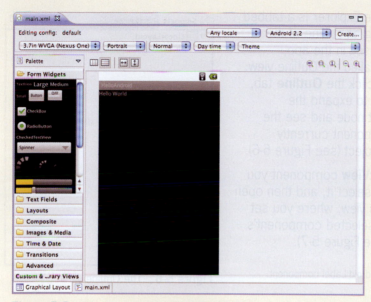

Figure 5-5 The `main.xml` file in the Graphical Layout view

The Graphical Layout view is the visual designer you use for the user interface. You can choose the emulator "skin" you want as well as orientation and theme, for example. Figure 5-5 shows the 3.7in FWVGA Slider theme in Portrait mode. Later, you can experiment to see what your apps look like in a variety of formats. You want your app to look good in as many configurations as possible. For now, the defaults are fine for developing your app.

Android is used on many devices that vary in look and feel, so when you build an Android app, you should test it on as many devices as possible. With MOTODEV Studio, you can do some multiple-device testing right in the emulator.

(continues)

(continued)

5. Under Package Explorer is a tabbed view containing an outline of the components used in the app, conveniently called the Outline view. If necessary, click the **Outline** tab, and then click to expand the **LinearLayout** node and see the TextView component currently used in the project (see Figure 5-6).

6. Click the **TextView** component you just added to select it, and then open the Properties view, where you set the currently selected component's properties (see Figure 5-7).

 A TextView is an Android Label component.

Figure 5-6   The Outline view

 If you can't find the Properties view, you can open it by clicking Window, Show View, Other, General, Properties from the menu.

(continues)

(continued)

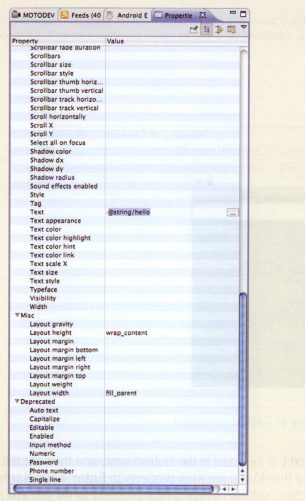

113

Figure 5-7 The Properties view with the TextView component selected

7. Click the **Text** property and delete the value, which sets the text of the TextView component to nothing. Don't worry—your app will set the text to the right value later. You're going to duplicate the behavior of the HelloAppInventor app you created in Chapter 4.

8. The left pane of the Graphical Layout view is a palette of available views for your app. Expand the **Text Fields** group, and then drag a **Plain Text** component to the UI in the middle (see Figure 5-8). The Plain Text component is the first Text Field available.

(continues)

(continued)

All the available views are subclasses of the `View` class, which you develop to create UI components. Because of polymorphism, subclasses can always be substituted where a superclass is expected.

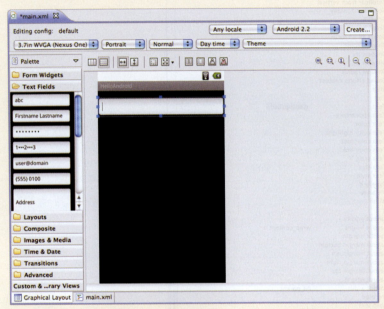

Figure 5-8   Dropping an EditText component

9.   Make sure **editText1** is selected in the Outline view, and then set the `Text` property to nothing (blank) and the `Hint` property to **Enter Your Name**. In the Miscellaneous section, set the `Layout width` property to **fill_parent** and the `Layout height` property to **wrap_content**. The UI should look like Figure 5-9.

There are a lot of properties, so make sure you set the correct ones!

(continues)

(continued)

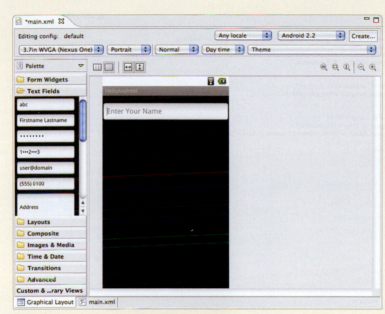

Figure 5-9   Adding an EditText component

A benefit of using an IDE with an integrated form designer is that it creates the necessary code as you design the UI visually. In this case, Studio modifies the `main.xml` file to reflect the changes you've made.

10.   Click the **main.xml** tab to see what's going on with the code (see Figure 5-10). As you can see, UI components are declared hierarchically in the XML file. All the View components are children of the LinearLayout container, and all properties of each component are stored in key/value pairs called **attributes** in XML.

(continues)

(continued)

```
main.xml
<?xml version="1.0" encoding="utf-8"?>
<LinearLayout xmlns:android="http://schemas.android.com/apk/res/android"
    android:orientation="vertical"
    android:layout_width="fill_parent"
    android:layout_height="fill_parent"
    >
<TextView
    android:layout_width="fill_parent"
    android:layout_height="wrap_content"/>

<EditText
    android:id="@+id/editText1"
    android:layout_width="fill_parent"
    android:layout_height="wrap_content" android:hint="Enter Your Name">

    <requestFocus />
</EditText>

</LinearLayout>
```

Graphical Layout   main.xml

Figure 5-10   The `main.xml` file reflecting changes made in the designer

11.   The next UI component you need is a Button. Click the **Graphical Layout** view,
      expand the **Form Widgets** group, and drag a Button component to the UI.
      In the Properties view, set the `Text` property to **Press Me**. Figure 5-11 shows
      the modified interface.

(continues)

(continued)

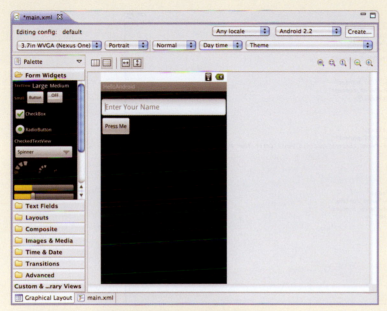

Figure 5-11   Adding a Button component to the UI

There's one more piece of code to write for the UI. Because you want to access the original TextView component provided by the New Project template, which displays "Hello World" by default, you need to supply an ID (by adding an `id` attribute) for the component to get access to it. The Graphical Layout and Editing views stay in sync regardless of where you do your editing.

12.   To supply an ID, click the **main.xml** tab. In the Editing view, add an `id` attribute for the TextView component inside the `<TextView>` tag (see the highlighted line in Figure 5-12) by entering this code:

```
android:id="@+id/textView1"
```

 The value used for the `id` attribute follows the Android naming conventions for UI components. Later, when you write code to modify what's displayed, the SDK creates a reference to the correct component based on the name. This process is called "inflating the UI," and it's discussed in more detail later in this section.

(continues)

(continued)

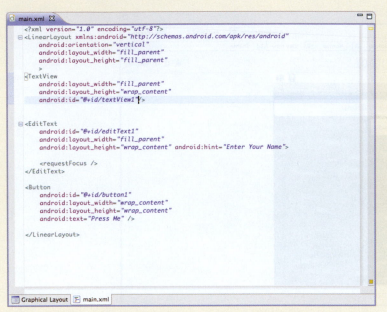

```xml
<?xml version="1.0" encoding="utf-8"?>
<LinearLayout xmlns:android="http://schemas.android.com/apk/res/android"
    android:orientation="vertical"
    android:layout_width="fill_parent"
    android:layout_height="fill_parent"
>
<TextView
    android:layout_width="fill_parent"
    android:layout_height="wrap_content"
    android:id="@+id/textView1" />
>

<EditText
    android:id="@+id/editText1"
    android:layout_width="fill_parent"
    android:layout_height="wrap_content" android:hint="Enter Your Name">

    <requestFocus />
</EditText>

<Button
    android:id="@+id/button1"
    android:layout_width="wrap_content"
    android:layout_height="wrap_content"
    android:text="Press Me" />

</LinearLayout>
```

Figure 5-12   Adding an `id` attribute to the TextView component

13. Save your work by clicking the disk icon at the top of the window. Double-click the **R.java** file to see how UI elements are accessed in code (see Figure 5-13). Take care not to modify this file, as incorrect code can corrupt your app.

References are made to each UI element with an `id` attribute. UI components with no `id` attribute can't be accessed, which makes sense for a label that never changes its display. However, if you plan to modify any component in your code, you must give it an `id` attribute. In this case, you need access to the text entered in the EditView component and the text displayed in the TextView component, and you trigger the display with the Button component.

(continues)

(continued)

```
main.xml        R.java
/* AUTO-GENERATED FILE.  DO NOT MODIFY.

   package com.helloandroid;

   public final class R {
       public static final class attr {
       }
       public static final class drawable {
           public static final int ic_launcher=0x7f020000;
       }
       public static final class id {
           public static final int button1=0x7f050002;
           public static final int editText1=0x7f050001;
           public static final int textView1=0x7f050000;
       }
       public static final class layout {
           public static final int main=0x7f030000;
       }
       public static final class string {
           public static final int app_name=0x7f040001;
           public static final int hello=0x7f040000;
       }
   }
```

Figure 5-13 The R.java file

 The R.java file defines a class named R that's declared as final. The final keyword in Java has multiple meanings. When you declare a variable final, it can't be changed. This is how constants work in Java. When you declare a method final, it can't be overridden; when you declare a class final, no subclasses can inherit from it.

Now that you have created the view for your app, it's time to add the functionality in the Controller tier. You do that by creating an event handler for the click event of the Button component in MainActivity.java. The Model tier for the app is the text the user enters.

14. Double-click **MainActivity.java** in Package Explorer to open it in the Editing view. Add the following import statements shown in bold:

```
import android.app.Activity;
import android.os.Bundle;
import android.view.View;
import android.widget.*;
```

(continues)

(continued)

You might need to expand the import section by clicking the + sign in the left margin of the Editing view.

As mentioned, the * character is a wildcard. When used in an `import` statement, it includes all classes in a package.

The `View` class is the superclass for all UI components. The widget package includes all the UI components.

15. Next, you add instance variables for each UI component. These variables enable you to manipulate UI elements while the app is running. Add the following code shown in bold just after the class declaration:

```
public class MainActivity extends Activity{
    /** Called when the activity is created. */
    private Button btn;
    private EditText edit;
    private TextView view;
```

16. Inside the `onCreate()` method, you need to instantiate the instance variables. To do this, you refer to the `R.java` class and use the inner `id` class to get pointers to the actual components. Add the following code shown in bold to the `onCreate()` method:

```
    super.onCreate(savedInstanceState);
    setContentView(R.layout.main);
    edit = (EditText)findViewById(R.id.editText1);
    view = (TextView)findViewById(R.id.textView1);
    btn = (Button)findViewById(R.id.button1);
```

`R.java` contains references to the components used to build the UI in the form designer as `id` attributes. Using `id` attributes defined in `R.java` to create objects is known as **inflating** the UI, which is the process of instantiating objects created in the form designer. So to access components from `main.xml`, you use the `findViewById()` method and pass a reference to the objects generated in `R.java`. Then you cast the objects to the correct object type. (Casting is the process of changing an object from one type to another. In Java, you can cast only objects existing in the same class inheritance tree.)

(continues)

(continued)

Finally, you need to assign a click event for the button. You create the event handler in the GUI container by implementing the OnClickListener interface in MainActivity.java. As you learned in Chapter 3, implementing an interface makes the MainActivity class an OnClickListener, too. There are four steps:

- Import the interface class.
- Implement the interface.
- Register the listener with the object that will handle the event.
- Write the code that handles the event.

17. First, add the following line to the import section of the code to import the interface class:

```
import android.view.View.OnClickListener;
```

18. Next, to implement the interface, you must perform two tasks. First, add the implements clause (in bold) to the class declaration, as follows:

```
public class MainActivity extends Activity implements OnClickListener{
```

19. When you add this line, Studio displays an error icon to the left of the line. Click the error icon and double-click **Add unimplemented methods** to add the onClick() method to your code and officially implement the OnClickListener interface.

20. Because the Button component is the object that triggers the event, you must register the listener with this component. Add the following code to the end of the onCreate() method to register the listener with the button:

```
btn.setOnClickListener(this);
```

 Note the this keyword in the preceding code line. The setOnClickListener() method expects an instance of a class that implements the OnClickListener interface. Because the MainActivity class does so, you can pass this to the method.

21. Last, you need to add code to the onClick() method that handles the event. When the user touches the button, a welcome message is displayed in two ways: in an alert and then in the view's TextView component. In Android, you

(continues)

(continued)

122

use the `Toast` class, which is part of the widget package, to display alerts. Modify the `onClick()` method as follows:

```
public void onClick(View v){
if(btn==v){
  String msg = "Welcome to Android, " + edit.getText()+ "!";
  Toast toast = Toast.makeText(this,msg,Toast.LENGTH_SHORT);
    toast.show();
    view.setText(msg);
  }
}
```

Remember that Android apps are written in Java. Java uses a single-inheritance model, meaning classes can extend only a single superclass. As you learned in Chapter 3, Java uses interfaces to simulate multiple inheritance. In this case, `MainActivity` is an Activity as well as an `OnClickListener` object. It can be treated as both types of objects because of the way Java handles multiple inheritance. The capability to be treated as an Activity is inherited through the `Activity` class. The capability to be treated as an `OnClickListener` is made possible by implementing all methods declared in the `OnClickListener` interface. Java classes can inherit from only a single class, but they can use multiple interfaces. After the `OnClickListener` interface is implemented, `MainActivity` *is* an Activity that can *behave* like an `OnClickListener`.

Running in the Emulator

HOW-TO 5-2

1. To start the emulator, click **Run** on the menu, point to **Run As**, and click **Android Application using MOTODEV Studio**. If you're asked to run the emulator as a Studio/Eclipse view, click **Yes**. If you're asked to save changes, click **Yes** in the Save Resources message box. The emulator starts in the same view as the Properties view. (Like the App Inventor emulator, it can take a long time to start.)

2. If you're having problems starting the emulator, click the **Device Management** tab at the bottom, and then click **Start** from the drop-down list associated with the Android device you want to start. After the emulator starts, your app is loaded. (You might have to unlock the screen, click the app name to load it, or both.) Enter your name in the text box and click the **Press Me** button (see Figure 5-14).

Detective Work

1. Modify the code so that the app displays the correct text when no name is entered.

2. Modify the code so that the message is displayed in the app's title bar after the button is pressed.

Working with MOTODEV Studio and Eclipse

As you've learned, MOTODEV Studio is an application plug-in written on top of Eclipse that makes Android-specific tools available to Eclipse. The benefit is that Studio can make use of all the features that make Eclipse a useful editor as well as all the tools available in the plug-in. You can think of Studio as a subclass of Eclipse: It adds functions to Eclipse to create a more specific tool. This section describes some helpful features that are available in MOTODEV Studio and Eclipse.

Figure 5-14 Hello Android after entering text and pressing the button

Eclipse is a full-strength editor with features included in most current code editors. One is **code folding**. You might have noticed the + and - signs in the left margin of the code editor, shown in Figure 5-15. You can use these symbols to show or hide blocks of code as necessary. They're similar to the expand and collapse features you're familiar with in other interfaces. This mechanism helps you make better use of available screen space and is especially helpful when you're working with large files.

```
⊞ import android.app.Activity;
```

```
⊟ import android.app.Activity;
  import android.os.Bundle;
  import android.view.View;
  import android.view.View.OnClickListener;
  import android.widget.*;
```

Figure 5-15 Folded and unfolded code

Eclipse also includes extensive context menus. You can right-click almost any object to see a list of its available features. For example, Figure 5-16 shows the context menu that's displayed when you right-click the Button object in the HelloAndroid MainActivity.java file. Because this object was right-clicked in the Editing view, the context menu includes a Source item that shows you additional things you can do with the Button object, including generating overriding methods. The more useful items include Add Import, which enables you to simply declare a type and import it into your project afterward, and Generate Getters and Setters, which generates read/write access code for an object.

↶ Undo Typing	⌘Z
Revert File	
💾 Save	⌘S
Open Declaration	F3
Open Type Hierarchy	F4
Open Call Hierarchy	^⌥H
Show in Breadcrumb	⌥⌘B
Quick Outline	⌘O
Quick Type Hierarchy	⌘T
Open With	▶
Show In	⌥⌘W ▶
Cut	⌘X
Copy	⌘C
Copy Qualified Name	
Paste	⌘V
Quick Fix	⌘1
Source	**⌥⌘S ▶**
Refactor	⌥⌘T ▶
Local History	▶
References	▶
Declarations	▶
📄 Add to Snippets...	
Run As	▶
Debug As	▶
Profile As	▶
Validate	
Team	▶
Compare With	▶
Replace With	▶
Preferences...	

Toggle Comment	⌘/
Remove Block Comment	⇧⌘\
Generate Element Comment	⌥⌘J
Correct Indentation	⌘I
Format	⇧⌘F
Format Element	
Add Import	⇧⌘M
Organize Imports	⇧⌘O
Sort Members...	
Clean Up...	
Override/Implement Methods...	
Generate Getters and Setters...	
Generate Delegate Methods...	
Generate hashCode() and equals()...	
Generate toString()...	
Generate Constructor using Fields...	
Generate Constructors from Superclass...	
Externalize Strings...	
▥ Fill Java Code Based on Android Layout...	

Figure 5-16   The context menu for a Button

The Refactor submenu has some useful tools, too. Of particular interest is Encapsulate Field, which you can use to generate getter and setter methods, declare access types, and generate method comments, all in a single step. Making use of features in the Source and Refactor submenus results in far fewer errors than writing code by hand.

 Refactoring is the process of rewriting your code to make it better without changing its behavior. "Making code better" is somewhat subjective, but generally it means making it more efficient, more reusable, or easier to read. When you refactor your code, you must take care never to break other code that uses the code you're refactoring.

As you learned when you implemented the OnClickListener interface, when you implement an interface or extend an abstract class, Eclipse can generate abstract method stubs, which are placeholder methods you can use and modify as needed (see Figure 5-17). This might not seem important, but some interfaces have dozens of methods to implement. Getting Eclipse to include stubs for you eliminates a lot of potential errors.

```
public class MainActivity extends Activity implements OnClickListener{
    private B  ⊕ Add unimplemented methods          1 method to implement:
    private E  ⊕ Make type 'MainActivity' abstract     – android.view.View.OnClickListener.onClick()
    private T  ⊞ Rename in file (⌘2 R)
               ⊞ Rename in workspace (⌥⌘R)
    /** Calle
    @Override
    public vo
        super
        setCo
        edit
        view
        btn =
        btn.s                                           Press 'Tab' from proposal table or click for focus
```

Figure 5-17 Adding unimplemented methods

The Outline view you used for the main.xml file is useful for looking at source code, too. This view is context sensitive, so it displays the members of a class differently than it does an XML file (see Figure 5-18).

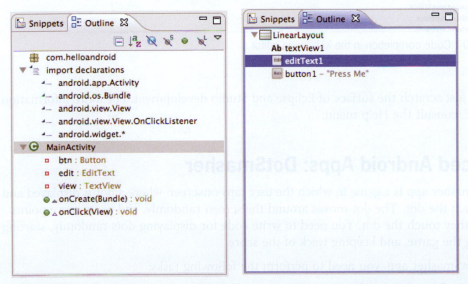

```
📄 Snippets  📑 Outline ✕          ⊟ ⊡
         ⊟ ↓ᴬz ⊠ ⊠ˢ ● ⊠ ▽

⊞ com.helloandroid
▼ ≡ import declarations
   ◢– android.app.Activity
   ◢– android.os.Bundle
   ◢– android.view.View
   ◢– android.view.View.OnClickListener
   ◢– android.widget.*
▼ ⊙ MainActivity
   ▫ btn : Button
   ▫ edit : EditText
   ▫ view : TextView
   ●△ onCreate(Bundle) : void
   ●△ onClick(View) : void
```

```
📄 Snippets  📑 Outline ✕          ⊟ ⊡
▼ ⬚ LinearLayout
   Ab textView1
   🆎 editText1
   🔘 button1 – "Press Me"
```

Figure 5-18 The Outline view for MainActivity.java on the left and main.xml on the right

Eclipse includes code completion features that are also context sensitive. So when you type the . character after an object reference in the Java code editor, Eclipse generates a list of available members for the object, as shown in Figure 5-19.

Similarly, when you type the : character after the android namespace in main.xml, Eclipse generates a list of available attributes for the object (see Figure 5-20).

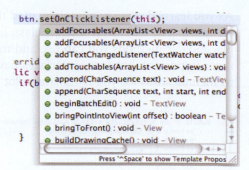

Figure 5-19   Code completion for the Hello Android button

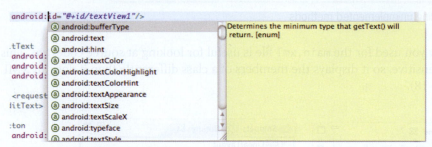

Figure 5-20   Code completion in the XML code editor

These tips just scratch the surface of Eclipse and Studio development. For more information on the IDE, consult the Help menu.

Advanced Android Apps: DotSmasher

The DotSmasher app is a game in which the user taps onscreen where a dot is displayed and tries to touch the dot. The dot moves around the screen randomly, and users score points each time they touch the dot. You need to write code for displaying dots randomly, starting and ending the game, and keeping track of the score.

For the DotSmasher app, you need to perform the following tasks:

1. Create a custom canvas that draws the dot and score onscreen.

2. Subclass the TimerTask class that supplies instructions to run repeatedly until the game ends.

3. Implement a MainActivity that instantiates the app's objects.

4. Provide a way to restart and end the game.

Most game programs follow the same recipe: The game must gather input from the user, process the input and any other data, and render objects onscreen. Usually, the program creates event handlers that listen for user input via the mouse, keyboard, or other input device and a **game loop** that manages data processing and rendering the display. After a game loop is started, it continues until it encounters some end condition.

Java provides some classes that make programming simple games easy. In this example, you use the Java `Timer` class to give the game loop a custom implementation of a Java `TimerTask`. You also create a custom canvas to handle all drawing onscreen.

HOW-TO 5-3

1. Start by creating a new Android project, naming it **DotSmasher**, clicking **Android 2.2** as the SDK target (because you don't need the newest Android features for this project), and clicking **Finish**.

2. In Package Explorer, click to expand the **res** node and then the **layout** node, and then double-click **main.xml** to open it. Click the **Graphical Layout** tab, and then click the **Hello World** label. Delete it by right-clicking it and clicking **Delete** (or pressing the Delete or Backspace key). This project handles drawing the score on the game screen, so you don't need the label. Save the **main.xml** file.

3. Right-click the **dotsmasher** package, point to **New**, and click **Class**. In the New Java Class dialog box, name the class **DotSmasherCanvas**.

4. Studio can help you extend a superclass and implement interfaces. Click the **Browse** button next to the Superclass text box to open the Superclass Selection dialog box. In the Choose a type text box, type **View**. Then click **View - android.view** in the Matching items list box, and click **OK**.

5. Click the **Add** button next to the Interfaces section to open the Implemented Interfaces Selection dialog box. In the Choose interfaces text box, type **OnTou** to start the interface name you want, and Studio tries to match it to existing interfaces that apply to the `View` class. Click **OnTouchListener** (see Figure 5-21), and then click **OK**.

The `OnTouchListener` interface does exactly what you think it does: It listens for touches. By using this interface, the `DotSmasherCanvas` class can provide event handlers for when users touch the canvas.

(continues)

(continued)

Figure 5-21 Selecting interfaces to implement

6. In the New Java Class dialog box, under "Which method stubs would you like to create?" click to select the **Inherited abstract methods** and **Constructors from superclass** check boxes, if necessary, to make sure methods that need to be implemented are included. The IDE generates the DotSmasherCanvas class and provides the extends and implements clauses in the declaration. In addition, it places required method stubs in the code. Less work for you is definitely better! The New Java Class dialog box should look like Figure 5-22. Click **Finish** to create the DotSmasherCanvas class.

(continues)

(continued)

Figure 5-22   The `DotSmasherCanvas` class

7. The `DotSmasherCanvas` class is responsible for drawing the dot onscreen, moving it around randomly, detecting whether the user hit the dot, and keeping score. To begin, add instance variables for the dot location and score inside the class declaration:

```
public class DotSmasherCanvas extends View implements OnTouchListener{
int dotX, dotY, score;
```

8. Next, you need getter and setter methods for these variables. Instead of typing all that code, right-click the preceding code line, point to **Source**, and click **Generate Getters and Setters**. In the dialog box that opens, click all three check boxes at the top (see Figure 5-23), and then click **OK**.

(continues)

(continued)

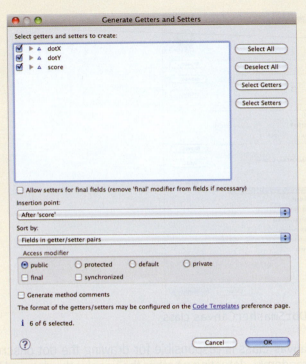

Figure 5-23 Generating getter and setter methods

The IDE inserts the following code for you:

```
public int getDotX(){
    return dotX;
}
public void setDotX(int dotX){
    this.dotX = dotX;
}
public int getDotY(){
    return dotY;
}
public void setDotY(int dotY){
    this.dotY = dotY;
}
public int getScore(){
    return score;
}
public void setScore(int score){
    this.score = score;
}
```

(continues)

(continued)

9. Because `DotSmasherCanvas` is responsible for moving the dot onscreen, you need a method to move the dot. Enter the following code for adding the `moveDot()` method to the `DotSmasherCanvas` class after the code the IDE just generated:

```
protected void moveDot(){
// create two random numbers
// assign random numbers to dotX, dotY
   Random generator = new Random();
   generator.setSeed(System.currentTimeMillis());
   int w = getWidth()-20; // to avoid covering score
   int h = getHeight()-40; // to avoid covering score
   float f = generator.nextFloat();
   dotX = (int)(f*w)%w;
   f = generator.nextFloat();
   dotY = (int)(f*h)%h;
}
```

10. When you type the code that uses the `Random` class, you might see an error message to the left. The problem is that the compiler doesn't know anything about the `Random` class, so you need to import this class before using it in your code. As shown in Figure 5-24, click the error icon and click **Import 'Random' (java.util)** to get Studio to insert the code for you. Again, less work is good.

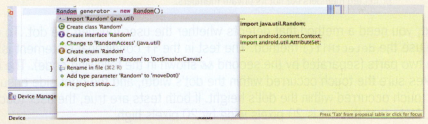

Figure 5-24 Using the IDE to import the `Random` class

Letting the IDE write as much code as possible is always a good idea. Your code will contain far fewer errors than if you typed it yourself.

There's nothing complicated about the `moveDot()` method. It doesn't actually move a dot onscreen. Instead, it creates a `Random` object and sets the seed to the current system time. Then the canvas width and height are stored in `w` and `h`. A few pixels are

(continues)

(continued)

subtracted from both values so that when the dot is drawn, it's guaranteed to be on the canvas, not covering the score.

The **Random** class doesn't create truly random numbers. Instead, it creates a floating-point decimal number between 0 and 1 based on the seed, using a complex algorithm. If you use the same seed, you get the same number. The convention is to use the current system time to get different numbers because this time is always changing.

moveDot() then asks for the next floating-point value from the Random object. The nextFloat() method returns a decimal number between 0 and 1. That number is then multiplied by the available width, and the decimal part is truncated by using the modulus (%) operator. The result is cast to an int and assigned to the dotX variable. The same process is followed with the dotY variable for the available height.

You might have noticed the **protected** keyword in the moveDot() method. You've already seen the **public** and **private** keywords used in Java code examples. Public data members are available to all classes in a program, and private data members are available only from within the current class. **Protected data members** are available to classes in the same package and to all subclasses. They enable you to access certain parts of code from subclasses without making that code available to classes outside the package. Subclasses can access the superclass's public and protected members but not its private members.

Next, you need a method that detects whether the user touched the dot. To do this, you use the detectHit() method. The test in the if conditional statement is divided into two parts (separated by the second && shown in the following code). The left side makes sure the touch occurred within the dot's width, and the right side ensures that the touch occurred within the dot's height. If both tests are true, the user touched the dot. Note that the dot is 20 pixels wide by 20 pixels high.

11. Enter the following code after moveDot() to add the detectHit() method:

```
protected boolean detectHit(int x, int y){
if((x>=dotX && x<=dotX+20) && (y>=dotY && y<=dotY+20)){
// You have a hit
  return true;
  }
  return false;
}
```

(continues)

(*continued*)

12. Next, you override the `onDraw()` method. When you do this, your code determines how the component is drawn onscreen. The `onDraw()` method is called every time the component is drawn onscreen. First, however, add the following line of code to the `import` section of the class to prevent any errors:

```
import android.graphics.*;
```

13. Then add the `onDraw()` method to the class definition:

```
protected void onDraw(Canvas canvas){
    canvas.drawColor(Color.BLACK);
    Paint dotPaint = new Paint();
    dotPaint.setColor(Color.RED);
    canvas.drawRect(dotX,dotY,dotX + 20,dotY + 20,dotPaint);
    canvas.drawText("Score: " + score,20,20,dotPaint);
}
```

 Overriding methods is a common practice in object-oriented programming. A method is overridden when a subclass gives a method the same signature, which hides the method used in the superclass. When the method is called, the OS finds the method in the subclass and ignores the implementation in the superclass. Method overriding enables you to supply custom methods in subclasses.

 A method signature includes the method name and its parameter list.

The `onDraw()` method first fills the background of the `DotSmasherCanvas`'s internal canvas with black. The `canvas` parameter is created for you. Next, a `Paint` object is created to do the painting on the canvas. Red is used to paint the dot and score, but you can use any color you like (except black, obviously). Then the dot and score are drawn on the canvas. The `drawRect()` method takes parameters as follows: `left`, `top`, `right`, `bottom`, `Paint` object. So the rectangle is determined by the parameters and drawn by the `Paint` object. The width and height are 20 pixels—the same number used by `detectHit()`.

14. Next, you need to modify the `onTouch()` method, which is called when the user touches the `DotSmasherCanvas` object onscreen. Modify this method as follows (adding the code shown in bold):

```
public boolean onTouch(View v, MotionEvent event){
    if(detectHit((int)event.getX(),(int)event.getY())){
```

(continued)

```
        score += 1;
        invalidate();
    }
    return false;
}
```

The preceding code increases the score whenever a hit is detected. The `invalidate()` method causes the component to be redrawn. When this happens, the system looks for an `onDraw()` method. Because the `onDraw()` method has been overridden, your custom drawing routine is called.

15. The only task left is modifying the constructor you use when creating the `DotSmasherCanvas` class from the `MainActivity`. When the component is created, place the dot randomly and register the touch listener so that the component can react to touch events. Modify the constructor that expects a `Context` object as follows:

```
public DotSmasherCanvas(Context context){
    super(context);
    moveDot();
    setOnTouchListener(this);
}
```

Now you can start work on the game loop, which is responsible for moving the dot around onscreen, detecting hits, and updating the score. First, you create a subclass of the Java `TimerTask` class that includes calls to the methods you want to call repeatedly in the `DotSmasherCanvas` class. Then you create a `Timer` object and schedule calls in `TimerTask` to be made repeatedly in the `MainActivity`.

16. To create a new class for `TimerTask`, right-click the **dotsmasher** package, point to **New**, and click **Class**. Name the class **DotSmasherTimerTask**.

17. Click the **Browse** button next to the Superclass text box. In the Choose a type text box, type **TimerTask**. Studio finds `java.util.TimerTask`. In the Matching items list box, click **TimerTask**, and click **OK**.

18. Under "Which method stubs would you like to create?" make sure the **Inherited abstract methods** check box is selected, and then click **Finish** to create the class.

`TimerTask` is an abstract class with one abstract method, `run()`, that you're required to implement. You need a reference to a `DotSmasherCanvas` object as an instance variable and in the constructor. Later, you create a `DotSmasherTimerTask` object by passing it a reference to the `DotSmasherCanvas` used in the app. Including this reference allows you to call the methods specified in `DotSmasherCanvas` that need to be called repeatedly in the `run()` method. Moving the dot and redrawing the screen

(continues)

(continued)

are all that need to be repeated. `DotSmasherCanvas` handles updating the score, drawing the dot, and listening for touches.

19. Modify the `DotSmasherTimerTask` class as follows:

```
package com.dotsmasher;
import java.util.TimerTask;
import com.dotsmasher.DotSmasherCanvas;

public class DotSmasherTimerTask extends TimerTask{
  DotSmasherCanvas canvas;
  public DotSmasherTimerTask(DotSmasherCanvas canvas){
    this.canvas = canvas;
  }
  @Override
  public void run(){
    canvas.moveDot();
    canvas.postInvalidate();
  }
}
```

Later, you create a `Timer` object in `MainActivity` and associate it with a `DotSmasherTimerTask`. `Timer` objects can schedule tasks specified in `TimerTask` objects repeatedly. `Timer` objects carry out code specified in the `run()` method of `TimerTask` objects.

 Why call `postInvalidate()` in the preceding code instead of just `invalidate()`? The answer is that you use `postInvalidate()` when you make the call from a separate thread. Because the `TimerTask`'s `run()` method is called on its own thread, you need to call `postInvalidate()` instead of `invalidate()`, as you did in `DotSmasherCanvas`.

20. It's finally time to implement the `MainActivity` class. The good news is that most of the heavy lifting is done in the `DotSmasherCanvas` class. In Package Explorer, double-click **MainActivity.java** to open it in the Editing view. First, you need to import the `Timer` class and the view package. To do this manually, add the following code to the `import` section:

```
import java.util.Timer;
import android.view.*;
```

21. Then add the instance variables for the class after the class declaration:

```
private Timer timer;
private DotSmasherCanvas canvas;
private DotSmasherTimerTask task;
```

(*continued*)

MainActivity.java is responsible for creating the objects the app needs and getting them started. Because MainActivity.java extends the Activity class, it has the life cycle methods you learned in Chapter 2—specifically, that the onCreate() method is called when the app is started. You're going to override onCreate() to create startup behavior in your app.

22. Modify the onCreate() method as follows:

```
/** Called when the activity is first created. */
@Override
public void onCreate(Bundle savedInstanceState){
   super.onCreate(savedInstanceState);
// setContentView(R.layout.main);
   setTitle("DotSmasher");
   canvas = new DotSmasherCanvas(getBaseContext());
   timer = new Timer();
   task = new DotSmasherTimerTask(canvas);
   timer.schedule(task, 0, 1500);
   setContentView(canvas);
}
```

This onCreate() method first calls the onCreate() method in the superclass. Doing so is always a good idea because the superclass might provide some initialization your Activity class needs. The next line is commented by adding two forward slashes (//) at the beginning; it's the line used to inflate the UI. You're not inflating the UI from the resource file, so this code line isn't necessary.

Next, the title is set for the app, and then objects for the app are instantiated. First, a DotSmasherCanvas object is created for the app. Next, a new Timer object is instantiated. Then a new DotSmasherTimerTask object is created, and a reference to the DotSmasherCanvas created previously is passed to it.

After the DotSmasherTimerTask object is created, you can pass it to the Timer object's schedule() method. The parameters for this method are a TimerTask object, a delay value, and a timeout value. The delay specifies how long, in milliseconds, to wait before calling the run() method in TimerTask, and the timeout specifies how often, in milliseconds, to call the run() method in TimerTask. So the call to schedule() makes the call to the run() method immediately and then every 1.5 seconds. This is how the game loop operates. Finally, the DotSmasherCanvas object is set as the app's content view.

(*continues*)

136

(continued)

A Context object is an interface to an app's environment. The Android OS creates it to give you access to app resources and classes.

23. To test your app, run it in the emulator. Right-click your project, point to **Run As**, and click **Android Application using MOTODEV Studio for Android**. Click **OK** in the Save Resources message box. If prompted to select a video device, click **OK** to continue. The emulator should start and run your app (see Figure 5-25).

You should be able to click the dot to simulate touches. If the dot is moving too quickly for you, increase the timeout specified in the Timer's schedule() method. You might need to experiment with the value to make the dot move slowly enough for you to touch but keep the game playable. Start by increasing the timeout to 3000 and adjust it from there.

Figure 5-25 DotSmasher running in the emulator

The DotSmasher app still has some problems; the most glaring is that there's no way to stop the game short of killing the emulator. To fix this problem, you add a menu item to exit the game and another to start a new game.

All Android phones include a menu button. In the emulator, it's labeled "MENU." Items for a context menu are generated dynamically, meaning they aren't instantiated until the menu button is pressed. You can design a context menu in XML and then inflate it when it's needed.

(continues)

(continued)

138

24. Right-click the **res** folder in your project, point to **New**, and click **Folder** to open the New Folder dialog box. In the Folder name text box, type **menu**, and then click **Finish**.

25. Then right-click the **menu** folder, point to **New**, and click **Android XML File**. In the File text box, type **game_menu.xml**. Make sure the **menu** option button is selected for the type of resource configuration (see Figure 5-26), and then click **Finish**.

Figure 5-26   The New Android XML File dialog box

26. Double-click the **game_menu.xml** file in Package Explorer to open it in the Graphical Layout view. Click the **Add** button, and then double-click **Item**. Studio adds the item to the list of menu elements. Click **item1**, and in the Attributes pane of the Graphical Layout view, set the Title attribute to **New Game** and the Title condensed attribute to **New**. Click the **Add** button again, and follow the same procedure to create a second menu item named item2. Click **item2**, and set the Title attribute to **Exit Game** and the Title condensed attribute to **Exit**.

(continues)

(continued)

27. To see the XML that's generated, click **game_menu.xml** in the lower-left corner of the Editing view. You should see the following code:

```xml
<?xml version="1.0" encoding="utf-8"?>
<menu xmlns:android="http://schemas.android.com/apk/res/android">
  <item android:id="@+id/item1" android:titleCondensed="New"
 android:title="New Game"></item>
  <item android:id="@+id/item2" android:titleCondensed="Exit"
 android:title="Exit Game"></item>
</menu>
```

Of course, you could have generated this code manually, but you'd have to know all the namespace and attribute information. Using the IDE is much easier.

28. Each time the user presses the menu button, the `onCreateOptionsMenu()` method is called, but you can override this method and provide your own behavior. To do this, add the following code to the `MainActivity` class in the `MainActivity.java` file:

```java
@Override
public boolean onCreateOptionsMenu(Menu menu){
  MenuInflater inflater = getMenuInflater();
  inflater.inflate(R.menu.game_menu, menu);
  return true;
}
```

In this code, the game menu is inflated from the file stored in the res folder and displayed to the user.

29. To actually make the menu items useful, you need to override and implement the `onOptionsItemSelected()` method, which is called each time the user touches a menu item. Add the following code to the `MainActivity` class:

```java
@Override
public boolean onOptionsItemSelected(MenuItem item){
// Handle item selection
switch (item.getItemId()){
  case R.id.item1:
    newGame();
    return true;
  case R.id.item2:
    quit();
    return true;
  default:
    return super.onOptionsItemSelected(item);
  }
}
```

(continues)

(continued)

140

The Java `switch` mechanism is a shorthand way to create `if/else` statements. The preceding code tests the `id` property of the `MenuItem` that was clicked. If this property matches the `id` property of the New Game button, `newGame()` is called. If it matches the `id` property of the Exit button, `quit()` is called. If there's no match, the call is passed to the superclass.

In Android SDK 4.0 (Ice Cream Sandwich), `switch` statements in library projects no longer compile. They must be converted to `if-else` statements. For more information, see *http://tools.android.com/tips/non-constant-fields*.

30. To include the `newGame()` and `quit()` methods, add the following code to `MainActivity`, inside the class definition:

```
void newGame(){
    canvas.setScore(0);
}

void quit(){
    timer.cancel();
    task = null;
    timer = null;
    canvas = null;
    finish();
}
```

Notice that all objects in the app are set to null before calling `finish()`. Doing so is best for memory management because it tags objects for garbage collection.

Figure 5-27   The DotSmasher menu items

31. Run your app in the emulator. When you click the menu icon, both menus should be displayed, as shown in Figure 5-27.

Clicking the New button simply resets the score to 0. Clicking the Exit button terminates the app and returns the user to the Home screen.

Detective Work

1. Implement a start/stop mechanism for the app. (*Hint*: The `Timer` class includes a `cancel()` method.)

2. Force the game to end after 30 seconds, and inform the user that the game has ended.

3. Devise a way for users to select a difficulty level. You might want to give them the options Easy, Medium, and Hard. You need to determine what defines the level of difficulty. You might increase the speed at which the dot moves, make the dot smaller, and so forth.

Packaging and Deploying Apps in MOTODEV Studio

The Android OS requires that the developer sign apps digitally before users install them. The good news is that no certification authority is necessary, and the process doesn't cost anything. Typically, developers self-sign their apps, and MOTODEV Studio makes this step easy with the Export Wizard.

HOW-TO 5-4

1. To sign your app, click **File**, **Export** from the menu. Click to expand the **Android** node, click **Export Android Application using MOTODEV Studio for Android**, and click **Next** to move to the Export Android Package Files window.

2. Because it's your first signed application in Studio, click the **Sign the package** check box, and then click the **Create new self-signed certificate** link. Fill in the necessary information, using Figure 5-28 as an example, and then click **Finish**. Make sure you use your own information, not what's shown in the figure.

(continues)

141

(*continued*)

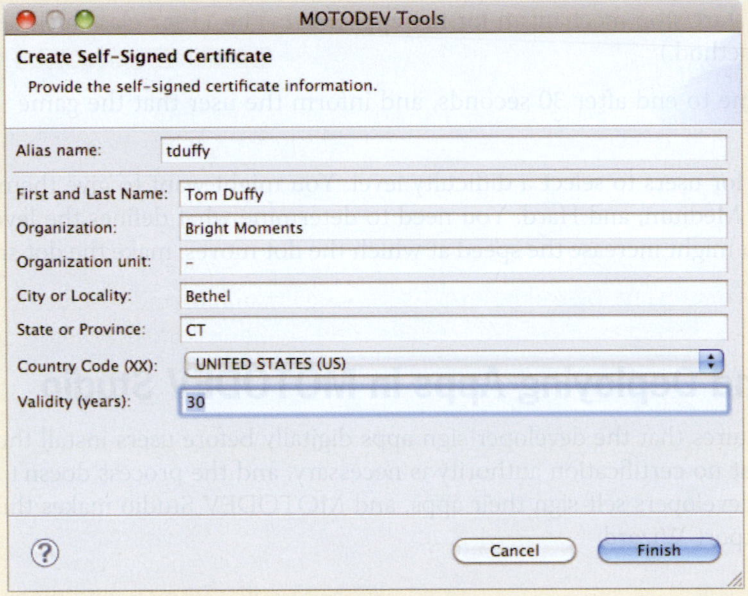

Figure 5-28   Creating a self-signed certificate

Studio creates your certificate, signs your app, and creates the Android Package (.apk) file that you distribute to your users. This file is created in a bin folder, which is in the destination folder specified in the Export Wizard.

Deploying your app couldn't be simpler. Just post the .apk file created by the Export Wizard to a Web site. Users can then download the file to their devices and install your app. As you learned in Chapter 4, apps not sold through the Android Market must have the unknown sources option selected on the user's device. This setting allows an app from anywhere to be installed on the device.

Deploying to the Android Market is easy, too. To sell a signed app on the Market, just follow these steps before uploading an app:

1. Sign up for the Android Market at *http://market.android.com/publish/signup*.

2. Create a developer profile.

3. Pay a $25 registration fee with a credit card, using Google Checkout.

4. Agree to the Android Market developer distribution agreement.

Advanced Android Apps: Where's My Phone?

This version of Where's My Phone mimics the App Inventor version. It shows you how to send and receive text messages, how to get a phone's location by using the Location API, and how to play sounds. In addition, it teaches you how to store and retrieve preferences for an app by using a password mechanism.

To refresh your memory, Where's My Phone? is a handy little app for users to run when they misplace their phones. Usually, they can find someone to send a text message to their phones. In this version of the app, the user needs to enter a password twice and then touch Start to store the password in the app's preferences and dismiss the UI so that the app runs in the background from the start. Like the Where's My Phone? app in Chapter 4, after the app is started, it listens for incoming text messages. When a message matching the specified phrase is received, location data is sent back to the message sender, and a sound is played.

HOW-TO 5-5

1. Start by creating a new Android project, and name it **WheresMyPhone**. In the Application name text box, type **Where\'s My Phone**, and then click **Finish**.

The application name is the text displayed on the device under the icon. Setting an application name that's tailored to your app enhances its professional look.

Notice the slash (\) character in "Where\'s My Phone." It's used as an escape character so that reserved characters, such as apostrophes, can be embedded in a `String` object.

2. After Studio creates the project, click to expand the **res** and **layout** nodes in Package Explorer, and then double-click the **main.xml** file to open it. The user interface for this project asks the user to set the password for the app. Using what you've learned previously, drag two **TextView** components, two **EditText** components, and a **Button** component to the screen so that it looks like Figure 5-29.

(continues)

144

(continued)

Figure 5-29   The Where's My Phone UI

3. It's time to write some code. Double-click **MainActivity.java** to open it in the Editing view. Start by importing the classes needed for the app:

```
import android.app.Activity;
import android.os.Bundle;
import android.content.SharedPreferences.Editor;
import android.view.*;
import android.view.View.OnClickListener;
import android.widget.*;
```

(continues)

(continued)

4. Add the following instance variables after the class declaration for the components you're accessing in code:

```
private Button start;
private EditText pword;
private EditText confirm;
```

5. In the `onCreate()` method, instantiate the objects by adding the following code:

```
start = (Button)findViewById(R.id.button1);
pword = (EditText)findViewById(R.id.editText1);
confirm = (EditText)findViewById(R.id.editText2);
```

6. Then add an `implements` clause to the class definition to listen for button clicks:

```
public class MainActivity extends Activity implements OnClickListener{
```

7. Adding the preceding line of code generates an error on the class declaration line. To eliminate the error, you need to implement the `onClick()` method of the `OnClickListener` interface as follows:

```
@Override
public void onClick(View v){
  String pass = pword.getText().toString();
  String conf = confirm.getText().toString();
// Check that user typed a password
  if(pass.length()==0){
    Toast.makeText(this, "Please enter a password", ↵
  Toast.LENGTH_SHORT).show();
    pword.requestFocus();
    return;
  }
// Make sure two fields match
  if(pass.equals(conf)){
// Fields match, store password in shared preferences
    Editor passwdfile = getSharedPreferences("passwd", 0).edit();
    passwdfile.putString("passwd",pass);
    passwdfile.commit();
    finish();

  }else{  // password mismatch - start over
    Toast.makeText(this, "Passwords must match", ↵
  Toast.LENGTH_SHORT).show();
    pword.setText("");
    confirm.setText("");
    pword.requestFocus();
    return;
  }
}
```

(continues)

(continued)

In the `onClick()` method, the first `if` condition checks for a 0-length string in the first edit field. If no password is entered, an alert is displayed and the user must start over, forcing him or her to enter a password. The `else` clause at the end is called when the passwords don't match. It notifies the user and resets the UI.

The interesting part is in the second `if` condition. If the passwords match, the value is stored in a key/value pair named `passwd` in the app's shared preferences. That way, it can be retrieved later to make sure that the findme message includes the password. The `finish()` method terminates the activity.

A `SharedPreferences` object is a mechanism for storing an app's primitive data. In Java, the primitive data types are `int`, `float`, `double`, `long`, `boolean`, and `String`. (Technically speaking, `String`s are objects, but they get preferential treatment in Java and can be treated as primitives.) The data is stored in key/value pairs. You use an editor to create and modify the data, and then call `commit()` to save it. The `getSharedPreferences()` method takes two arguments: the `SharedPreferences` object and a mode. The default value for the mode is 0, which equates to "private." To retrieve data, use getter methods based on data types, such as `getInt()` and `getString()`.

8. The only thing left to do in `MainActivity` is to register the button with the listener. Add the following line to the end of the `onCreate()` method:

    ```
    start.setOnClickListener(this);
    ```

9. To test your program logic in the emulator, right-click your project in Package Explorer, point to **Run As**, and click **Android Application using MOTODEV Studio**. Click **OK** in the Save Resources message box to save your changes. At this point, not much is going on, but the button clears the activity from the screen.

It's time to write the code that actually performs the app's actions. You need to create an object that listens for text messages, decides whether they're findme messages, and then reacts to them by sending the phone's location back to the sender. This is a perfect task for a Broadcast Receiver, which responds to systemwide broadcasts, such as the battery running low or a text message arriving. Broadcast Receivers have a limited life cycle; they're valid only within the scope of the `onReceive()` method. When the broadcast they're waiting for occurs, the OS calls `onReceive()`. When this method returns, the receiver is terminated. For this app, the Broadcast Receiver waits for findme messages and reacts to them in the `onReceive()` method.

An advantage of developing Android apps is that you have access to all the functions built into the platform. For example, you can send and receive text messages

(continued)

via program code without user intervention. Being able to do so is a double-edged sword, however, because developers could easily create malicious apps. To address this potential problem, Android uses an extensive permission mechanism. In essence, users must grant permission for your app to access system resources.

10. In Package Explorer, right-click the **wheresmyphone** package, point to **New**, and click **Android Broadcast Receiver**. In the New Android Broadcast Receiver Wizard, click the **Choose** button in the Permission section. Scroll down, click the **SEND_SMS** permission (see Figure 5-30), and click **OK**.

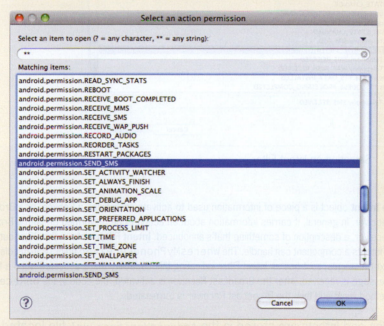

Figure 5-30 Adding permission for sending text (SMS) messages

11. To add the permission for receiving text messages to the Broadcast Receiver, click **Choose** again in the Permission section, click the **RECEIVE_SMS** permission, and then click **OK**.

12. In the Intent Filter section, click the **Choose** button next to the Action list box, scroll down, click the **SMS_RECEIVED** action (see Figure 5-31), and then click **OK**.

(continues)

(continued)

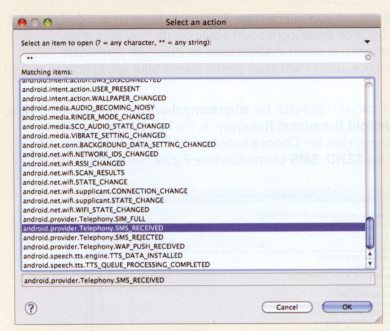

Figure 5-31   Selecting an Intent Filter

 An **Intent** object is a piece of information used to activate an Activity, a Service, or a Broadcast Receiver. In general, it carries information about an action to be performed or, with a Broadcast Receiver, a description of something that's announced. **Intent Filters** inform the OS about the kinds of Intents a component can handle. The `WheresMyPhoneReceiver` object can handle incoming text messages, so it has an Intent Filter indicating this capability that's activated when a text message is received. After the Broadcast Receiver is activated, the code in the `onReceive()` method runs, and then the Broadcast Receiver is terminated.

Permissions and Intents are stored in the `AndroidManifest.xml` file located in the root of every Android app. This specially structured XML file tells the OS how to run and interact with your app. Using the IDE means you don't usually have to deal with the manifest file.

13.   Finally, name the Broadcast Receiver **WheresMyPhoneReceiver** (see Figure 5-32), and then click **Finish**.

(continues)

(continued)

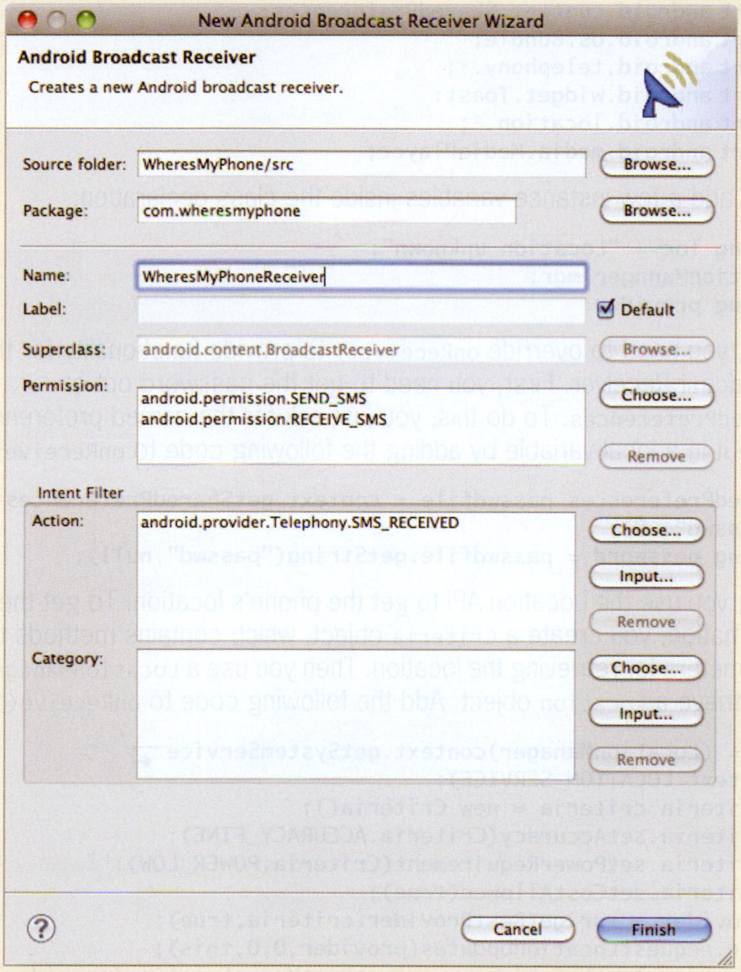

Figure 5-32   The New Android Broadcast Receiver Wizard

14. After the Broadcast Receiver is created, it opens in the Editing view automatically. If it doesn't, double-click **WheresMyPhoneReceiver.java** to open it. First, add the necessary statements to the `import` section:

```
import android.content.BroadcastReceiver;
import android.content.Intent;
import android.content.Context;
```

(continues)

(continued)

```
import android.content.SharedPreferences;
import android.os.Bundle;
import android.telephony.*;
import android.widget.Toast;
import android.location.*;
import android.media.MediaPlayer;
```

15. Then add a few instance variables inside the class declaration:

```
String loc = "Location unknown";
LocationManager mgr;
String provider;
```

16. Next, you need to override `onReceive()` to provide functionality for the Broadcast Receiver. First, you need to get the password out of `SharedPreferences`. To do this, you just ask for the named preference and store it in a local variable by adding the following code to `onReceive()`:

```
SharedPreferences passwdfile = context.getSharedPreferences↵
("passwd", 0);
String password = passwdfile.getString("passwd",null);
```

17. Next, you use the Location API to get the phone's location. To get the location information, you create a `Criteria` object, which contains methods to set parameters for retrieving the location. Then you use a `LocationManager` object to retrieve a `Location` object. Add the following code to `onReceive()`:

```
mgr = (LocationManager)context.getSystemService↵
(Context.LOCATION_SERVICE);
    Criteria criteria = new Criteria();
    criteria.setAccuracy(Criteria.ACCURACY_FINE);
    criteria.setPowerRequirement(Criteria.POWER_LOW);
    criteria.setCostAllowed(true);
    provider = mgr.getBestProvider(criteria,true);
    mgr.requestLocationUpdates(provider,0,0,this);
    Location lastLocation = mgr.getLastKnownLocation(provider);
    if(lastLocation!=null)
        loc = "Findme Latitude: " + lastLocation.getLatitude() +↵
    "Longitude: " + lastLocation.getLongitude();
```

18. Because of the error icon shown on the `requestLocationUpdates()` call, you need to implement the `LocationListener` interface. This interface provides a means for the Broadcast Receiver to register for changes in location. Add the `implements` clause to the class declaration, as shown:

```
public class WheresMyPhoneReceiver extends BroadcastReceiver↵
    implements LocationListener
```

(continues)

(continued)

19. Next, you need to implement the methods declared in the `LocationListener` interface. To do this, click the error icon and click **Add unimplemented methods**. You must include all the methods in the `LocationListener` interface, but you override only one of the methods: `onLocationChanged()`. You can leave the others as is because they don't add any functionality to the app.

20. Modify the `onLocationChanged()` method as follows:

```
@Override
public void onLocationChanged(Location location){
// Get location and store in loc
if(location == null){
  location = mgr.getLastKnownLocation(provider);
}
loc = "Findme Latitude: " + location.getLatitude() + "\nLongitude: "↵
 + location.getLongitude();
}
```

The `onLocationChanged()` method fires every time the phone's location changes. All it does is rebuild the display string.

21. To use the Location API, you need to declare a permission in the `AndroidManifest.xml` file. You could have done that when creating the class, but then you wouldn't have learned this method. Double-click the **AndroidManifest.xml** file, and then click the **Permissions** tab at the bottom (see Figure 5-33). You should see the permissions you set earlier.

(continues)

(*continued*)

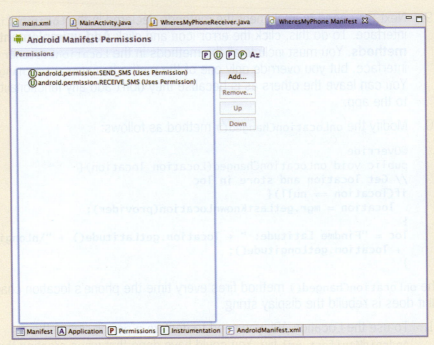

Figure 5-33 The Permissions tab for the `AndroidManifest.xml` file

22. Click the **Add** button. In the dialog box that opens, click **Uses Permission** in the list box (see Figure 5-34), and then click **OK**.

Figure 5-34 Adding a permission

(*continues*)

(continued)

23. In the text box at the top, type **android.permission.ACCESS_FINE_LOCATION**, and then click **OK**, if necessary, to add the permission to the list (see Figure 5-35).

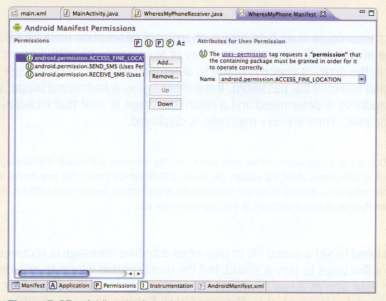

Figure 5-35 Adding the Location permission

You can view the XML code to verify that the permission was added:

```
<uses-permission
android:name="android.permission.ACCESS_FINE_LOCATION">
</uses-permission>
```

24. It's time to receive the text message and do something with it. Add the following to the end of the `onReceive()` method:

```
// Get the messages - PDU = protocol description unit
Bundle bundle = intent.getExtras();
Object[] pdusObj = (Object[]) bundle.get("pdus");
SmsMessage[] messages = new SmsMessage[pdusObj.length];
for (int i = 0; i<pdusObj.length; i++) {
  messages[i] = SmsMessage.createFromPdu ((byte[])pdusObj[i]);
}
for (SmsMessage msg : messages){
// Make sure it's a findme message
if (msg.getMessageBody().contains("findme:" + password)){
  String to = msg.getOriginatingAddress();
```

(continued)

```
    SmsManager sm = SmsManager.getDefault();
    sm.sendTextMessage(to, null, loc, null, null);
    Toast.makeText(context,"Location sent to: " + to + " using
  provider: " + provider, Toast.LENGTH_LONG).show();
    }
  }
```

SMS messages come in as byte arrays of protocol description units (PDUs), and these byte arrays are converted to an array of SmsMessage objects. For each message in the array, a check is made to determine whether the message is "findme" and includes the password. If the message is a findme message, the sender's address is determined and a return message is sent that includes the phone's location. Then a Toast message is displayed.

PDUs are an encapsulation of the data sent in an SMS message and include the message itself as well as information about the sender, the sender's SMS service center, the timestamp, and more. This metadata is passed along with the message in the form of hexadecimal numbers. The SmsMessage object decodes all this information for you.

25. You need to set a sound file to play when a findme message is received. There are a few ways to play a sound, but the most reliable way is to include the file with your app as a raw resource. To do this, right-click the **res** folder in the Package Explorer, point to **New**, and click **Folder**. Name the folder **raw**, and click **Finish**.

26. Next, copy the **keys1.mp3** file used in the Chapter 4 App Inventor project to the raw folder by using the file system (in Explorer or Finder, depending on the OS you're using). Navigate to the **~workspace/WheresMyPhone/res/raw** folder and drop the file there. (You can also get the file at *www.bright-moments.com/keys1.mp3*.)

27. After dropping the file, you still need to create a reference to the file in your project. Right-click the **raw** folder, point to **New**, and click **Other**. Then click to expand the **General** node, click **File** (see Figure 5-36), and then click **Next**.

(continues)

(continued)

Figure 5-36 Adding a file to your project

28. Click the **Advanced** button, click the **Link to file in the file system** check box, and then click the **Browse** button. Find and click the **keys1.mp3** file (see Figure 5-37), and then click **Finish**.

(continues)

(*continued*)

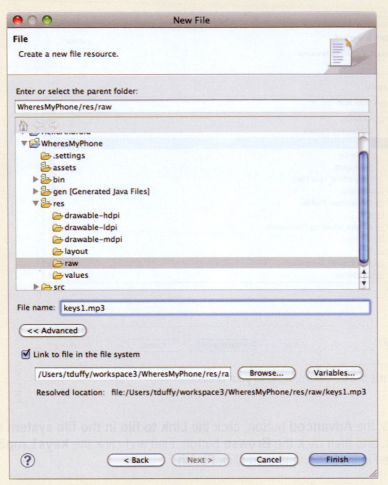

Figure 5-37   Adding the sound file `keys1.mp3`

29.   Then add the following code under the call to `Toast.makeText()`:

```
MediaPlayer mp = MediaPlayer.create(context, R.raw.keys1);
mp.start();
```

Now you can inflate the sound file from the resources. That's far easier than trying to track down the file in the file system.

30.   It's time to test your app. In Package Explorer, right-click the project, point to **Run As**, and click **Android Application using MOTODEV Studio for Android**. The emulator should start. Type the password once and again to confirm (see Figure 5-38), and then click **Start**.

(*continues*)

(continued)

31. Click the **Emulator Control** tab. Scroll down to the Location Controls section, enter some data (see Figure 5-39), and then click **Send**. This step fixes the emulator's location.

Figure 5-38 Where's My Phone running in the emulator

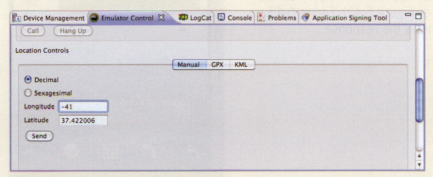

Figure 5-39 Setting the emulator's location

(continues)

(continued)

32. Scroll to the Telephony Actions section, and send a text message to the emulator. Make sure to send the correct password after the `findme:` text. In this example, `findme:1234` was sent (see Figure 5-40).

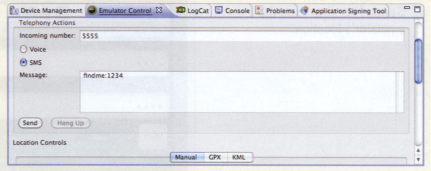

Figure 5-40   Sending the emulator a text message

The emulator then plays the sound file and shows the alert (see Figure 5-41).

33. Of course, you have no way of knowing whether the response was sent to the sender. To do that, you need to start a second emulator. For this example, start the emulator instance you used with App Inventor. Send a text message to the instance running your app from the new instance (see Figure 5-42). Figure 5-43 shows the response.

Figure 5-41   Where's My Phone showing the alert

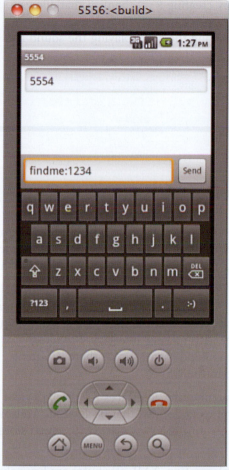

Figure 5-42   Sending a findme message to Where's My Phone from a second emulator

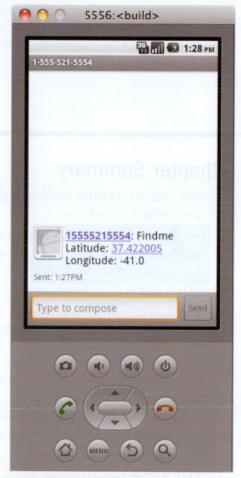

Figure 5-43   The Where's My Phone response

Notice that you never actually start the Broadcast Receiver. Instead, you actually kill the `MainActivity` of the app! So how does this work? Remember, the `AndroidManifest.xml` file registers the Broadcast Receiver and informs the OS. When users install your app, the OS starts the Broadcast Receiver and waits for findme messages, even after the `MainActivity` is terminated.

Detective Work

1.   Ensure that the user's password is at least six characters long.

2.   Sometimes users need to find their phones without a sound being played. Create a mechanism so that the phone doesn't play the sound file or display the `Toast` message.

3. Enhance the Where's My Phone app more by creating a mechanism that allows users to designate which parts of the app take place when a findme message is received. You might allow users to toggle showing the alert, playing the sound file, and sending the location.

Chapter Summary

- Motorola MOTODEV Studio is a plug-in for the IBM Eclipse IDE that's used for developing Android apps.

- In Eclipse, a workspace is a set of files on disk to help organize development projects, a workbench is an arrangement of specific windows in the IDE, a perspective is an editor that enables you to work with specific file types, and a view is a window that displays a certain aspect of a project.

- Android can activate four types of components: Activities, Services, Broadcast Receivers, and Content Providers. Activities are visual components that the user sees when running your app. Services can be thought of as activities with no user interface. Broadcast Receivers wait for things to happen outside the app and then react to them. Content Providers make certain parts of an app available to the OS.

- Android programming was developed when designing user interfaces for small devices was a code-heavy process. The Android OS developers decided that because an Android app's view is hierarchical, the natural choice for creating the view was XML, which stores and displays data hierarchically.

- XML is a tag-based language designed to store information. XML attributes are key/value pairs stored in XML elements. Android uses attributes for UI object properties.

- The `main.xml` file in the Layout folder defines an app's UI. UI components are declared hierarchically in this file.

- You subclass the `View` class (the superclass for all UI components) to create UI components.

- Inflating the UI is the process of instantiating objects designed in the Graphical Layout view.

- Java follows a single-inheritance model and uses interfaces to simulate multiple inheritance. Java classes can inherit only from a single class, but they can use multiple interfaces. You must implement all methods declared in the interface you're creating.

- Eclipse includes many helpful features, such as code folding, multiple views, code generation, and code completion.

- Studio can help you extend a superclass and implement interfaces in the New Java Class dialog box.

- Overriding methods is a common practice in object-oriented programming; a method in a subclass hides a method with the same signature in a superclass.

- Menu items are instantiated dynamically. They don't exist until the corresponding button is pressed. You can design a menu in XML and then inflate it when it's needed.

- The Android OS requires that developers sign all applications digitally before users install them.

- `AndroidManifest.xml` is a specially structured XML file that tells the OS how to run and interact with your app.

- Android makes use of an extensive permission mechanism. Users must grant permission for your app to access system resources.

- An Android Intent is a piece of information used to activate an Activity, a Service, or a Broadcast Receiver. Intent Filters inform the system about the kinds of Intents a component can handle.

- Override the `onReceive()` method to provide functionality for Broadcast Receivers.

Key Terms

attributes—Key/value pairs stored in XML elements.

code folding—An IDE feature used to show or hide blocks of code with a click.

Extensible Markup Language (XML)—A tag-based language designed to store information.

game loop—Code that manages data processing and rendering the display in a game app.

inflating—The process of instantiating objects created in the form designer.

Intent—A piece of information used to activate an Activity, Service, or Broadcast Receiver in an Android app.

Intent Filters—Objects that inform the system about the kinds of Intents a component can handle. *See also* Intent.

MOTODEV Studio—The Motorola IDE for developing Android apps.

perspective—An editor in Eclipse that enables you to work with specific file types.

protected data members—Data members available to classes in the same package and to all subclasses.

refactoring—The process of rewriting code to make it better without changing its behavior.

view—A window in Eclipse that displays a certain aspect of a project.

workbench—An arrangement of specific windows in Eclipse.

workspace—In Eclipse, a set of files on disk used to help organize development projects.

161

Review Questions

1. MOTODEV Studio displays all project assets in which of the following?

   a. Graphical Layout view
   b. Package Explorer
   c. Properties view
   d. Outline view

2. MOTODEV Studio's form designer is called which of the following?

   a. Graphical Layout view
   b. Package Explorer
   c. Properties view
   d. Outline view

3. Which of the following is used to build user interfaces for Android apps? (Choose all that apply.)

   a. HTML
   b. Java
   c. XML
   d. Objective-C

4. Instantiating objects created in the form designer is called which of the following?

   a. Inflating
   b. Rebirthing
   c. Rebuilding
   d. All of the above

5. Which class do you use to display an alert in an Android app to users?

   a. Activity
   b. Toast
   c. Intent
   d. Filter

6. Protected data members are available to which of the following? (Choose all that apply.)

   a. All subclasses
   b. All classes in the same package
   c. All superclasses
   d. Implemented interfaces

7. Which of the following is the process of rewriting code to improve it?

   a. OOP
   b. Inheritance
   c. Polymorphism
   d. Refactoring

8. Giving a method the same signature in a subclass as in a superclass is called which of the following?

   a. Overriding
   b. Overloading
   c. Constructor
   d. Refactoring

9. A method signature contains which of the following? (Choose all that apply.)

   a. The method name

   b. The parameter list

   c. The return type

   d. The class that contains the method

10. The Java `switch` mechanism replaces which of the following?

    a. Conditional statements   c. Primitives

    b. Loops   d. Instantiation

11. A `SharedPreferences` object provides a mechanism for doing which of the following?

    a. Polling users

    b. Sharing contact information

    c. Storing and retrieving primitive data

    d. Setting the home screen for a device

12. Which of the following is true of the `AndroidManifest.xml` file? (Choose all that apply.)

    a. It's a standard file that's the same for every app.

    b. It tells the OS how to interact with your app.

    c. It includes permissions required for your app.

    d. It includes Intent Filters for your app.

13. A Broadcast Receiver:

    a. Must be started by an Activity

    b. Waits for things outside your app to happen

    c. Can be thought of as an Activity with no UI

    d. None of the above

14. Which of the following describes an Intent? (Choose all that apply.)

    a. A bundle of information

    b. A pointer to an Activity

    c. Activates Activities, Services, and Broadcast Receivers

    d. The same thing as a Service

15. Which of the following classes do you subclass for UI objects?

    a. `Activity`
    b. `BroadcastReceiver`
    c. `View`
    d. `Service`

16. Which of the following components informs the OS about what kinds of Intents it can handle?

    a. Services
    b. Activities
    c. Intent Filters
    d. Broadcast Receivers

Up for Discussion

1. Discuss the Java `protected` keyword. Do you think it's necessary? Why or why not?

2. Android has an extensive system of granting permission for functionality. Discuss how this works—or doesn't. What could happen if users weren't given a chance to grant or deny permission for certain activities?

3. Discuss overriding methods. What does it mean in terms of dynamic invocation?

4. Discuss what "inflating the UI" means. How is it done? What do you think of the process? Is it easy to figure out? Imagine doing it without an IDE. Is it still easy to do?

5. Discuss the DotSmasher app in terms of the MVC design pattern. What parts of this app correspond to the Model, View, and Controller tiers?

Programming Exercises

1. Create an Android app that displays the area and circumference for circles. Create a `Circle` class that performs the calculations, and instantiate a `Circle` object in the main activity based on a user-entered radius.

2. Create an Android app that displays the area and perimeter for rectangles. Create a `Rectangle` class that performs the calculations, and instantiate a `Rectangle` object in the main activity based on user-entered length and width values.

3. Create an Android app in MOTODEV Studio that converts temperature from degrees Fahrenheit to degrees Celsius. Ask users for the temperature in degrees Fahrenheit. Write a `TempConverter` class to perform the calculations, and instantiate a `TempConverter` object with the user input. Use the following formula for the conversion:

    $C = 5/9(F - 32)$

4. Create an Android app in MOTODEV Studio that converts temperature from degrees Celsius to degrees Fahrenheit. Ask users for the temperature in degrees

Celsius. Write a `TempConverter` class to perform the calculations, and instantiate a `TempConverter` object with the user input. Use the following formula for the conversion:

$F = 9/5 * C + 32$

5. Combine Programming Exercises 3 and 4 so that users can choose between converting Fahrenheit to Celsius and vice versa. Be sure to include the `TempConverter` class and instantiate a `TempConverter` object for each calculation.

6. Create an app that calculates payroll. Allow the user to enter the number of hours worked and an hourly wage. The wage should be "time and a half" for hours worked over 40 in a week. Display the amount to be paid to the user.

CHAPTER 6

Apple iOS

In this chapter, you learn to:

◎ Write code with Objective-C

◎ Compare Objective-C syntax and metaphors with Java syntax and metaphors

◎ Manage memory in Objective-C

◎ Describe the iOS development process

◎ Use Xcode and Interface Builder to create iOS apps

◎ Make use of delegates

◎ Use the Delegate and Model-View-Controller design patterns

◎ Run apps in the iOS simulator

In this chapter, you learn how to use Apple's development tools—Xcode and Interface Builder—to create iOS apps with Objective-C. Xcode 4 is the code editor you use, coupled with the iOS SDK, to write Objective-C code, compile it, run it in the included simulator, and debug any errors that occur. Xcode 4 now includes Interface Builder, a tool for creating user interfaces for apps. It's the only IDE available to create apps for iOS, and it runs only on Intel-based Macs with OS X 10.6.7 or later installed.

Xcode and Interface Builder are bundled with OS X on Mac computers. The version that comes on your Mac depends on the OS X version. The newest version—OS X 10.7, code-named Lion—ships with Xcode 4 with the iOS SDK 5. Xcode 4 and the iOS SDK 5 can be downloaded for OS X 10.6 (code-named Snow Leopard).

If you have an older Mac running OS X 10.5 or earlier, however, you aren't out of luck. Xcode 3 and the iOS SDK 4 are available free. Xcode 3 isn't compatible with OS X 10.7 but works beautifully on OS X 10.6. If you're using Xcode 3, the screenshots and steps in this chapter will be slightly different.

Both Xcode 3 and Xcode 4 include the most recent iOS SDK. All the code you write in this chapter is compatible with any iOS device. The concepts are far more important than what version of the tool you're using.

Apple hosts information about transitioning to Xcode 4 at *http://developer.apple.com/library/mac/#documentation/IDEs/Conceptual/Xcode4TransitionGuide/Introduction/Introduction.html*.

An Objective-C Primer

Objective-C is the programming language used to develop in both Mac OS X and iOS. It's a superset of ANSI C, so it includes the C language as well as other libraries and tools, much as C++ extends the C language. It's also an object-oriented language that makes use of inheritance, polymorphism, and encapsulation—the three pillars of object-oriented programming.

So why do you need a primer? You might not, but Objective-C looks so much different from the other languages used in this book that it warrants a short discussion, at least. To begin, Objective-C uses some different metaphors than most other languages. So, for example, in Objective-C you send messages to objects rather than call methods on them. Although each Objective-C class includes an interface in a header file, an Objective-C interface is different from a Java or C# interface. Objective-C interfaces provide the API for a single class, whereas Java and C# interfaces can be implemented by many classes. You learned in Chapter 3 that Objective-C classes are said to conform to protocols rather than implement interfaces as do Java and C# classes.

There are a few aspects of Objective-C worth mentioning. Objective-C is **weakly typed**. That is, you don't have to determine an object's type at design time. You can add methods to any object you want, including objects for which you don't have the source code. This alternative to subclassing is called adding a **category** to a class. The interesting part of categories is that any methods you add through a category become part of the class definition. There's no concept of public, protected, and private access. In Objective-C, everything is public.

Encapsulation is more a guideline than a rule in Objective-C. Because all data members are public in Objective-C, you can access them directly. Your code will be far more manageable, however, if you use encapsulation.

The best way to see this is through an example. The following code is a Java class that represents a circle. This `Circle` class is simpler than those you've seen in previous chapters; the validation routines have been left out to keep it as readable as possible. The class is stored in `Circle.java`:

```java
public class Circle{
  private double radius;
  public double getRadius(){
    return radius;
  }
  public void setRadius(double radius){
    this.radius = radius;
  }
  public Circle(double radius){
    this.radius = radius;
  }
  public double getArea(){
    return Math.PI * radius * radius;
  }
  public double getPerimeter(){
    return Math.PI * 2 * radius;
  }
  public static void main(String args[]){
    Circle myCircle = new Circle(2.0);
    System.out.println("Area: " + myCircle.getArea() + " Circumference: "
 + myCircle.getPerimeter());
  }
}
```

When you compile and run `Circle.java`, you get the following output:

```
run:
Area: 12.566370614359172 Circumference: 12.566370614359172
```

To accomplish the same task in Objective-C, you need two files: an interface file (more commonly called a header) with an `.h` file extension and an implementation file with an `.m` file extension. The **header file** declares the class's public API, and the **implementation file** defines the class behavior. The header file is stored in `Circle.h`, shown here:

```
@interface Circle : NSObject{
  double radius;
}
  -(double) radius;
  -(void) setRadius: (double) r;
  -(double) getArea;
  -(double) getPerimeter;
  -(id) initWithRadius: (double) r;

@end
```

The implementation file is stored in `Circle.m`, shown here:

```
#import "Circle.h"
#import <Foundation/Foundation.h>


@implementation Circle : NSObject
-(double) radius{
  return radius;
}
-(void) setRadius: (double) r{
  radius = r;
}
-(double) getArea{
  return M_PI * radius * radius;
}
-(double) getPerimeter{
  return M_PI * radius * 2;
}
-(id) initWithRadius: (double) r{
  radius = r;
  return (self);
}

int main (int argc, const char *argv[]){
  NSAutoreleasePool *pool = [[NSAutoreleasePool alloc] init];
  Circle *myCircle = [[Circle alloc] initWithRadius:2.0];
  NSLog([NSString stringWithFormat:@"Area: %f Circumference: %f",
[myCircle getArea], [myCircle getPerimeter]]);
  [myCircle release];
  [pool release];
  return(0);
}

@end
```

Technically, you're allowed to put both the header and implementation in a single file. This works for very small files but gets unwieldy for larger classes. The convention is to split them into two files.

Building and running `Circle.m` results in the following output:

```
Running...
2012-07-30 10:03:00.645 Circle[2662:a0f] Area: 12.566371 ⏎
 Circumference: 12.566371

Debugger stopped.
Program exited with status value:0.
```

It's usually not a good practice to include the `main()` method in data classes. As you learned in Chapter 3, there's usually only one class in any program with a `main()` method. The `main()` method instantiates all objects and gets them to work together. In this case, it's included in each `Circle` class so that you can see the differences in how they're used. In addition, because there's only a single class, it makes sense to just create classes that are executable.

The following are some points to remember about Objective-C code:

- Objective-C is case sensitive.

- The – character indicates an instance method, one that's called by an object on its own data. Although it's not used in `Circle.h`, you use the + character to indicate a class method. The Java equivalent is a `static` method.

- The `main()` method in Objective-C code doesn't have a + or – sign at the front, which indicates it's a C method, not an Objective-C method.

- The * character, when used for declaring a variable, indicates that the variable is a pointer to an object.

- Technically speaking, you don't call methods on objects in Objective-C. Instead, you send messages to objects, and then the objects call their own methods. So [`myCircle getPerimeter`] can be translated roughly as "Send `myCircle` the `getPerimeter` message, and use the result that's returned."

- Notice the auto-release pool as well as the `alloc` and `release` messages. In Objective-C, you're responsible for allocating and initializing memory and, eventually, releasing it.

- Objective-C includes the `id` object type for use when you don't know or need to know the type of data you're working with. Java is strongly typed, so it has no late-binding equivalent.

- The NS prefix for objects stands for NextStep, the company that built the original Objective-C libraries used for Mac development. OS X is a descendant of NextStep. When you see the NS prefix, you're looking at code developed by NextStep.

Objective-C uses **infix notation** for writing code, which generally means method names and parameters are intertwined. Usually, the name of the first parameter is included with the method name. To see how this works, compare the constructors. In Java, this is the constructor:

```
Circle myCircle = new Circle(2.0);
```

In Objective-C, it's the following:

```
Circle *myCircle = [[Circle alloc] initWithRadius:2.0];
```

A benefit of infix notation is that it includes the names of arguments in the message. Sometimes Java method calls include many arguments, and keeping track of them can be difficult. You'll find yourself searching through the documentation to figure out which argument goes where, especially if all the arguments are the same type. Objective-C code is easier for people to read because it specifies the argument names.

Objective-C recently introduced the concept of automatic garbage collection: the process the OS uses to manage memory. Both Java and C# handle this task for you automatically; the Java and .NET runtimes remove unused objects from memory. Objective-C programs written to target OS X 10.5 or later can be configured to collect garbage for you. However, iOS doesn't include automatic garbage collection, so you need to manage memory in your code. In some ways, Objective-C is a trip back in time for most developers, especially those trained in high-level newer languages, such as Java and C#. Managing memory can be a tricky undertaking. The benefits, however, are reducing your app's footprint and improving its performance substantially.

Back to the Beginning

iOS development and Objective-C are different enough from the other types of development covered in this book that it is in your best interest to go back to the beginning and create the most basic application of all: displaying a string onscreen. That's right—you're going to write a Hello World app for the iPhone.

The iOS development process is, however, identical to that in almost all platforms:

- Create the project.
- Design the UI.
- Write code.
- Build and test.
- Tune performance.

Except for what you learned in Chapter 3, tuning performance is beyond the scope of this book, but you work through the first four steps for every app you write, regardless of the platform or language.

 Make sure you have followed the installation and setup instructions in Appendix A before proceeding.

HOW-TO 6-1

The default location for Xcode after installation is the Developer/Applications folder in the root of the file system (see Figure 6-1). If you haven't already, drag Xcode to the Dock to make starting it easier.

Figure 6-1 The default location for Xcode

1. Start Xcode, and in the welcome window, click **Create a new Xcode project** (see Figure 6-2).

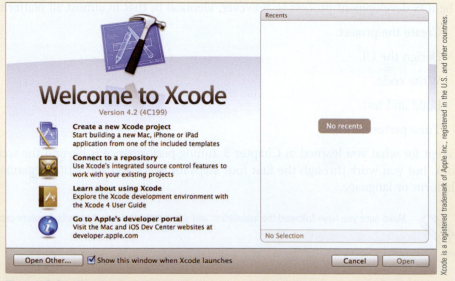

Figure 6-2 The Xcode welcome window

(continues)

(continued)

2. Click the **Empty Application** template (see Figure 6-3), and then click **Next**. Name the project **HelloWorldXcode4**, click **Next**, and save it to a location of your choice. (Your window might look slightly different from what's shown here.)

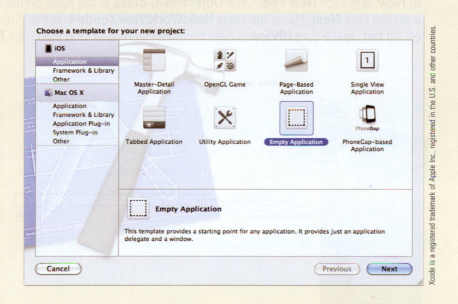

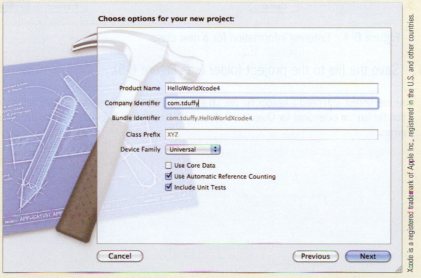

Figure 6-3   Starting a new project in Xcode 4

(continued)

3. The Empty Application template includes a `window` object for you to use. To actually display something in the `window` object, you must add an instance of a `UIView` object by creating a subclass of `UIView`. Click **File** on the menu, point to **New**, and click **New File**. Click **Objective-C class** in the pane on the right, and then click **Next**. Name the class **HelloWorldViewXcode4**. In the "Subclass of" list box, make sure **UIView** is selected (see Figure 6-4), and then click **Next**.

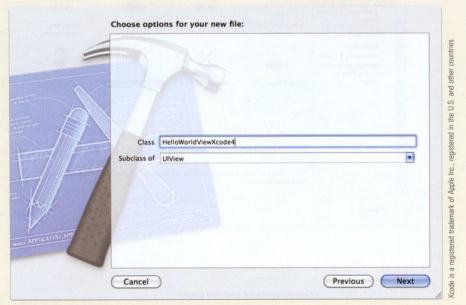

Xcode is a registered trademark of Apple Inc., registered in the U.S. and other countries.

Figure 6-4   Entering information for a new class

4. Save the file to the project folder (see Figure 6-5).

As mentioned, you need a header file (an `.h` extension) that specifies the interface and an implementation file (an `.m` extension) for Objective-C classes. Getting Xcode to create the files eliminates possible errors.

(continues)

(continued)

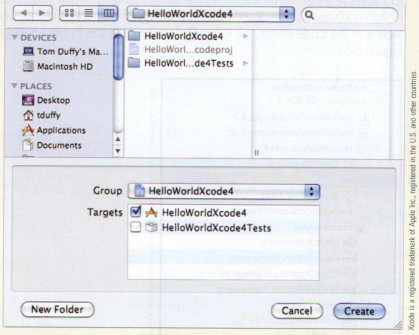

Figure 6-5   Saving the `HelloWorldViewXcode4` class

The next development phase is creating the UI. For this project, you do it with code instead of an interface designer. To draw Hello World onscreen, you must override the `drawRect:` method, which handles drawing the rectangle represented by the view onscreen. It's similar to overriding `onDraw()` in an Android app.

5.   Click **HelloWorldViewXcode4.m** to open it in the code editor. Find the commented `drawRect:` method (green, by default), and replace it with the following code:

```
-(void)drawRect:(CGRect) rect{
    NSString *hello    = @"Hello, World!";
    CGPoint  location  = CGPointMake(10, 20);
    UIFont   *font     = [UIFont systemFontOfSize:24.0];
    [[UIColor whiteColor] set];
    [hello drawAtPoint:location withFont:font];
}
```

This code is straightforward. It creates the string and the location where it will be drawn, specifies the font and color for the display, and draws the string onscreen.

(continues)

(continued)

6. iOS apps rely heavily on the Delegate design pattern. When you created the HelloWorldXcode4 app, Xcode created an application delegate for you. To view it in the code editor, click **AppDelegate.m** in the Project Navigator (see Figure 6-6).

Figure 6-6   Selecting the `AppDelegate.m` file in the Project Navigator

 Recall from Chapter 3 that delegates perform work on behalf of another object. `AppDelegate` is the delegate for the `HelloWorldXcode4` app object, so it performs tasks on behalf of the app. As you learned in Chapter 2, the application delegate is where life cycle events for the app occur.

7. Next, you need to tell the application delegate to add the view to the window. If necessary, click **AppDelegate.m** to open it in the code editor. If you don't see the file, expand the **HelloWorldXcode4** node in the Project Navigator. To let the delegate know about your custom view, you must import the header file. Add the following code after the existing `#import` statement:

```
#import "HelloWorldViewXcode4.h"
```

As you type, Xcode completes your code with possible endings. You can use the Tab key to accept the current suggestion. Note that Xcode accepts only the stub that matches, not the entire selection, so you might have to press Tab more than once. To see the entire list of possible endings, you press Esc.

(continues)

(continued)

8. Next you need to instantiate the view and add it to the window. Still in the `HelloWorldAppDelegate.m` file, add the following code to the `application: didFinishLaunchingWithOptions:` method, just before the `makeKeyAndVisible` message to the `self.window` object:

```
HelloWorldViewXcode4 *view = [[HelloWorldViewXcode4 alloc]
  initWithFrame : [self.window frame]];
[self.window addSubview:view];
```

9. Save both files, and then click **Run** on the Xcode toolbar. If prompted to save your work, click **Save All**. The simulator should start and display the string you added (see Figure 6-7).

Figure 6-7 Running Hello World in the simulator

 The default simulator in Xcode 4 is the iPad 5.0 simulator. To use the iPhone simulator, click the "Set the active scheme" button, and then click iPhone 5.0 Simulator.

(continues)

(continued)

If you change devices while your app is running, you might need to navigate back to it. Click the dot on the right, above the Safari icon, to find the home screen housing your app. Then double-click your app to restart it.

Moving Forward: Hello iPhone!

This project builds on the Hello World app from the previous section and is closer to what you do with real-world apps. It also introduces you to Interface Builder, Xcode 4's UI designer.

HOW-TO 6-2

1. Start a new project in Xcode. Click the **Empty Application** template, and then click **Next**. Name the project **HelloiPhone**, and save it in a location of your choice. Xcode should open and populate the project for you.

2. Exploring some resources Xcode generates can give you some insight into how iPhone apps work. In the Project Navigator, click to expand the **Frameworks** folder to see what frameworks Xcode has included in your project. So far, your app uses the Core Graphics, Foundation, and UIKit frameworks.

A **framework** is a collection of assets, including header files, images, sounds, and libraries, for performing a certain task. Frameworks are a convenient way to deploy code and enable you to focus on what your app does instead of how to do it. Cocoa Touch, for example, includes the function of drawing onscreen so that you don't have to. Apple includes many frameworks with the SDK and on Apple devices.

3. Next, expand the **Supporting Files** folder to see your app's **property list (plist)** file, used to set global parameters for an app. Click the file to open it in the code editor (see Figure 6-8). For the apps in this book, the plist file is updated for you automatically, so you don't need to deal with it.

(continues)

(continued)

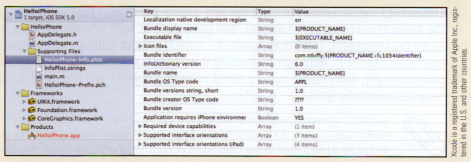

179

Figure 6-8 `HelloiPhone-Info.plist` in the list of project files

4. In the Project Navigator, click the **.pch** file under the Supporting Files folder to open it in the code editor. It's the prefix header for all files in the project. Its code, which specifies that the Foundation and UIKit frameworks are available for every class in the project, is as follows:

```
// Prefix header for all source files of the 'HelloiPhone' target in
   the 'HelloiPhone' project
//
#import <Availability.h>
#ifndef __IPHONE_3_0
#warning "This project uses features only available in iOS SDK 3.0
   and later."
#endif
#ifdef __OBJC__
   #import <UIKit/UIKit.h>
   #import <Foundation/Foundation.h>
#endif
```

5. The `main.m` file is the entry point for the application, and it's executed by the iPhone runtime. Click it to see the code, shown here:

```
//   main.m
//   HelloiPhone
//
//   Created by Tom Duffy on 11/22/11.
//   Copyright (c) 2011 NCC. All rights reserved.
//
#import <UIKit/UIKit.h>
#import "AppDelegate.h"
int main(int argc, char *argv[]){
   @autoreleasepool{
      return UIApplicationMain(argc, argv, nil, NSStringFromClass
   ([AppDelegate class]));
   }
}
```

(continues)

(continued)

The main() method exists to start the app, create the UIApplication object by calling the UIApplicationMain() function, and pass control, with any parameters, to the AppDelegate object. Note that Xcode 4's default project settings use automatic reference counting. Although technically it isn't the same as automatic garbage collection, you don't have to worry about releasing objects you create. iOS apps don't support automatic garbage collection.

 Automatic reference counting is available only in iOS 5 and later. If you need to support devices running older versions of iOS, clear the Use Automatic Reference Counting check box when you set options for a new project. In that case, you're responsible for releasing objects you no longer use.

6. So what does UIApplicationMain() do? To find out, click the **Organizer** button at the upper right and click the **Documentation** tab. In the left pane, click the search icon, and type **UIApplicationMain**. Click **UIApplicationMain** in the Reference node, and then click the link to **UIApplicationMain** in the Application Launch section. The Organizer opens the reference docs and displays the documentation for the UIApplicationMain() function (see Figure 6-9).

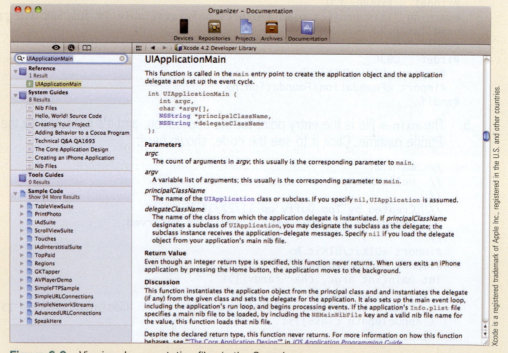

Figure 6-9   Viewing documentation files in the Organizer

(continues)

(continued)

Running into problems when viewing documentation in Xcode is a known issue. To solve the problem, download the documentation to view it locally on your system. To do this, click Preferences on the Xcode menu. Click the Documentation toolbar icon, click the Documentation button just below the toolbar, and then click Check and Install Now. You might need to submit authentication credentials more than once to install the documentation. You can also click the "Check for and install updates automatically" check box. Finally, you can always view documentation in your browser by going to *https://developer.apple.com/library/ios/navigation/*.

If you read the entry, you see that `UIApplicationMain()` simply runs your app and loads the main window, if any. Take a look at the plist file again. You can see that the `MainWindow.xib` file is the main window and is loaded when the app starts.

Your app gets one and only one `UIApplicationMain` object, which instantiates the view and fires life cycle events (explained in Chapter 2) at specified times. The `AppDelegate` object is created for you in the project folder—in this case, the HelloiPhone folder. This object is where you write code for the life cycle events your app supports.

Recall that a delegate is an object that does work on behalf of another object. When developing for iOS, you use the Delegate design pattern extensively. Delegating is an alternative to subclassing. So instead of inheriting from the `UIApplicationMain` class, you create a delegate to do the work. `UIApplicationMain` calls the life cycle methods on its delegate, and you provide the life cycle methods in the delegate.

A common development cycle for iOS apps is to create a subclass of the `UIViewController` class, get a `View` object from the `UIViewController`, and display it in a window. `UIViewController` objects do exactly what their name indicates: They control a view and display it onscreen. Instead of configuring the user interface, the application delegate typically creates a `UIViewController` object. The delegate asks the `UIViewController` for its `View` object (which `UIViewController` creates on demand) and adds it as a subview of the `window` object.

The **view controller** (the `UIViewController` object in the preceding discussion) is responsible for setting up and configuring the view when asked and for brokering requests between the model and view. Instead of creating the view directly, you do it via the view controller. You handle most UI events in the view controller.

(continues)

(*continued*)

7. To create the view, click the **HelloiPhone** project at the top of the Project Navigator. Then click **File** on the menu, point to **New**, and click **New File**. The file is placed in the directory you select. If you selected the project folder, Xcode determines where to put the file based on the type of file you create.

8. If necessary, click **Cocoa Touch** on the left, under the iOS section, and then click the **UIViewController subclass** template on the right (see Figure 6-10). Click **Next**.

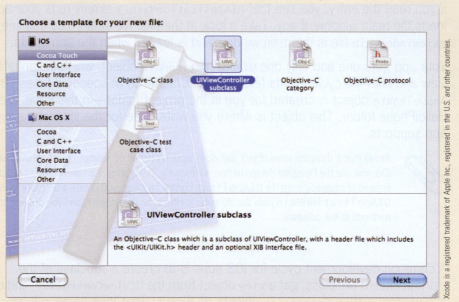

Figure 6-10   Creating a `UIViewController` subclass

9. Name the file **HelloiPhoneViewController** (see Figure 6-11). Click **Next** and then **Create** to save the file and let Xcode add it to the project.

(*continues*)

(*continued*)

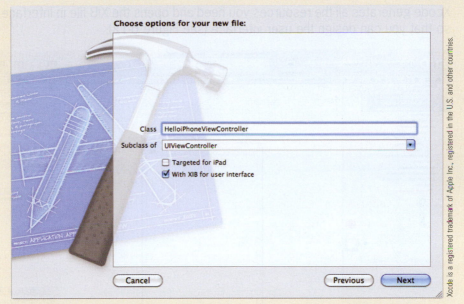

Choose options for your new file:

Class	HelloiPhoneViewController
Subclass of	UIViewController

☐ Targeted for iPad
☑ With XIB for user interface

Cancel   Previous   Next

Xcode is a registered trademark of Apple Inc., registered in the U.S. and other countries.

Figure 6-11 Entering options for `HelloiPhoneViewController`

  A **target** is a set of instructions for building a project, such as the HelloiPhone app. Targets can be edited in Xcode, but this process is beyond the scope of this book.

(*continues*)

(continued)

Xcode generates all the resources you need and opens the XIB file in Interface Builder so that you can design the user interface (see Figure 6-12).

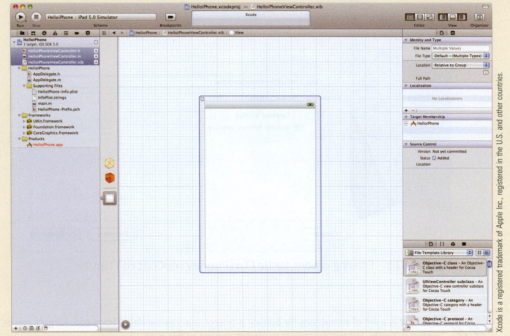

Figure 6-12   `HelloiPhoneViewController.xib` in Interface Builder

10.   Click to select the view (the blue box in Figure 6-12), if necessary. Then open the Objects Library in the lower-right pane. If you can't find it, click **View** from the menu, point to **Utilities**, and click **Show Object Library**. It displays objects that can be used with the selected object. In this case, the view object is selected, so the Objects Library displays UI elements you can add to the view (see Figure 6-13).

(continues)

(continued)

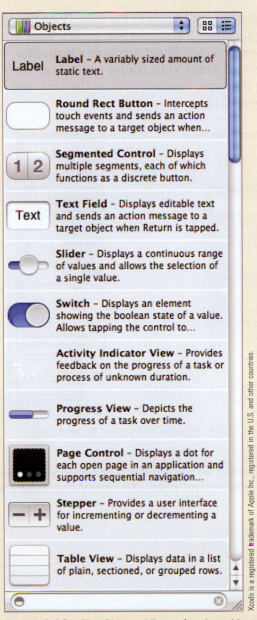

Figure 6-13   The Objects Library for view objects

(continues)

(continued)

11. Drag a **Text Field** from the Objects Library to the view. Open the Attributes Inspector in the upper-right corner. If you can't find it, click **View** from the menu, point to **Utilities**, and click **Show Attributes Inspector**. Set the `Placeholder Text` property to **Enter Your Name** and the `Capitalization` property to **Words**. Drag the sizing handles to resize the Text Field almost as wide as the view (see Figure 6-14).

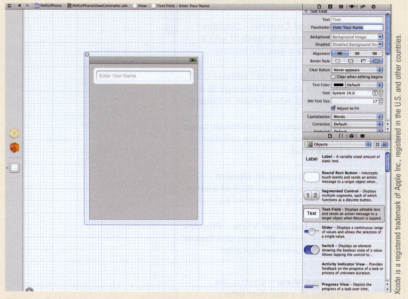

Figure 6-14   Dragging a Text Field to the view and setting its attributes

 You might have noticed that blue guidelines are displayed when you move and resize components. Pay attention to these guidelines because they help you adhere to the iPhone UI guide so that your apps look more like native apps.

(continues)

(continued)

12. Drag a **Round Rect Button** to the view, and set its `Title` property to **Press Me**. Drag a **Label** to the view, and resize it to the same size as the Text Field. Set its `Text` property to nothing by deleting the default value. You write the code to fill in the label in a moment. When you're finished, the view should look similar to Figure 6-15.

To make the connection between the nib file and your app, you need to specify outlets in the header file. An **outlet** is an instance variable that can be connected to a UI component. You use the keyword `IBOutlet` in the `@property` directive to create outlets in your code.

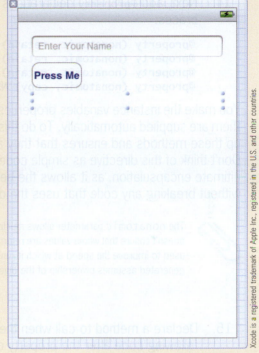

Figure 6-15 The HelloiPhone user interface

 `IBOutlet` and `IBAction` are reserved keywords that tell the compiler to look for connections to the nib file. `IBOutlet` is actually declared as `Nothing`, and `IBAction` is defined to return `void`.

13. Click the **HelloiPhoneViewController.h** file. Add the following instance variables inside the interface declaration:

```
{
UITextField *textField;
UILabel *label;
NSString *string;
UIButton *button;
}
```

(continues)

(continued)

14. Next, add `@property` declarations for the instance variables outside the curly braces:

```
@property (nonatomic, retain) IBOutlet UITextField *textField;
@property (nonatomic, retain) IBOutlet UILabel *label;
@property (nonatomic, retain) IBOutlet UIButton *button;
@property (nonatomic, copy) NSString *string;
```

You make the instance variables properties to make sure getter and setter methods for them are supplied automatically. To do this, you use an `@property` directive, which sets up these methods and ensures that they adhere to Objective-C naming conventions. Don't think of this directive as simple code generation and replacement. Using it is the ultimate encapsulation, as it allows the behavior of getters and setters to change without breaking any code that uses the directive.

The `nonatomic` parameter allows multiple threads to access a property concurrently; however, it doesn't ensure that whole values are returned. Because this app isn't multithreaded, `nonatomic` is used to improve the speed at which it runs. The `retain` parameter makes sure the setter that's generated assumes ownership of the object's reference count while the setter executes.

15. Declare a method to call when the user presses the button by adding the following code after the property declarations:

```
-(IBAction)sayHello:(id)sender;
```

16. The view controller can also handle button events if it adopts the `UITextFieldDelegate` protocol. To declare this, change the `@interface` declaration to the following:

```
@interface HelloiPhoneViewController : UIViewController ↵
  <UITextFieldDelegate>{
```

The complete interface code should look like the following (comments are omitted):

```
#import <UIKit/UIKit.h>

@interface HelloiPhoneViewController : UIViewController ↵
  <UITextFieldDelegate>{
  UITextField *textField;
  UILabel *label;
  NSString *string;
  UIButton *button;
}
```

(continues)

(continued)

```
@property (nonatomic, retain) IBOutlet UITextField *textField;
@property (nonatomic, retain) IBOutlet UILabel *label;
@property (nonatomic, retain) IBOutlet UIButton *button;
@property (nonatomic, copy) NSString *string;

-(IBAction)sayHello:(id)sender;
@end
```

 Notice that the instance variables are declared inside the curly braces, but properties and methods are declared outside them.

17. You can wire UI components to code by dragging and connecting them in Interface Builder. Click **HelloiPhoneViewController.xib** in the Project Navigator. Ctrl-click the **File's Owner** icon (a wireframe cube) to the left of the design area. The file's owner is the class that instantiates it. In this case, it's `HelloiPhoneViewController`. A list of the outlets you created is displayed (see Figure 6-16).

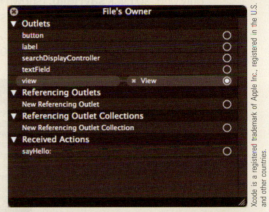

Figure 6-16 The File's Owner dialog box showing outlets and received actions

18. Drag from the circle next to the `button` outlet to the Button component in the view window. A blue line is drawn as you drag. Xcode indicates which components you can release the mouse button over. Because you're dragging from an instance of a `UIButton` (the name of this component is the "button" listed in the dialog box), Xcode allows you to release the mouse button only over the Button component. When you do, the circle next to the `button` outlet is filled, as shown in Figure 6-17.

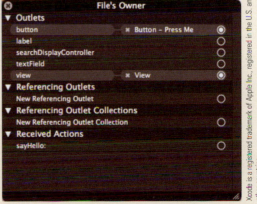

Figure 6-17 Connecting the `button` outlet to the view's Round Rect Button

(continues)

190

(continued)

19. Repeat this process for the Text Field component: Drag from the circle next to the `textField` outlet and release the mouse button over the Text Field component in the view window. Repeat the process again for the Label component.

20. To register to hear events from the button, you must drag in the other direction. Ctrl-click the button in the view window. A list of available events for this component is displayed. Find the Touch Up Inside event, and click and hold the circle to the right.

21. This time, drag over to the File's Owner icon and release the mouse button. When you do, a dialog box opens where you can choose an action. In this case, there's only one, so click **sayHello:** (shown in Figure 6-18). This modifies the button's list of events. Now when the user presses the button, the `sayHello:` message is sent to the file's owner; in this case, it's `HelloiPhoneViewController.m`. The good news is it's where the code you write is stored.

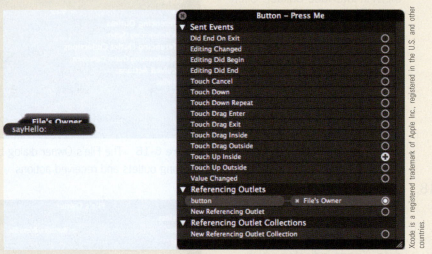

Figure 6-18   Connecting the view's Round Rect Button to the `sayHello:` method

22. To dismiss the virtual keyboard from the view when the user is done, the Text Field component sends a message to its delegate (the view controller). Ctrl-drag from the Text Field to the File's Owner icon, and click **delegate** in the Outlets list (see Figure 6-19).

Figure 6-19   Available outlets for the Text Field component

(continues)

(continued)

Three things need to be done with the view controller:

- Synthesize the properties for the instance variables and manage their memory footprint.

- Implement the `sayHello:` message.

- Make sure the keyboard is dismissed when the user is done with it.

23. Back in Xcode, click **HelloiPhoneViewController.m** and add the following code after the `@implementation` directive:

```
@synthesize textField;
@synthesize label;
@synthesize string;
@synthesize button;
```

Recall that synthesizing properties inserts getter and setter methods into the compiled code. Use `@synthesize` when you want to use the default getters and setters. Don't use `@synthesize` if you're supplying your own getters and setters.

24. Next, create the `sayHello:` message by adding the following code:

```
-(void)sayHello:(id)sender{
  self.string = textField.text;
  NSString *greeting = [[NSString alloc]
initWithFormat:@"Hello, %@!", self.string];
  label.text = greeting;
}
```

You might be wondering why you need the string instance variable. It's a good question. The answer is that the string variable represents the app's model (data). Simply put, you shouldn't be storing data in UI components. The view controller manages communication between the model and the UI, so data should be stored there.

Next, you need to dismiss the keyboard when the user presses the Done button. In an iOS app, the keyboard becomes the first responder when input is entered in a text field. "First responder" is the iOS equivalent of receiving focus in an app. Because you can't message the keyboard directly, the solution is to get focus off the text field when the user is done with it. You do this by getting the Text Field component to relinquish its first responder status. The good news is that Text Field components call the `textFieldShouldReturn:` method when the user taps the Return button. This method

(continued)

192

is included in the `UITextFieldDelegate` protocol, which you adopted in `HelloiPhoneViewController.h`. So all you need to do is to override this method in the `HelloiPhoneViewController.m` file.

25. Add the following code to `HelloiPhoneViewController.m` at the end of the file but before the `@end` directive:

```
-(BOOL)textFieldShouldReturn:(UITextField *)theTextField{
  [textField resignFirstResponder];
  return YES;
}
```

In more complex apps with more than a single text field, you should check which text field triggered the event and then react accordingly. Your code might look something like this:

```
if (theTextField == textField){
  [textField resignFirstResponder];
}else if (theTextField == someOtherTextField){
  [someOtherTextField resignFirstResponder];
} // more code here...
return YES;
```

26. To create an instance of `HelloiPhoneViewController`, click the **AppDelegate.h** file in the Project Navigator. Add a forward declaration to the top of the file, just after the `#import` statement:

`@class HelloiPhoneViewController;`

 Use the `@class` directive only when you refer to objects of the type used in the directive as a pointer and when the compiler doesn't need to know any inheritance information. If you need to make use of any of the object's members, you must tell the compiler where these members are defined. In this case, use `#import`.

27. Then add an instance variable at the beginning of the `@interface` section:

```
{
    HelloiPhoneViewController *helloiPhoneViewController;
}
```

28. Add the following code to the end of the file to make the instance variable a property:

`@property (nonatomic, retain) HelloiPhoneViewController` ↵
   `*helloiPhoneViewController;`

(continues)

(continued)

29. When you've finished, save your work. Your code for the `HelloiPhoneAppDelegate.h` file should look like the following (comments omitted):

```objc
#import <UIKit/UIKit.h>
@class HelloiPhoneViewController;
@interface AppDelegate : UIResponder <UIApplicationDelegate>{
   HelloiPhoneViewController *helloiPhoneViewController;
}
@property (strong, nonatomic) UIWindow *window;
@property (nonatomic, retain) HelloiPhoneViewController
   *helloiPhoneViewController;
@end
```

So far, you have just added a reference to `HelloiPhoneViewController` as a property to the application delegate. You still need to create an instance of `HelloiPhoneViewController` and set it as the value of the property. You do that in the implementation file.

30. Click **AppDelegate.m** to open it in the code editor. To import the `HelloiPhoneViewController.h` file, add the following line to the `#import` section:

    #import "HelloiPhoneViewController.h"

31. Then synthesize the `helloiPhoneViewController` property by adding the following line to the `@synthesize` section:

    @synthesize helloiPhoneViewController;

32. Scroll down to the `application:didFinishLaunchingWithOptions` method, and add the following code to the method right before the `[self.window makeKeyAndVisible];` statement:

```objc
HelloiPhoneViewController *viewController =
   [[HelloiPhoneViewController alloc]
   initWithNibName:@"HelloiPhoneViewController"
   bundle:[NSBundle mainBundle]];
[self setHelloiPhoneViewController:viewController];
```

 Recall from Chapter 3 that `application:didFinishLaunchingWithOptions:` is fired during app initialization, just before the UI is displayed.

(continues)

(continued)

In the preceding code, first you create an instance of the view controller. It uses the `alloc` method, but because this project uses automatic reference counting, you aren't responsible for releasing the object when you're finished with it.

The `init` method specifies the name of the nib file the controller should load and the bundle in which it's located. A **bundle** is an abstraction of a file system location that groups code and resources that can be used in an application. The advantages of using bundles instead of finding resources yourself in the file system are that bundles provide a convenient and simple API (because the `bundle` object can find a resource just by name) and can offer localization services (resources in multiple languages) for you. The code then sets the newly created view controller as the `HelloiPhoneViewController` property for the application delegate.

33. Add the following code after the preceding code block you added:

```
UIView *controllerView = [helloiPhoneViewController view];
[self.window addSubview:controllerView];
```

This code gets a `UIView` object by sending the `view` message to the view controller object. Then the `UIView` is added as a subview. Here's the complete listing for the application delegate stored in `HelloiPhoneAppDelegate.m`:

```
//  AppDelegate.m
//  HelloiPhone
//
//  Created by Tom Duffy on 11/22/11.
//  Copyright (c) 2011 NCC. All rights reserved.
//

#import "AppDelegate.h"
#import "HelloiPhoneViewController.h"

@implementation AppDelegate

@synthesize window = _window;
@synthesize helloiPhoneViewController;
-(BOOL)application:(UIApplication *)application
 didFinishLaunchingWithOptions:(NSDictionary *)launchOptions
{
   self.window = [[UIWindow alloc]
 initWithFrame:[[UIScreen mainScreen] bounds]];
// Override point for customization after application launch.
   self.window.backgroundColor = [UIColor whiteColor];
   HelloiPhoneViewController *viewController =
 [[HelloiPhoneViewController alloc]
 initWithNibName:@"HelloiPhoneViewController"
 bundle:[NSBundle mainBundle]];
```

(continues)

(continued)

```
    [self setHelloiPhoneViewController:viewController];
    UIView *controllerView = [helloiPhoneViewController view];
    [self.window addSubview:controllerView];

    [self.window makeKeyAndVisible];
    return YES;
}

-(void)applicationWillResignActive:(UIApplication *)application
{
/*
Sent when the application is about to move from active to inactive
 state. This can occur for certain types of temporary interruptions
 (such as an incoming phone call or SMS message) or when the user
 quits the application and it begins the transition to the
 background state.
Use this method to pause ongoing tasks, disable timers, and throttle
 down OpenGL ES frame rates. Games should use this method to
 pause the game.
*/
}

-(void)applicationDidEnterBackground:(UIApplication *)application
{
/*
Use this method to release shared resources, save user data,
 invalidate timers, and store enough application state information
 to restore your application to its current state in case it is
 terminated later.
If your application supports background execution, this method is
 called instead of applicationWillTerminate: when the user quits.
*/
}

-(void)applicationWillEnterForeground:(UIApplication *)application
{
/*
Called as part of the transition from the background to the inactive
 state; here you can undo many of the changes made on entering
 the background.
*/
}
```

(continues)

(continued)

```
-(void)applicationDidBecomeActive:(UIApplication *)application
{
/*
Restart any tasks that were paused (or not yet started) while the
 application was inactive. If the application was previously in the
 background, optionally refresh the user interface.
*/
}

-(void)applicationWillTerminate:(UIApplication *)application
{
/*
Called when the application is about to terminate.
Save data if appropriate.
See also applicationDidEnterBackground:.
*/
}

@end
```

Notice the life cycle methods in the application delegate class. You can add functionality to react to any life cycle event in the appropriate method.

The view controller sits in the Controller tier and handles interaction between the user and app. The View tier is designed in the .xib file with Interface Builder. In this simple app, the Model tier is the data the user enters. As mentioned, iOS apps use the Delegate design pattern extensively, but they also rely heavily on the MVC design pattern to separate data from how it's displayed to users.

34. Finally, test your app by clicking **Run** on the Xcode toolbar. If prompted to save your work, click **Save All**. Xcode starts the iPhone simulator and runs your app. If Xcode starts the iPad simulator, switch to the iPhone simulator by using

Figure 6-20   Displaying the welcome message

(continues)

(*continued*)

> the steps described at the end of How-To 6-1. Enter your name in the text box, and then click the **Return** button on the keyboard to dismiss it. Finally, click the **Press Me** button to display the message (see Figure 6-20).

 Detective Work

1. Modify the code so that the app displays the correct text when no username is entered.

2. Modify the code so that the text displayed in the button reads "Thank you, *name*!" (replacing *name* with the name the user enters) after the button is touched. Make sure the button is displayed correctly if no name is entered.

Troubleshooting

You might encounter some problems when creating apps for iOS. When you do, the first place to look is in your code. Objective-C is a forgiving language, especially at compile time, and Xcode generates warnings and errors. Treat warnings as though they're errors because they can create headaches at runtime that are hard to track down.

Objective-C is case sensitive, so many errors can be traced to simple typing errors. When you're "borrowing" code, copying and pasting it into Xcode instead of typing it yourself is a good idea because it eliminates another possibility for human error.

The iOS development process adds another layer of complexity with Interface Builder and nib files. In most cases, the UI is encoded in nib files that include the connections you made between objects in Interface Builder. If you don't make the correct connections in Interface Builder, your code doesn't behave as expected. Sometimes the fix is as simple as saving the nib file to update changes. Sometimes, however, it isn't.

In addition, sometimes Xcode doesn't rebuild your project after you've made changes. If you think this is the problem, first click Product, Clean from the menu to remove any compiled objects from your project. These objects are re-created when you click Build, Go from the menu.

Advanced iOS Apps: ButtonChaser

ButtonChaser is the iPhone version of DotSmasher. It uses a label and a button to accomplish the same thing DotSmasher did with graphics and gives you a chance to practice using Interface Builder. There are a few reasons for "upgrading" to UI components:

*   The app looks more professional and looks like a native app.

*   Handling button touches is more natural than detecting hits.

*   Labels are more natural for displaying text.

198

HOW-TO 6-3

1. Start a new project in Xcode, click the **Empty Application** template, and click **Next**. Name the project **ButtonChaser**, and save it wherever you like.

2. Create a new `UIViewController` subclass, and name the file **ButtonChaserViewController**. If the `ButtonChaserViewController.xib` file doesn't open automatically, click it in the Project Navigator.

3. The Button Chaser app requires only a Round Rect Button and a Label. Drag one of each from the Objects Library to the view window, and arrange them with the Label at the bottom and the Button in the middle.

4. Next, set a few properties:

   - Label: Set the `Text` property to **Score: 0**, and click to select the **Clears Graphics Context** check box, if necessary.

   - Round Rect Button: Use the sizing handles in the view window to resize the button to 30.0 by 30.0.

Save your work. The UI should look like Figure 6-21.

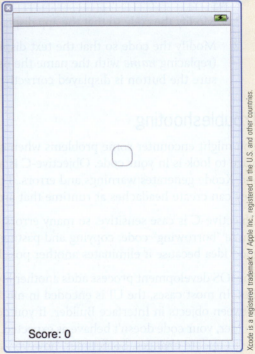

Figure 6-21 The ButtonChaser user interface

Xcode is a registered trademark of Apple Inc., registered in the U.S. and other countries.

5. Click the **ButtonChaserViewController.h** file to open it, and add the following instance variables to the header file:

```
{
UIButton *button;
UILabel *scoreLabel;
int score;
NSTimer *timer;
}
```

(continues)

(continued)

6. Next, add `@property` directives to the instance variables that require getters and setters. Note that the `score` variable doesn't need these methods.

```
@property (nonatomic, retain) IBOutlet UILabel *scoreLabel;
@property (nonatomic, retain) IBOutlet UIButton *button;
@property (nonatomic, retain) NSTimer *timer;
```

7. Finally, add a method to call when the user presses the button:

```
-(IBAction)processHit:(id)sender;
```

The header file should look like this (comments omitted):

```
@interface ButtonChaserViewController : UIViewController
{
    UIButton *button;
    UILabel *scoreLabel;
    int score;
    NSTimer *timer;
}
@property (nonatomic, retain) IBOutlet UILabel *scoreLabel;
@property (nonatomic, retain) IBOutlet UIButton *button;
@property (nonatomic, retain) NSTimer *timer;
-(IBAction)processHit:(id)sender;
@end
```

8. Save the file, and then click **ButtonChaserViewController.xib** to reopen it. Ctrl-click the **File's Owner** icon, and using what you learned in the previous project, make connections between the `scoreLabel` outlet and the Label component and between the `button` outlet and the Round Rect Button component (see Figure 6-22).

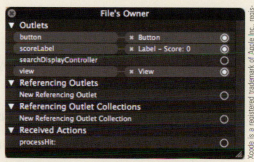

Figure 6-22 Making connections between outlets and UI components

9. Right-click the **Round Rect Button** component in the view window. Drag from the Touch Up Inside event to the File's Owner icon. Release the mouse button and click the **processHit:** method (see Figure 6-23).

(continues)

(continued)

200

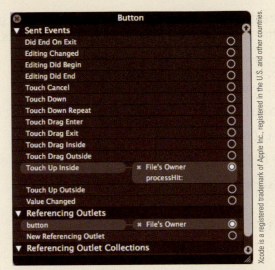

Figure 6-23   Selecting the `processHit:` method

10. Click the **ButtonChaserViewController.m** file to open it. Add the following code after the `@implementation` directive to synthesize the properties:

```
@synthesize scoreLabel;
@synthesize button;
@synthesize timer;
```

11. Create the `processHit:` method by adding the following to the class definition:

```
-(void)processHit:(id)sender{
  score += 1;
  NSString *scoreString = [[NSString alloc]
 initWithFormat:@"Score: %d", score];
  scoreLabel.text = scoreString;
}
```

12. Next, you need to create a method, called from inside the timer, that moves the button around the screen randomly. Add the following code for the `moveButton:` method, which takes an `NSTimer` object as a parameter. This parameter is automatically the timer that calls the method.

```
-(void)moveButton:(NSTimer *)timer{
  float availableWidth = self.view.bounds.size.width;
  float availableHeight = self.view.bounds.size.height;
  float btnX = random() % (int)(availableWidth - 60);
  float btnY = random() % (int)(availableHeight - 60);
  [button setFrame:CGRectMake(btnX, btnY, 30.0, 30.0)];
}
```

(continues)

(continued)

The parameters for **CGRectMake** are passed in parentheses, not separated by colons. This tells you that **CGRectMake** is a C function, not an Objective-C method. The "CG" stands for Core-Graphics, one of the frameworks included in the project.

201

13. To initialize the random number generator, find the `viewDidLoad:` method and add the following code after the `[super viewDidLoad]` message:

```
srandom(time(0));
```

14. In Chapter 3, you learned that the `viewDidLoad:` method fires right after the view is loaded. You can use this method to perform any initialization when loading the UI from a nib file. This method is also where you initialize the timer to move the button around. Add the following after the call to `srandom()` in `viewDidLoad:`

```
timer = [NSTimer scheduledTimerWithTimeInterval:1.5 target:self
    selector:@selector(moveButton:) userInfo:nil repeats:YES];
```

`scheduleTimerWithTimeInterval` is a class method that returns an instance of an `NSTimer` object. In the preceding code, it starts calling the `moveButton:` method every 1.5 seconds. Remember that the timer is passed as the argument—hence the semicolon with no argument in the call to `moveButton:`. Following is the complete code for `ButtonViewController.m`:

```objc
#import "ButtonChaserViewController.h"

@implementation ButtonChaserViewController
@synthesize scoreLabel;
@synthesize button;
@synthesize timer;
-(void)processHit:(id)sender{
  score += 1;
  NSString *scoreString = [[NSString alloc]initWithFormat:@"Score:
%d", score];
  scoreLabel.text = scoreString;
}
-(void)moveButton:(NSTimer *)timer{
  float availableWidth = self.view.bounds.size.width;
  float availableHeight = self.view.bounds.size.height;
  float btnX = random() % (int)(availableWidth - 60);
  float btnY = random() % (int)(availableHeight - 60);
  [button setFrame:CGRectMake(btnX, btnY, 30.0, 30.0)];
}
```

(continues)

(continued)

```
-(id)initWithNibName:(NSString *)nibNameOrNil bundle:(NSBundle
  *)nibBundleOrNil
{
  self = [super initWithNibName:nibNameOrNil bundle:nibBundleOrNil];
  if (self) {
// Custom initialization
  }
  return self;
}
-(void)didReceiveMemoryWarning
{
// Releases the view if it doesn't have a superview.
  [super didReceiveMemoryWarning];
// Release any cached data, images, etc. that aren't in use.
}

#pragma mark - View lifecycle
-(void)viewDidLoad
{
  [super viewDidLoad];
  srandom(time(0));
  timer = [NSTimer scheduledTimerWithTimeInterval:1.5 target:self
  selector:@selector(moveButton:) userInfo:nil repeats:YES];
// Do any additional setup after loading the view from its nib.
}
-(void)viewDidUnload
{
  [super viewDidUnload];
// Release any retained subviews of the main view.
// for example, self.myOutlet = nil;
}
-(BOOL)shouldAutorotateToInterfaceOrientation:
  (UIInterfaceOrientation)interfaceOrientation
{
// Return YES for supported orientations
  return (interfaceOrientation == UIInterfaceOrientationPortrait);
}
@end
```

15. Next, you need to instantiate the view controller in the application delegate and add it to the delegate's view. Click **AppDelegate.h** to open it, and add the following @class directive to the file:

```
#import <UIKit/UIKit.h>
@class ButtonChaserViewController;
```

(continues)

(continued)

16. Add an instance variable:

```
@interface AppDelegate : UIResponder <UIApplicationDelegate>
{
    ButtonChaserViewController *buttonChaserViewController;
}
```

17. Add an @property directive:

```
@property (strong, nonatomic) UIWindow *window;
@property (nonatomic, retain) ButtonChaserViewController↵
  *buttonChaserViewController;
```

18. Click **AppDelegate.m** to instantiate the view controller and add it to the view. The first step is synthesizing the buttonChaserViewController property, as shown:

```
@synthesize window = _window;
@synthesize buttonChaserViewController;
```

19. Then import the ButtonChaserViewController class:

```
#import "AppDelegate.h"
#import "ButtonChaserViewController.h"
```

20. Enter the following code in the application: didFinishLaunchingWithOptions method just before the [self.window makeKeyAndVisible]; message:

```
// Instantiate a ButtonChaserViewController based on the nib file
ButtonChaserViewController *viewController =↵
  [[ButtonChaserViewController alloc] initWithNibName:↵
@"ButtonChaserViewController" bundle:[NSBundle mainBundle]];
// Assign it to the instance variable
[self setButtonChaserViewController:viewController];
// Create a UIView from the instance variable's view
UIView *controllerView = [buttonChaserViewController view];
// Show the UIView by adding it as a subview of the window object
[self.window addSubview:controllerView];
```

(continues)

(continued)

21. Test your app by clicking **Run** on the toolbar. If prompted to save your work, click **Save All**. Figure 6-24 shows the results.

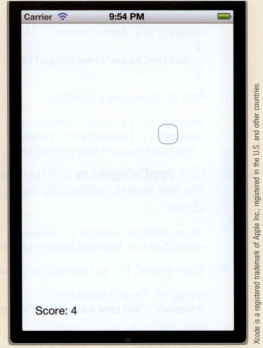

Score: 4

Figure 6-24 Running ButtonChaser in the simulator

 ## Detective Work

1. Create a start/stop mechanism for the app. (*Hint*: The NSTimer class includes an invalidate: method.)

2. Force the game to end after 30 seconds, and inform the user that the game has ended. (*Hint*: Create a variable that keeps track of how many times the button moves. If you know how often the button moves and for how long it should move [30 seconds], you can calculate how many moves to make before ending the game.)

3. Create a way for users to select a difficulty level. You might want to give them the choices Easy, Medium, and Hard. Then you need to determine what defines the level of difficulty. You might increase the speed at which the button moves or make the button smaller, for example.

Working with the iOS Development Tools

One helpful feature of Xcode is the code completion mechanism. As you learned in the first project in this chapter, when you start typing, Xcode displays suggestions for completing the current statement. The suggested code is shown in gray, and you use the Tab key to accept the current suggestion. To see all the options, use the Esc key (see Figure 6-25). You can then double-click the option you want to insert it into your code.

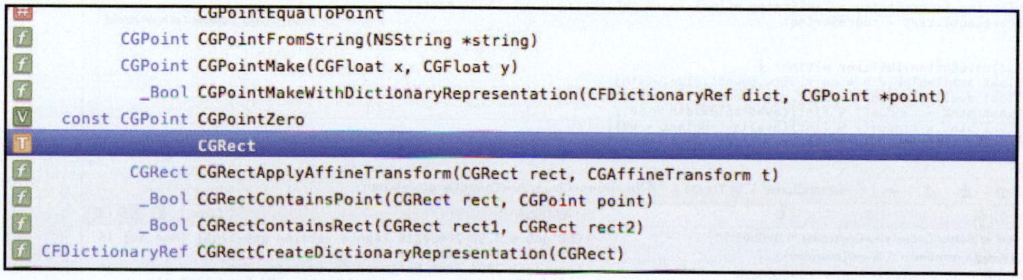

Figure 6-25 Xcode listing available options

Xcode includes good debugging tools, and finding them is easy. By default, they're visible under the main code editor window when a source code file is open. If you can't find the Debug view, click the middle button of the three View buttons on the toolbar.

One use of these debugging tools is setting breakpoints in your code to examine what's happening when program execution reaches that line. To do this, click in the gutter next to the line where you want to set the breakpoint. When you run your project, execution stops at that line. You can examine local variables while execution is halted. The typical debugging tools are available (see Figure 6-26): Step Over, Step Into, and Step Out.

206

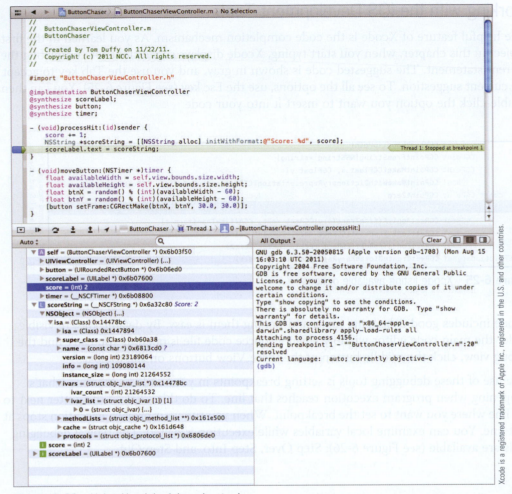

Figure 6-26 Using Xcode's debugging tools

With the iPhone simulator, you can choose which SDK version to target as well as the device: iPad, iPhone, or iPhone (Retina). You can simulate shakes, rotations, memory warnings, and incoming calls. The Home and Lock buttons function as they do on devices. You can find all these features in the simulator's Hardware menu.

Keep in mind that there's no camera in the simulator, and although you can simulate rotation, there's no Accelerometer feature. All location services return the address and coordinates of the running computer's IP address. There are no iPod, iTunes, Calendar, Mail, SMS, Phone, or Maps apps in the simulator, but you can use their services in your apps. In addition, the Settings app is severely limited, and there's no proximity sensor. If your app requires any of these features, you need to test it on an actual device.

Packaging and Deploying iOS Apps

Packaging iOS apps couldn't be easier. In the upper-left corner of the Xcode window is a drop-down list for configuring your app. Click your app's name and choose Edit Scheme. You can also click Product, Edit Scheme from the menu. Then click the Archive tab on the left, and change the build configuration to Release (see Figure 6-27). Finally, select Product, Archive from the menu to build your app.

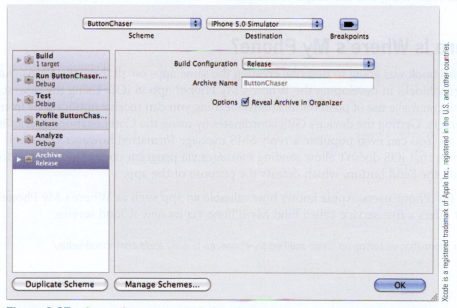

Figure 6-27 Generating an app ready for release

 For more information on packaging and deploying apps, go to *http://developer.apple.com/library/mac/ #documentation/ToolsLanguage/Conceptual/Xcode4UserGuide/DistApps/DistApps.html.*

Deploying your app is another matter. To make your app available on the iTunes App Store, you need to enroll in the iOS developer program for a fee of $99. There are other levels of enrollment (and cost), but they generally apply to companies and corporations. The $99 program is enough for most developers.

 For more information on the iOS developer program, visit *http://developer.apple.com/programs/ios/.*

Like other vendors, Apple requires you to get a secure code-signing certificate for your code. You need to apply for a certificate before any deployment, sign your code, and upload it through iTunes. In addition, you should supply screenshots, icons, and so forth to make your app look as professional as possible. All the information you need to deploy your app is available after you join the iOS developer program.

Currently, Apple charges a 30% fee for paid apps. If you decide to make your app free, Apple won't charge you. Of course, you can still make money with a free app by adding advertising to it, but that topic is beyond the scope of this book.

So Where Is Where's My Phone?

Originally, this book was going to describe creating the same apps on all three platforms, but there were roadblocks in developing the Where's My Phone? app in iOS. Using the newest iOS SDK, you can make use of push notifications, meaning you can receive notifications from incoming servers. Getting the device's GPS coordinates by using the CoreLocation libraries is fairly easy, too. You can even populate a reply SMS message formatted however you want. The problem is that iOS doesn't allow sending messages via program code. The user has to actually touch the Send button, which defeats the purpose of the app.

Fortunately for iPhone users, Apple knows how valuable an app such as Where's My Phone? can be, so it offers a free service called Find My iPhone via its new iCloud service.

 For information on setting up iCloud and Find My iPhone, go to *www.apple.com/icloud/setup/*.

Using the Core Location Framework

In this section, you create a simple app that makes use of the CoreLocation framework to see how to get an iOS device's location.

HOW-TO 6-4

1. Start a new project in Xcode, click the **Single View Application** template (see Figure 6-28), and click **Next**.

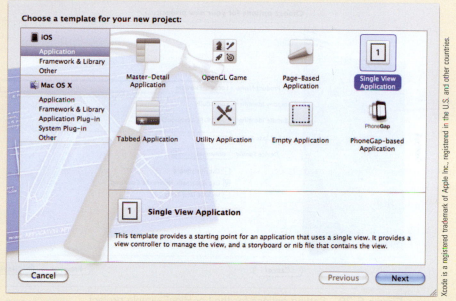

Figure 6-28 Selecting the Single View Application template

The Single View Application template generates a view controller class for you. You don't have to add it yourself.

(continues)

(continued)

2. Name the project **LocationExample**, and click to clear the **Use Storyboard** check box (see Figure 6-29). Click **Next**, and save the project.

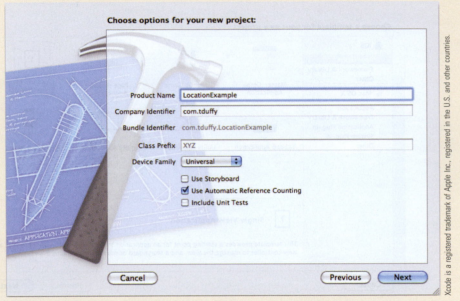

Figure 6-29   Setting options for the LocationExample project

3. Before you can use the Core Location services, you must add the CoreLocation framework to your project. Click your project (the first item) in the Project Navigator. Under TARGETS, click **LocationExample**, and then click the **Build Phases** tab. Expand the **Link Binary With Libraries** node (see Figure 6-30). Finally, click the + sign at the bottom of the list.

Figure 6-30   Adding an existing framework, step 1

(continues)

(continued)

4. In the resulting dialog box, click **CoreLocation.framework** (see Figure 6-31) and click **Add**.

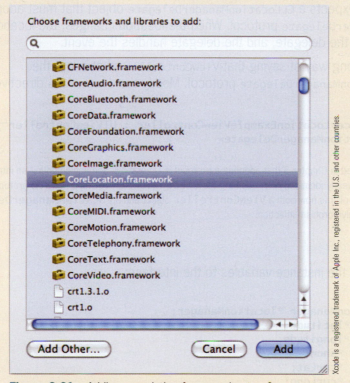

Choose frameworks and libraries to add:

- CFNetwork.framework
- CoreAudio.framework
- CoreBluetooth.framework
- CoreData.framework
- CoreFoundation.framework
- CoreGraphics.framework
- CoreImage.framework
- **CoreLocation.framework**
- CoreMedia.framework
- CoreMIDI.framework
- CoreMotion.framework
- CoreTelephony.framework
- CoreText.framework
- CoreVideo.framework
- crt1.3.1.o
- crt1.o

Add Other...   Cancel   Add

Xcode is a registered trademark of Apple Inc., registered in the U.S. and other countries.

Figure 6-31   Adding an existing framework, step 2

In the Project Navigator, you can drag the CoreLocation framework into the Frameworks folder. The framework might turn red in the Link Binary With Libraries list, but Xcode works out the new location of the framework files, and they should still work fine.

5. Click **LocationExampleViewController.h** to open it in the code editor. At the top of the file, import the CoreLocation framework by adding the following line:

```
#import <CoreLocation/CoreLocation.h>
```

(continues)

(continued)

The CoreLocation framework works as a callback mechanism. In general, you instantiate a `CLLocationManager` (or location manager), set some properties, and then send it the `startUpdatingLocation` message. One property you set is the `Delegate` property, which expects a `CLLocationManagerDelegate` object that must adopt the `CLLocationManagerDelegate` protocol. When the location changes, the location manager notifies the delegate, and the delegate handles the event.

6. That's a long way of saying that `ViewController` must adopt the `CLLocationManagerDelegate` protocol. Modify the `@interface` directive as follows:

```
@interface LocationExampleViewController : UIViewController ↵
  <CLLocationManagerDelegate>
```

You learned in Chapter 3 that adopting a protocol in Objective-C and implementing an interface in Java are nearly identical. After adopting the **CLLocationManagerDelegate** protocol, the view controller is now both a **ViewController** object *and* a **LocationManagerDelegate** object. Polymorphism in action!

7. Next, add the instance variables to the interface:

```
{
CLLocationManager *locationManager;
UILabel *latitude;
UILabel *longitude;
UIButton *show;
NSString *curLat;
NSString *curLong;
}
```

8. Then declare the properties and Interface Builder outlets for use in designing the UI:

```
@property (nonatomic, retain) CLLocationManager *locationManager;
@property (nonatomic, retain) IBOutlet UILabel *latitude;
@property (nonatomic, retain) IBOutlet UILabel *longitude;
@property (nonatomic, retain) IBOutlet UIButton *show;
```

9. Finally, declare the method that's fired when the user asks for the device's location:

```
-(IBAction)showLocation;
```

(continues)

(continued)

10. It's time to design the UI. Click the **ViewController_iPhone.xib** file to open it in Interface Builder. Drag four **Label** components and a **Round Rect Button** to the view window so that the UI looks like Figure 6-32.

11. The two empty labels in the UI are going to be used to display latitude and longitude values. Ctrl-click the **File's Owner** icon to display the outlets and actions. Click the circle to the right of the latitude outlet and drag to the empty Label component at the top. Repeat the process for the longitude outlet and the bottom empty Label component.

12. Click the circle to the right of the show outlet and drag to the Round Rect Button. Then Ctrl-click the **Round Rect Button** in the view window to see the available events. Click the circle to the right of Touch Up Inside and drag to the File's Owner icon. Click to select the **showLocation** action.

13. When you have finished, Ctrl-click the **File's Owner** icon to open the File's Owner dialog box. It should look like Figure 6-33.

14. Save your work. Click **ViewController.m**, and add the following code after the `@implementation` directive to synthesize the properties:

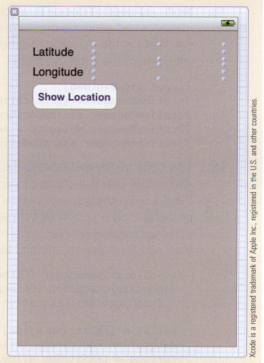

Figure 6-32 The LocationExample user interface

Figure 6-33 The File's Owner dialog box

```
@synthesize longitude, latitude, locationManager, show;
```

(continues)

(continued)

15. Next, you need to decide in which life cycle event to create the location manager and send the message to start updating the location. A good candidate is the `viewDidLoad` method. Modify it as shown (you might need to uncomment the entire method):

```
[super viewDidLoad];
locationManager = [[CLLocationManager alloc] init];
locationManager.desiredAccuracy = kCLLocationAccuracyBest;
locationManager.delegate = self;
[locationManager startUpdatingLocation];
```

16. This code simply instantiates the location manager and sets the accuracy. Remember that you declared `LocationExampleViewController` would adopt the `CLLocationManagerDelegate` protocol. Assigning `self` to the `Delegate` property makes sense. Of course, you need to implement the `CLLocationManagerDelegate` protocol's methods for it to be useful. To do that, add the following method to the class before the `@end` directive:

```
-(void)locationManager:(CLLocationManager *)manager
  didUpdateToLocation:(CLLocation *)newLocation
    fromLocation:(CLLocation *)oldLocation
{
  curLat = [[NSString alloc] initWithFormat:@"%g",↵
 newLocation.coordinate.latitude];
  curLong = [[NSString alloc] initWithFormat:@"%g",↵
 newLocation.coordinate.longitude];
}
```

The `locationManager:didUpdateToLocation:fromLocation:` method is declared in `CLLocationManagerDelegate`. Adding it here sends the code you write to the application delegate. In this case, it just updates the `curLat` and `curLong` instance variables.

17. To create a second method from the `CLLocationManagerDelegate` protocol to handle errors, add the following code:

```
-(void)locationManager:(CLLocationManager *)manager↵
  didFailWithError:(NSError *)error
{
  latitude.text = @"An error occurred";
  longitude.text = [error localizedFailureReason];
}
```

(continues)

(continued)

18. This simple error handler runs if the location manager runs into problems. Next, you need to write the event handler for location updates. Add the `showLocation` method:

```
-(void)showLocation{
    latitude.text = curLat;
    longitude.text = curLong;
}
```

All this method does is set the text of labels to the values stored in `curLat` and `curLong`. `showLocation` is called when the user presses the button.

19. Save your work, and then click **Run** on the toolbar to run your app in the simulator. If prompted to save your work, click **Save All**. If you're asked for permission to use your current location, click **OK**. Clicking the Show Location button displays the location of Apple's headquarters (see Figure 6-34).

20. You can control the simulator's location by clicking **Debug** from the menu, pointing to **Location**, and clicking **Custom Location**. In the Custom Location dialog box (see Figure 6-35), enter any values you like.

Figure 6-34 The LocationExample app running in the simulator

 Valid values for latitude are numbers from -90 to 90, and for longitude, they're from -180 to 180. You can't enter invalid values in the Custom Location dialog box.

(continues)

216

(continued)

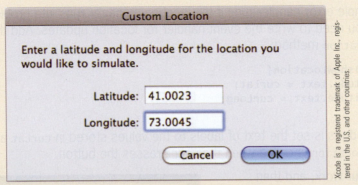

Custom Location

Enter a latitude and longitude for the location you would like to simulate.

Latitude: 41.0023

Longitude: 73.0045

Cancel   OK

Xcode is a registered trademark of Apple Inc., registered in the U.S. and other countries.

Figure 6-35   Setting a custom location for the simulator

21. Verify the new custom location by clicking the **Show Location** button again. Figure 6-36 shows the results.

Xcode is a registered trademark of Apple Inc., registered in the U.S. and other countries.

Figure 6-36   Showing a custom location

Chapter Summary

- Objective-C is the programming language used to develop both Mac OS X and iOS apps. It's a superset of ANSI C, so it includes the C language as well as other libraries and tools, much as C++ extends the C language. It's also an object-oriented language that makes use of inheritance, polymorphism, and encapsulation.

- In Objective-C, you send messages to objects rather than call methods on them. Objective-C is weakly typed, meaning you don't have to determine an object's type at design time.

- Typically, two files are created for each Objective-C class: a header file to declare the class's public API and an implementation file to define the class behavior.

- In Objective-C, you're responsible for allocating and initializing memory and, eventually, releasing it. Objective-C uses a reference counter to manage memory, so as long as an auto-released object has something pointing to it, it's retained in memory. When the count reaches 0, the object is released.

- If you don't use automatic reference counting, and you create an object by using `alloc`, `copy`, or `new`, you're responsible for its memory management.

- Objective-C includes the `id` object type for use when you don't know or need to know the type of the data you're working with.

- Objective-C uses infix notation for writing code, meaning method names and parameters are intertwined.

- A bundle is an abstraction of a file system location that groups code and resources to be used in an application.

- A category is an Objective-C mechanism for adding methods to an existing class, even if you don't have the source code for the class.

- An outlet is an instance variable that can be connected to a UI component.

- A framework is a collection of classes and resources used to perform a certain task.

- `UIApplicationMain` is the object that instantiates the view and fires life cycle events at specified times.

- A common development cycle for iOS apps is to subclass `UIViewController`, get a `View` object from `UIViewController`, and put the view in a `window` object.

- The view controller is responsible for setting up and configuring the view when asked and for brokering requests between the model and view. The View tier is designed in the `.xib` file by using Interface Builder.

- To make an app available on the iTunes App Store, you must be enrolled in the iOS developer program.

- The location manager uses a combination of GPS, Wi-Fi, and cellphone towers to get a device's location.

Key Terms

bundle—An abstraction of a file system location that groups code and resources to be used in an application.

category—An Objective-C mechanism for adding methods to an existing class, even if you don't have the source code for the class.

framework—A collection of classes, used for performing certain tasks.

header file—A file with an .h extension in Objective-C that's used to declare a class's public API.

implementation file—A file with an .m extension in Objective-C that's used to define class behavior.

infix notation—A notation system used in Objective-C code that intertwines the method name and parameters.

Objective-C—The programming language used to develop apps in both Mac OS X and iOS.

outlet—An instance variable that can be connected to a UI component.

property list (plist)—The file used to set global parameters for an app.

target—A set of instructions for building a product.

view controller—An object, usually a subclass of `UIViewController`, that's responsible for setting up and configuring the view when asked and for brokering requests between the model and view.

weakly typed—In Objective-C, a weakly typed object means you don't have to determine its type at design time.

Review Questions

1. Which of the following statements about Objective-C is true? (Choose all that apply.)

    a. It's the programming language used to create apps on Macs and iOS devices.

    b. It's a procedural programming language.

    c. It's a superset of ANSI C.

    d. It makes use of inheritance but not polymorphism.

2. A weakly typed object must be declared at design time. True or False?

3. Which of the following files is created for an Objective-C class? (Choose all that apply.)

    a. Header

    c. Implementation

    b. Delegate

    d. Directive

4. In Objective-C, the `id` type indicates which of the following?

    a. You don't know the type of the object.

    b. The object isn't instantiated.

    c. The class handles instantiation.

    d. All of the above

5. In infix notation, method names and parameters are intertwined. True or False?

6. The Empty Application template includes which of the following? (Choose all that apply.)

    a. A `window` object   c. A property list file

    b. A main class   d. A `UIView` object

7. The `drawRect:` method does which of the following? (Choose all that apply.)

    a. Handles drawing the rectangle represented by the view onscreen

    b. Is similar to `onDraw()` in Android apps

    c. Draws only rectangles

    d. Is called when the view redraws itself

8. Which of the following statements about an application delegate is true? (Choose all that apply.)

    a. It works on behalf of the `UIApplication` class.

    b. It's where life cycle event handlers are created.

    c. It draws the view onscreen.

    d. It's the entry point of a program.

9. A framework is which of the following?

    a. A predefined app template

    b. A collection of classes for performing a specific task

    c. A list of properties for a given object

    d. An object

10. You use the plist file to do which of the following?

    a. Set global properties for an app.

    b. Access a collection of classes for performing a specific task.

    c. Create an entry point for the OS to run your app.

    d. Show the view.

11. A `UIViewController` object is used to do which of the following?

 a. Control a view and display it onscreen.

 b. Serve as the entry point for the OS to run your app.

 c. Form a collection of assets for performing a specific task.

 d. Handle life cycle events.

12. When should you use the `@class` directive? (Choose all that apply.)

 a. When you refer to objects of that type only as a pointer

 b. When the compiler doesn't need to know any inheritance information

 c. As a means of wiring components together in Interface Builder

 d. When you don't know what else to do

13. A bundle is a group of properties for an object. True or False?

14. Which of the following statements about a view controller is true? (Choose all that apply.)

 a. It's responsible for setting up and configuring the view when asked.

 b. It's responsible for brokering requests between the model and view.

 c. It's where you handle most UI events for your app.

 d. It serves as the entry point for an app.

15. What does the `@synthesize` directive do?

 a. Implements getters and setters for variables declared with the `@property` directive

 b. Combines the application delegate with the view controller

 c. Adds constructors to classes

 d. Bypasses the `UIView`

16. An outlet is which of the following? (Choose all that apply.)

 a. An instance variable

 b. A way to connect instance variables to UI components

 c. A memory management device

 d. Where you develop Xcode plug-ins

17. Core Location services are provided as which of the following?

 a. Application delegate

 b. View controller

 c. Framework

 d. Property list file

Up for Discussion

1. It's been said that developing iOS applications represents a step backward for most developers. What does this statement mean? Is it true? Explain your answer.

2. Compare delegation and subclassing. Which do you prefer, and why?

3. Compare Android and iOS development. Which do you prefer, and why?

4. Analyze current market trends for smartphones. If you were developing an app today, which platforms would you support? Explain your answer.

Programming Exercises

1. Create an iOS app that displays the area and circumference for circles, and write a `Circle` class that performs the calculations. Instantiate a `Circle` object in the view controller class based on a user-entered radius.

2. Create an iOS app that displays the area and perimeter for rectangles, and write a `Rectangle` class that performs the calculations. Instantiate a `Rectangle` object in the view controller class based on user-entered length and width values.

3. Create an iOS app that converts temperature from degrees Fahrenheit to degrees Celsius. Ask users for the temperature in degrees Fahrenheit. Write a `TempConverter` class to perform the calculations, and instantiate a `TempConverter` object with the user input. Use the following formula for the conversion:

   $C = 5/9(F - 32)$

4. Create an iOS app that converts temperature from degrees Celsius to degrees Fahrenheit. Ask users for the temperature in degrees Celsius. Write a `TempConverter` class to perform the calculations, and instantiate a `TempConverter` object with the user input. Use the following formula for the conversion:

   $F = 9/5 * C + 32$

5. Combine Programming Exercises 3 and 4 so that users can choose between converting Fahrenheit to Celsius and vice versa. Be sure to include the `TempConverter` class and instantiate a `TempConverter` object for each calculation.

6. Create an iOS app that calculates payroll. Allow the user to enter the number of hours worked and an hourly wage. The wage should be "time and a half" for hours worked over 40 in a week. Display the amount to be paid to the user.

CHAPTER 7

Microsoft Windows Phone 7

In this chapter, you learn to:

- ◎ Compare C# with Java and Objective-C
- ◎ Work with properties in C#
- ◎ Use Visual Studio 2010 Express
- ◎ Create Silverlight apps for Windows Phone 7
- ◎ Use the XAML language to create user interfaces for Windows Phone 7 apps
- ◎ Code events and event handlers with Visual Studio 2010
- ◎ Use the Delegate design pattern to create events and event handlers in C#
- ◎ Run apps in the Windows Phone 7 emulator
- ◎ Package and deploy Windows Phone 7 apps
- ◎ Create and send an SMS (text) message
- ◎ Use the Windows Phone 7 Location service

Windows Phone 7 is the newcomer to the smartphone playing field. Although Microsoft has been in the smartphone game for a while, earlier entries were attempts to squeeze desktop features of Windows into small devices and didn't pay off. Windows Phone 7, however, is a new OS designed specifically for smartphones; it features tight integration with Microsoft Office and Outlook.

Windows Phone 7 uses **C#**, the most advanced programming language of all the platforms discussed in this book. If Objective-C is a step backward from the industry-standard Java, C# is, in many ways, a look into the future. It has incorporated the best of Java and addressed many shortfalls.

Windows Phone 7 also uses Microsoft **Visual Studio 2010** as its IDE, which is easy to use and powerful. Microsoft helps developers create useful apps because it recognized long ago that users adopt platforms because of the apps they run. As you've learned, Apple has used this concept to dominate the small-device market.

Windows Phone 7 apps come in two types: Silverlight and XNA Games. You can build both types of apps with the Windows Phone 7 SDK and Visual Studio 2010 Express for Windows Phone 7, but this book covers only Silverlight apps. **Silverlight** is a development platform for creating interactive apps for the Web, desktops, and mobile devices. This free plug-in powered by the .NET Framework is compatible across several browsers, devices, and OSs. The Silverlight for Windows Phone version supports core Silverlight features and adds capabilities specific to Windows Phone 7. Silverlight features that don't make sense for small devices have been omitted. Its features include the following:

- Hardware-accelerated video with multicodec digital rights management (DRM) and Internet Information Services Smooth Streaming support

- Vector and bitmap graphics

- Multitouch support with Accelerometer, a control that responds to motion

- Camera and microphone support

- The Notification service for pushing information to the phone, regardless of whether an app is running

- Integration with the core Windows Phone 7 Series features, such as hubs

A Quick Look at C#

C# is an object-oriented programming language, so it supports encapsulation, inheritance, and polymorphism in much the same way that Java does. In Chapter 6, you saw the difference between writing a `Circle` class in Java and Objective-C. In this chapter, you see a C# `Circle` class and compare it with the Java and Objective-C classes. First, here's the C# code:

```
using System;

namespace Circle
{
  public class Circle
  {
    private double radius;
    public Circle(double radius)
    {
      this.Radius = radius;
    }

    public double Radius
    {
      get
      {
        return radius;
      }
      set
      {
        radius = value;
      }
    }

    public double getArea()
    {
      return Math.PI * radius * radius;
    }

    public getCircumference()
    {
      return 2 * Math.PI * radius;
    }

    static void Main(string[] args)
    {
      Circle myCircle = new Circle(2.0);
      Console.WriteLine("Area: " + myCircle.getArea() + " Circumference: "↵
 + myCircle.getCircumference());
    }
  }
}
```

At first glance, the C# class looks like the Java version, with a few minor differences. First, there's no header file. Both Java and C# include the class interface and implementation in the same file. C# uses the keyword using, and Java and Objective-C use import. A C# **namespace** is analogous to a Java package and is a convenient way to bundle assets for reuse. The closest thing to packages and namespaces in Objective-C is a framework, but you don't typically add classes to existing frameworks.

Inheritance in C# is nearly identical to that in Java and Objective-C. You can extend a single subclass but implement as many interfaces as you'd like. Interface implementation combined with inheritance makes it possible to incorporate polymorphism. C# uses a colon (:) to indicate inheritance, as Objective-C does, but Java uses the keyword `extends`, as shown in this example:

```
public class Circle extends Shape{
// Circle implementation
}
```

In C#, using inheritance looks like this:

```
public class Circle : Shape
{
// Circle implementation
}
```

Encapsulation in C# is a middle ground between Java and Objective-C. In Java, you declare private members and grant access by using public getter and setter methods. You have no direct access to the underlying property. In Objective-C, everything is public, and Apple handles creating properties through the `@property` directive. C# balances these two approaches by allowing you to restrict access to data *and* create and implement your own properties.

The `Circle` class shown previously illustrates creating properties in C#. Note that the data—the `radius` variable—is declared as private, and the property, `Radius`, is declared as public. In addition, getter and setter methods are provided in the property, which enables you to perform validation to make sure you get meaningful data input. Finally, notice that the `Radius` property is easier to use. In C#, you would write the following:

```
myCircle.Radius = 2.0;
```

The Java equivalent is as follows:

```
myCircle.setRadius(2.0);
```

The difference is subtle but significant. Using C# properties enables you to use the simpler assignment of a value instead of passing a value to a method. In addition, you still get all the encapsulation features of using getters and setters.

 C#, like Java and Objective-C, is case sensitive. For example, note the difference between the `radius` variable and the `Radius` property shown earlier.

Microsoft encourages you to use the Model-View-Controller (MVC) design pattern. Most of the sample code it shows uses this design pattern, although the Delegate design pattern is used extensively, too, especially in the event model. **Event delegates** are objects that handle interactions between data and the component firing the event.

Your First Windows Phone 7 App: Hello Windows!

Enough background—it's time to write your first app!

HOW-TO 7-1

1. Start Visual Studio from the Windows Start menu, and click **File, New Project** from the menu or click the **New Project** toolbar button to start a new project.

2. In the New Project dialog box, click to expand **Visual C#** on the left, and click the **Windows Phone Application** template in the middle pane, if necessary. Type **HelloWindows** in the Name text box at the bottom (see Figure 7-1), and then click **OK**. If prompted to select a platform, click **Windows Phone OS 7.1**, and click **OK**. Visual Studio creates what's called a **solution**, a group of files containing one or more projects. In this case, a new solution is created with the HelloWindows project loaded.

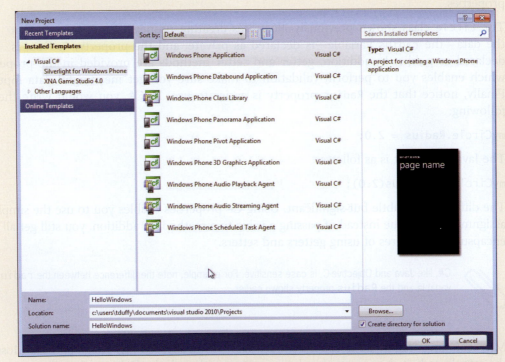

Figure 7-1 Creating the HelloWindows project

(continues)

(*continued*)

 Much as Android uses XML to describe UIs, Windows Phone 7 uses **Extensible Application Markup Language (XAML)**, an XML vocabulary consisting of predefined XML elements that's designed to contain and describe user interface components. XAML is easy for people to read and edit; however, in Windows Phone 7 apps, you design UIs almost exclusively with the visual designer.

3. If the Properties window isn't visible at the lower right, click the **Properties Window** button on the toolbar to make it visible (see Figure 7-2).

Figure 7-2 The Visual Studio interface with the Properties window open

 You can also click View on the menu and point to Other Windows to find and open a specific window.

4. In the form designer, click the **TextBlock** component displaying "MY APPLICATION," and in the Properties pane, click the **Text** property and type your name. Press **Enter** or click another property to see the results, shown in Figure 7-3.

(*continues*)

(continued)

In Windows Phone 7, TextBlocks are multiline label components, used simply to display text.

5. To set the app's title, click the **TextBlock** containing "page name" in the form designer. Set its `Text` property to **Hello Windows Phone 7** and its `FontSize` property to **32**.

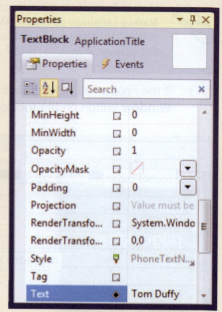

Figure 7-3 Changing the `Text` property of a TextBlock

(continues)

(continued)

6. Next, place your cursor over the toolbox icon at the upper-left corner of the design area. The Toolbox list shows Windows Phone Controls, and you can select available components (see Figure 7-4). Click the **TextBlock** component in this list, and drag it to the form designer.

The area where you drop a component can be very small. Don't worry about a component's size or placement when you drop it in the form designer. You can always resize and move it later.

7. Drag the **TextBlock** to the top of the form designer, and then resize it so that it takes up most of the width. As in iOS Interface Builder, guidelines appear to help you with placement. Set its Text property to **Enter Your Name**.

8. Next, drag a **TextBox** to the form designer, position it under the TextBlock, and resize it to take up most of the width. TextBox components can be edited, meaning users can enter text in them, so set its Text property to nothing (blank).

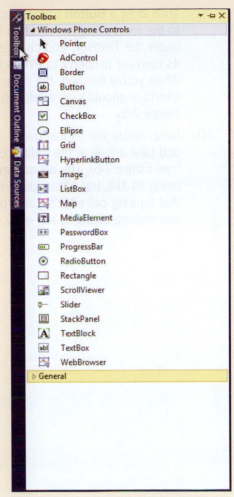

Figure 7-4   Displaying the Toolbox list of controls

(continues)

(continued)

230

9. Then drag a **Button** component to the form designer, position it under the TextBox, and change its Content property to **Press Me**. When you're finished, the user interface should look similar to Figure 7-5.

10. Next, resize the middle pane, and take a look at the XAML code (see Figure 7-6). The advantage of using an XML-based language is that figuring out what's going on and making changes are easy.

Figure 7-5   The HelloWindows user interface

(continues)

(continued)

```
<phone:PhoneApplicationPage
    x:Class="HelloWindows.MainPage"
    xmlns="http://schemas.microsoft.com/winfx/2006/xaml/presentation"
    xmlns:x="http://schemas.microsoft.com/winfx/2006/xaml"
    xmlns:phone="clr-namespace:Microsoft.Phone.Controls;assembly=Microsoft.Phone"
    xmlns:shell="clr-namespace:Microsoft.Phone.Shell;assembly=Microsoft.Phone"
    xmlns:d="http://schemas.microsoft.com/expression/blend/2008"
    xmlns:mc="http://schemas.openxmlformats.org/markup-compatibility/2006"
    mc:Ignorable="d" d:DesignWidth="480" d:DesignHeight="768"
    FontFamily="{StaticResource PhoneFontFamilyNormal}"
    FontSize="{StaticResource PhoneFontSizeNormal}"
    Foreground="{StaticResource PhoneForegroundBrush}"
    SupportedOrientations="Portrait" Orientation="Portrait"
    shell:SystemTray.IsVisible="True">

    <!--LayoutRoot is the root grid where all page content is placed-->
    <Grid x:Name="LayoutRoot" Background="Transparent">
        <Grid.RowDefinitions>
            <RowDefinition Height="Auto"/>
            <RowDefinition Height="*"/>
        </Grid.RowDefinitions>

        <!--TitlePanel contains the name of the application and page title-->
        <StackPanel x:Name="TitlePanel" Grid.Row="0" Margin="12,17,0,28">
            <TextBlock x:Name="ApplicationTitle" Text="Tom Duffy" Style="{StaticResource PhoneText
            <TextBlock x:Name="PageTitle" Text="Hello Windows Phone 7" Margin="9,-7,0,0" Style="{S
        </StackPanel>

        <!--ContentPanel - place additional content here-->
        <Grid x:Name="ContentPanel" Grid.Row="1" Margin="12,0,12,0">
            <TextBlock Height="30" HorizontalAlignment="Left" Margin="12,6,0,0" Name="textBlock1"
            <TextBox Height="72" HorizontalAlignment="Left" Margin="12,42,0,0" Name="textBox1" Tex
            <Button Content="Press Me" Height="72" HorizontalAlignment="Left" Margin="129,120,0,0"
        </Grid>
    </Grid>

    <!--Sample code showing usage of ApplicationBar-->
    <!--<phone:PhoneApplicationPage.ApplicationBar>
        <shell:ApplicationBar IsVisible="True" IsMenuEnabled="True">
```

Figure 7-6 The XAML code for the HelloWindows UI

Now for the fun part. Visual Studio makes it easy to get your components to interact with each other. There are no event listeners, as in Java, or wiring of components, as in Interface Builder. Simply double-click a component in the form designer, and Visual Studio produces the code needed to create an event handler for the component's default action.

11. If necessary, resize the code editor so that you can see the form designer, and double-click the **Button** component in the form designer. The default action for a button is the `click` event, so Visual Studio opens the code file where you can edit the `click` event. To do that, type the following code inside the `button1_Click()` method:

```
textBlock1.Text = "Hello, " + textBox1.Text + "!";
```

(continues)

232

(continued)

> 12. That's it! You're ready to test your app. Make sure **Windows Phone Emulator** (not Windows Phone Device) is selected in the drop-down list on the toolbar, and click the **Debug** button (a small green triangle) to the left of this list box.

Running in the Emulator

When you're ready to test your app, Visual Studio starts the emulator and loads your app. In addition, it makes your app the active app.

HOW-TO 7-2

1. Click the **TextBox** component and enter your name (see Figure 7-7).

Figure 7-7 Entering text in the app

(continues)

(continued)

2. Next, click the **Press Me** button. The welcome message should be displayed (see Figure 7-8).

3. Controls for the emulator are at the upper right, just outside the emulator window. Position the mouse cursor over them to make them visible (see Figure 7-9). The X is the button that closes the emulator; it mimics the phone's power button. You can also minimize and rotate the emulator window, zoom in or out, and display additional tools.

 You don't have to close the emulator between each app run. In fact, leaving it running is recommended because starting the emulator takes a *long* time, as with the Android emulator. Visual Studio reloads your app each time you run it.

Figure 7-8 Clicking the button displays the welcome message

Figure 7-9 The Windows Phone 7 emulator controls

Detective Work

1. Modify the code so that the app displays the correct text when no username is entered.

2. Modify the code so that the welcome message is displayed in the app's title after the user presses the Press Me button.

3. Modify the code so that the button's label reads "Thank you."

Working with Visual Studio 2010

Microsoft was a pioneer in adding code completion to its developer tools. In Visual Studio, this feature is called **IntelliSense**. This powerful tool helps you in every phase of code writing, from choosing which object to work with to choosing properties and methods and browsing documentation. No matter where you are in the process of working with code, IntelliSense never loses the context. Other IDEs sometimes "forget" where they are as you type commands, but that never happens in Visual Studio. To insert an IntelliSense suggestion, press Tab, and to hide the IntelliSense window, press Esc.

IntelliSense includes a useful parameter list feature. When you begin calling a method, IntelliSense lists all available signatures for the method with the parameters and their data types (see Figure 7-10). You can scroll the list and choose the signature you want to use. After you select a signature, IntelliSense includes placeholders for each parameter. The parameter in bold represents the next parameter needed as you type. The parameter list is displayed automatically after you type an open parenthesis and closes when you add a closing parenthesis. You can also close the list by pressing Esc.

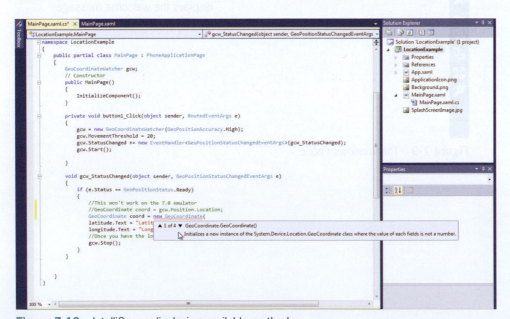

Figure 7-10 IntelliSense displaying available methods

Visual Studio also includes debugging features. To add a breakpoint, for example, right-click a line in the code editor, point to Breakpoint, and click Insert Breakpoint. Figure 7-11 shows other options in this menu. Figure 7-12 shows the visual indicator that you have inserted a breakpoint.

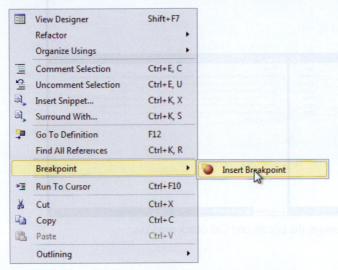

	View Designer	Shift+F7
	Refactor	▶
	Organize Usings	▶
	Comment Selection	Ctrl+E, C
	Uncomment Selection	Ctrl+E, U
	Insert Snippet...	Ctrl+K, X
	Surround With...	Ctrl+K, S
	Go To Definition	F12
	Find All References	Ctrl+K, R
	Breakpoint	▶	🔴 Insert Breakpoint
	Run To Cursor	Ctrl+F10
	Cut	Ctrl+X
	Copy	Ctrl+C
	Paste	Ctrl+V
	Outlining	▶

Figure 7-11   The context menu for debugging features

```
String nameString = textBox1.Text;
String welcomeMsg = "";
String btnMsg = "";
```

Figure 7-12   A breakpoint indicator

When you run your app in the emulator and reach the code line with the breakpoint inserted, Visual Studio halts the app on the line where you've set the breakpoint and displays the Locals and Call Stack windows (see Figure 7-13). You can use the Locals window to examine any variables in your app and the Call Stack window to examine the sequence of method calls. In addition, the Debug toolbar is displayed. You can use it to resume execution, step into or over blocks of code, and perform many other debug functions. The code editor updates and displays the current line of code, based on the debug action you take.

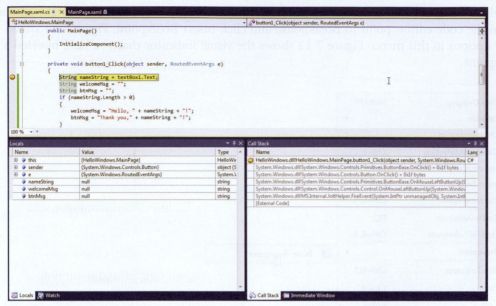

Figure 7-13 Hitting a breakpoint displays the Locals and Call Stack windows

Advanced Windows Phone 7 Apps: ButtonChaser

The ButtonChaser app for Windows Phone 7 mimics the iOS version. You use UI components for the game elements. The Windows Phone version, however, is much simpler to create than the iOS version because Visual Studio is easier to work with. The general idea behind the app remains the same. You want to move the button around onscreen randomly and detect when the user touches the button. If the user touches the button, you increment the score.

HOW-TO 7-3

1. Start a new project, and click the **Windows Phone Application** template. Name the project **ButtonChaser**, and click **OK**. If necessary, display the Properties window.

2. To display the game score, click the **TextBlock** component displaying "MY APPLICATION." In the Properties window, set the Text property to **Score: 0** and change the Text property of the page name text box to **Button Chaser**. Open the Toolbox, and drag a **Button** component to the form designer. Set the width

(continues)

(continued)

and `Height` properties to **72**, and delete the text stored in the `Content` property. Your UI should look like Figure 7-14.

3. Now it's time to write some code. In the Solution Explorer, expand the **MainPage.xaml** node, and double-click **MainPage.xaml.cs** to open it in the code editor. To create instance variables for the app, add the following code after the class declaration:

Figure 7-14   The ButtonChaser UI

```
Random random;
int aWidth;
int aHeight;
int score;
DispatcherTimer timer;
```

The instance variables you added represent the objects needed. You use the `Random` object to generate random numbers for placing the button. `aWidth` and `aHeight` are the game area's width and height, and the `score` variable is self-explanatory. You use the `DispatcherTimer` object to move the button at regular intervals. The red squiggly line you see under the timer declaration means the `DispatcherTimer` class is packaged in a namespace you haven't declared yet.

4. At the bottom of the namespace list (all the `using` declarations), add the following line:

```
using System.Windows.Threading;
```

To calculate the game area's width and height, you use the `ContentPanel` object because it's the container for the Button component. This object is supplied for you by default, and technically, it's where you've been dropping components all along. All UI components in the Windows Phone SDK include `Height` and `Width` properties as well as read-only `ActualWidth` and `ActualHeight` properties. You should use the latter two properties because they represent the onscreen object's actual size after it has been drawn onscreen.

The bigger question is where do you put the code to access properties? Your first instinct might be to place code inside the constructor, but if you try it, you'll see that UI components don't have sizes until they are rendered onscreen. So you can't access the dimensions of the `ContentPanel` object and the Button component until after

(continues)

238

(continued)

they're drawn onscreen. Fortunately, the ContentPanel object includes a SizeChanged event that fires every time the ContentPanel size changes, including the first time it's rendered onscreen.

5. Click the **MainPage.xaml** tab, if necessary, to open the form designer and access the UI components. Click near the button but not on it to select the ContentPanel. In the Properties window, click the **Events** tab, scroll down the list, and double-click the **SizeChanged** event (see Figure 7-15).

6. Visual Studio registers the event, creates the method stub for you, and opens the code editor so that you can modify the event code as follows:

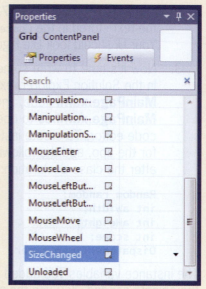

Figure 7-15 Selecting the ContentPanel's SizeChanged event

```
private void ContentPanel_SizeChanged(object sender,
  SizeChangedEventArgs e)
{
aWidth = (int)e.NewSize.Width;
aHeight = (int)e.NewSize.Height;
}
```

This code gets the ContentPanel's NewSize value from the SizeChangedEventArgs object (named e and supplied by the event) and assigns the Width and Height values to the aWidth and aHeight variables. The NewSize object stores its Width and Height values as doubles, so in the preceding code, they're cast to ints for assignment.

7. Next, you need to initialize the Random and DispatcherTimer objects. The logical place to do this is inside the constructor. Add the following code to the constructor after the InitializeComponent() call:

```
random = new Random();
timer = new DispatcherTimer();
```

8. To modify the timer to suit your needs, you need to set the Interval property, which represents the timer's delay. Add the following line to the constructor after the code you just entered:

```
timer.Interval = new TimeSpan(0,0,0,0,1000);
```

(continues)

(continued)

In this code line, the `Interval` property takes a `TimeSpan` object, which can be created in a number of ways. To be more precise, you use the `TimeSpan` constructor that accepts five arguments for days, hours, minutes, seconds, and milliseconds. The preceding code sets the `Interval` property to 1 second.

9. The `DispatcherTimer` class includes a `Tick` event that fires every time the 1-second interval you just set passes, and you add the code you want to repeat at intervals in the `Tick` event handler. Visual Studio uses a delegate method—in this case, the `+=` operator—to wire events to event handlers. To add the `Tick` event, begin typing the following at the end of the constructor:

```
timer.Tick +=
```

10. After you type the `+=` operator, IntelliSense displays a suggested delegate. Press **Tab** to accept it. Then click the **timer_Tick** parameter, and Visual Studio asks whether you want to implement the event handler (see Figure 7-16). Press **Tab** to have Visual Studio create the method with the correct signature.

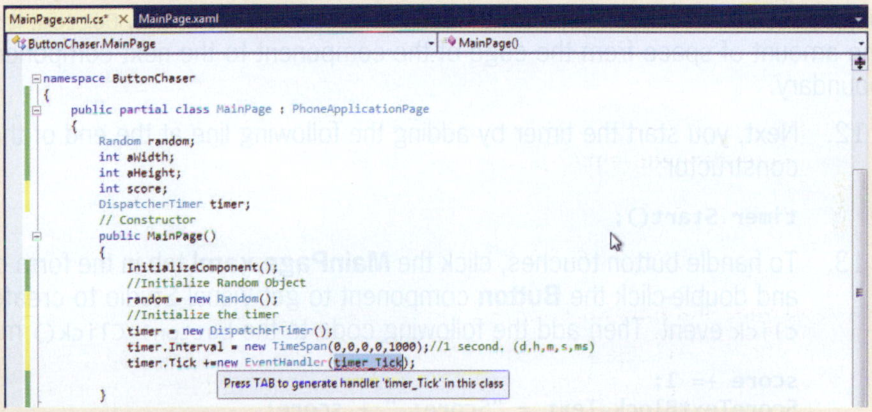

Figure 7-16 IntelliSense helps you use the `EventHandler` object correctly

The `EventHandler` object is a delegate for the timer. Essentially, this code says that each time the `Tick` event fires, the code in the `timer_Tick` method is called. Because the `timer_Tick` method is passed as a parameter to the `EventHandler` constructor, it must have a special signature that includes a reference of type `object` named `sender` that represents the event's origin and a reference to an `EventArgs` object that describes the event's properties.

(continues)

(continued)

11. Visual Studio creates the `EventHandler` delegate with a placeholder `throw` clause. Replace this statement with the following code that runs each time the `Tick` event occurs:

```
int x = random.Next(aWidth) - (int)button1.ActualWidth;
int y = random.Next(aHeight) - (int)button1.ActualHeight;
if (x < 10)
x = 10;
if (y < 10)
y = 10;
button1.Margin = new Thickness(x, y, 0, 0);
```

The first two statements create top and left coordinates (x and y) for the button. Passing an `int` as a parameter to the `Next()` method of a `Random` object returns an `int` between 0 and the parameter, which is essentially the maximum value. The button's width is subtracted from the random number to keep it from disappearing off the game area's right or bottom edge. The next two conditional statements make sure the button doesn't disappear off the top or left edge. Next, the x and y values are assigned to the `Left` and `Top` values of the button's `Margin` property. The `Margin` object uses a `Thickness` object with four values: `Left`, `Top`, `Right`, `Bottom`. It specifies the amount of space from the edge of the component to the next component or boundary.

12. Next, you start the timer by adding the following line at the end of the constructor:

```
timer.Start();
```

13. To handle button touches, click the **MainPage.xaml** tab in the form designer, and double-click the **Button** component to get Visual Studio to create the `click` event. Then add the following code to the `button1_Click()` method:

```
score += 1;
ScoreTextBlock.Text = "Score: " + score;
```

(continues)

(continued)

14. To rename the TextBlock that keeps the score, click the **TextBlock** with "ApplicationTitle" in the MainPage.xaml tab, and then type **ScoreTextBlock** in the text box at the top of the Properties window (see Figure 7-17).

15. Click the **Debug** toolbar button to run the program in the emulator. Figure 7-18 shows the results.

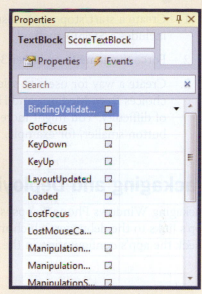

Figure 7-17 Renaming the Text-Block in the Properties window

Figure 7-18 Running the ButtonChaser app

Detective Work

1. Create a start/stop mechanism for the app. (*Hint*: The `DispatcherTimer` class includes a `Stop()` method.)

2. Force the game to end after 30 seconds, and inform the user that the game has ended.

3. Create a way for users to select a difficulty level. You might want to give them the choices Easy, Medium, and Hard. Then you need to determine what defines the level of difficulty. You might increase the speed at which the button moves or make the button smaller, for example.

Packaging and Deploying Windows Phone 7 Apps

Packaging Windows Phone 7 apps is painless. You simply change a setting to eliminate your app's links to the debugger, which makes the deployed code smaller and faster, and then check the app's configuration in the Solution Explorer.

HOW-TO 7-4

If the emulator is still running your project, quit the emulator.

1. First, click the ButtonChaser app's solution in the Solution Explorer. (It's usually the top node in the tree, as shown in Figure 7-19.) In the Properties window, click the **Active config** list arrow, and click the **Release|Any CPU** option.

(continues)

(continued)

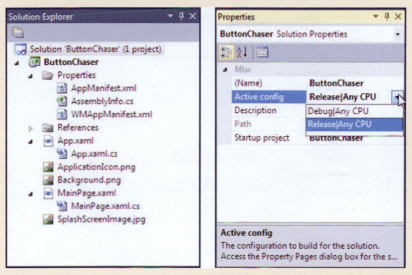

Figure 7-19   Setting your project's active configuration to the release version

2. To check your project's settings, right-click the project (usually the second node) in the Solution Explorer and click **Properties** to open the dialog box shown in Figure 7-20. Click the **Build** tab on the left. The Output path text box shows where the project's release version is stored. The default path is Bin/ Release. You can also click the Configuration drop-down list at the top to toggle between release and debug configurations, for example.

(continues)

(continued)

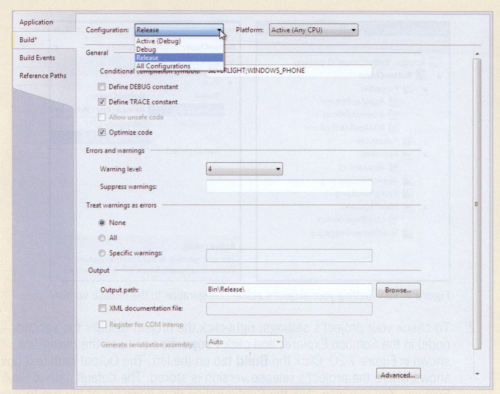

Figure 7-20   Checking the project's configuration settings

3. Next, right-click your project in the Solution Explorer and click **Build (or Rebuild)**. Visual Studio creates the files needed to deploy your app. The .xap file is the one you submit for publication on the Windows Phone Marketplace (see Figure 7-21).

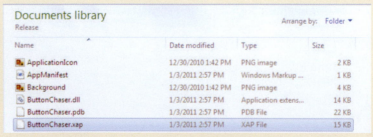

Figure 7-21   Selecting the .xap file to deploy

To deploy your app, you need an App Hub annual membership ($99 fee), which allows you to submit Silverlight and XNA apps for Windows Phone 7 as well as XNA games for Xbox LIVE. You can sign up for a free membership, and then pay the subscription fee when you're ready to submit your app. The subscription fee grants you access to the Marketplace, but distributing your apps locally is free. The App Hub subscription includes a dashboard for managing apps as well as a submission mechanism, download tracking, and earnings tracking.

To sign up for an App Hub membership, go to *http://create.msdn.com/en-US/*. To find out more about App Hub and how to submit apps, visit *http://create.msdn.com/en-US/home/about/how_it_works*.

The submission process is straightforward. After you've developed your app, submit it via the App Hub dashboard. Microsoft then processes the file to ensure that it meets its certification guidelines. If your app passes, it's made available on the Marketplace immediately. If it fails, you're told why and are given a chance to fix it.

Again, Where Is Where's My Phone?

Like iOS, Windows Phone 7 doesn't allow apps to send SMS messages without user initiation. You can build and populate a text message, but you can't send it via programming code. An argument can be made that this feature is a good thing because it prevents apps from sending potentially confidential data wirelessly without users knowing it. In addition, some phone plans still charge per message for text messages, so letting developers send messages could mean huge costs for the user.

You can, however, create an app that includes the capability to send messages. Sending an SMS message in code is fairly easy. You can use the SmsComposeTask object to create, populate, and send a text message, as shown in this example:

```
SmsComposeTask smsComposeTask = new SmsComposeTask();
smsComposeTask.To = "8005555555";
smsComposeTask.Body = "Message goes here.";
smsComposeTask.Show();
```

Data could come from TextFields instead of string literals. Then you could use the preceding code in a button click event, for example, to get the user to send the message by clicking a button in your app.

SmsComposeTask is a **launcher**, an object that starts a system service. You can use a variety of launchers in apps to initiate all kinds of services or to create an e-mail, play media, and load a Web page.

For more information on launchers, go to *http://msdn.microsoft.com/en-us/library/ ff769550%28v=VS.92%29.aspx*.

Using the Location Service

It's even easier to get the location of a Windows Phone 7 device than an Android or iOS device. The following project shows you how the Location service works.

HOW-TO 7-5

1. Start a new Windows Phone Application project and name it **LocationExample**. Design the UI so that it includes two TextBlocks to display latitude and longitude and a button to start the service. In the Properties window, rename the TextBlocks as **latitude** and **longitude** and change their Text properties to **Latitude:** and **Longitude:**. Set the button's Content property to **Get Coords** (see Figure 7-22).

2. To use the Location service, you must add a reference to the System.Device library. A **reference** is a collection of assets stored in a Dynamic Link Library (.dll) file, much like an Objective-C framework. Right-click the **LocationExample** project in the Solution Explorer, and click **Add Reference**. In the Add Reference dialog box, click the **.NET** tab, click **System.Device** in the list of components (see Figure 7-23), and click **OK**.

Figure 7-22   The LocationExample UI

(continues)

(continued)

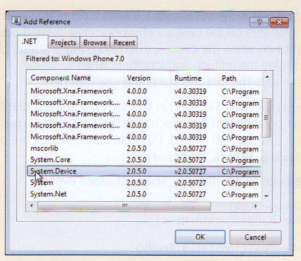

Figure 7-23 The Add Reference dialog box

3. In the form designer, double-click the **Button** component to open the code editor and create the `click` event. Add the following reference to the `System.Device.Location` namespace at the top of the code (with the rest of the `using` statements):

   ```
   using System.Device.Location;
   ```

4. Inside the class declaration, add an instance variable to hold the Location service monitor; the `GeoCoordinateWatcher` object keeps track of location changes:

   ```
   GeoCoordinateWatcher gcw;
   ```

5. Next, add the following code to the `button1_click` event:

   ```
   gcw = new GeoCoordinateWatcher(GeoPositionAccuracy.High);
   gcw.MovementThreshold = 20;
   gcw.StatusChanged += new EventHandler
     <GeoPositionStatusChangedEventArgs>(gcw_StatusChanged);
   gcw.Start();
   ```

This code instantiates a `GeoCoordinateWatcher` object named `gcw` with the highest accuracy for the device. It then sets the `MovementThreshold` property, which is used to set the distance from a specified point that triggers a location update. In this case, it's set at 20 meters.

(continues)

248

(continued)

The next line is the interesting one in the `click` event. It adds a delegate `EventHandler` object to listen for status changes on the `GeoCoordinateWatcher` named `gcw`. Essentially, it defines what to do when the `GeoCoordinateWatcher`'s status changes. For this simple app, you display the latitude and longitude when `GeoCoordinateWatcher` is ready. The last line starts the `gcw` watcher.

After you start the `GeoCoordinateWatcher` (gcw, in this case), you must use the `StatusChanged` event to get position updates. Each time the `GeoCoordinateWatcher`'s status changes, the code in this method is fired. Possible status values are `Disabled` (or unsupported), `Initializing`, `NoData`, and `Ready`.

6. Enter the following code to add the `gcw_StatusChanged` event:

```
void gcw_StatusChanged(object sender,
 GeoPositionStatusChangedEventArgs e)
{
  if (e.Status==GeoPositionStatus.Ready)
  {
    GeoCoordinate coord = gcw.Position.Location;
    latitude.Text = "Latitude: "+coord.Latitude.ToString("0.000");
    longitude.Text = "Longitude: "+coord.Longitude.ToString("0.000");
// After you have the location, stop the service to conserve power
    gcw.Stop();
  }
  if (e.Status==GeoPositionStatus.Disabled ||
  e.Status==GeoPositionStatus.NoData)
  {
    latitude.Text = "GPS Disabled";
    longitude.Text = "";
    gcw.Stop();
  }
}
```

If the `gcw` watcher's status is ready, the latitude and longitude are calculated and displayed in the corresponding labels. If the status is disabled or there's no data, you inform the user. In either case, stop the service to conserve battery power. Remember that the `gcw` watcher is started in the button's `click` event, so users can start it again whenever they want.

The Initializing status is superfluous in this app. You could notify the user that the service is initializing, but it's not needed for this simple example.

(continues)

(*continued*)

7. Run the app in the emulator, and place the cursor over the upper-right corner to display the emulator controls. Click the **>>** control to open the Additional Tools dialog box. Click the **Location** tab to load Bing Maps. When you click a location in the map, the data is fed to the emulator. Click the **Get Coords** button in the LocationExample app to display the location's latitude and longitude (see Figure 7-24).

Figure 7-24   LocationExample running in the emulator

Chapter Summary

- Windows Phone 7 is the latest Microsoft OS for smartphones. Apps for Windows Phone 7 are written with the C# programming language in Visual Studio 2010.

- C# is an object-oriented programming language supporting encapsulation, inheritance, and polymorphism. It includes the class interface and implementation in the same file, and a C# namespace is used to bundle assets for reuse. C# enables you to restrict access to data and create and implement your own properties.

- Silverlight is a development platform for creating interactive apps for the Web, desktops, and mobile devices. The Windows Phone 7 version supports core Silverlight features, adds capabilities specific to Windows Phone 7, and omits features that aren't used for small devices.

- XAML is an XML vocabulary designed to contain and describe user interface components.

- A C# namespace is analogous to a Java package and is a convenient way to bundle assets for reuse. The closest thing to a namespace in Objective-C is a framework.

- A Visual Studio solution is a group of files containing one or more projects.

- Code completion in Visual Studio is called IntelliSense.

- In Windows Phone 7, UI components don't have sizes until they are rendered onscreen.

- Visual Studio uses the Delegate design pattern via a delegate method to wire events to event handlers.

- Event delegates are objects that handle interactions between data and components that trigger events.

- A launcher is an object that starts a system event. Windows Phone 7 includes many launchers, such as those that send e-mail, play media, or show a Web page.

- A reference is a Visual Studio bundle of resources stored in a `.dll` file. You add references to projects to make use of their functionality.

- In Windows Phone 7, apps can't send SMS messages without user initiation.

Key Terms

C#—The programming language used to create Windows Phone 7 apps.

event delegates—Objects that handle interactions between data and the component firing the event.

Extensible Application Markup Language (XAML)—An XML vocabulary designed to contain and describe user interface components.

IntelliSense—The code-completion feature in Visual Studio.

launcher—An object that starts a system service.

namespace—A C# feature used to bundle assets for reuse.

reference—A collection of assets stored in a Dynamic Link Library (`.dll`) file.

Silverlight—A development platform for creating interactive apps for the Web, desktops, and mobile devices.

solution—A group of files in Visual Studio containing one or more projects.

Visual Studio 2010—The IDE used to create Windows Phone 7 apps.

Windows Phone 7—The latest Microsoft OS for smartphones, desktops, and mobile devices. It includes all the tools found on smartphones and features tight integration with Microsoft Office and Outlook.

Review Questions

1. When creating Windows Phone 7 apps, which programming language do you use?

   a. Java

   b. C++

   c. Objective-C

   d. C#

2. Silverlight apps can be created for which of the following? (Choose all that apply.)

   a. Web pages

   b. Windows phones

   c. Desktops

   d. iPhone

3. Both Objective-C and C# include the class interface and implementation in the same file. True or False?

4. The C# keyword `using` is closest to which keyword in Java and Objective-C?

   a. `@property`

   b. `implements`

   c. `extends`

   d. `import`

5. In C#, a namespace is which of the following?

   a. A way to bundle assets

   b. A location for naming a component

   c. A memory location

   d. The entry point for a program

6. Which of the following is true of C# properties? (Choose all that apply.)

   a. They provide a public interface for private data.

   b. They're written and maintained by Microsoft.

   c. They're written by the developer.

   d. They allow private, public, and protected access.

7. IntelliSense includes which of the following features? (Choose all that apply.)

a. Bundling assets

b. Code completion

c. Launcher objects

d. Breakpoints

8. A Visual Studio solution is:

a. A deployed app

b. A group of files containing one or more projects

c. A file on the Microsoft Web site

d. None of the above

9. Which Visual Studio window lists a project's assets?

a. Call Stack window

b. Locals window

c. Solution Explorer

d. Properties window

10. Which Visual Studio window do you use to set objects' attributes?

a. Call Stack window

b. Locals window

c. Solution Explorer

d. Properties window

11. In Visual Studio, which of the following objects serves as a container for where you drop components?

a. `FormContent`

b. `Container`

c. `ContentPanel`

d. `DrawHere`

12. In C#, a reference is which of the following?

a. A collection of files stored in a DLL

b. A pointer to an app

c. A user interface component

d. A book, such as a dictionary

13. Which of the following handles interactions between data and the component firing the event?

a. Application objects

b. Event delegates

c. XAML objects

d. The `main()` method

14. Objects that start system services are called:

a. Starters

b. System objects

c. Launchers

d. None of the above

15.   You submit `.xap` files for publication on the Windows Phone Marketplace. True or False?

16.   The Location service is provided as which of the following?
   a.   Component
   b.   Reference
   c.   Framework
   d.   Package

Up for Discussion

1.   Compare C#, Java, and Objective-C. In what way is C# a look into the future?

2.   Compare Visual Studio 2010, Xcode, and MOTODEV Studio. Which IDE do you prefer, and why?

3.   How is Apple different from Microsoft and Google in the smartphone market? Which company strategy is the most successful? Explain your answer.

4.   Microsoft and Apple don't allow apps to send SMS messages without user initiation, but Google does. Which policy is best, and why?

Programming Exercises

1.   Create a Windows Phone 7 app that displays the area and circumference for circles, and write a `Circle` class that performs the calculations. Instantiate a `Circle` object based on a user-entered radius.

2.   Create a Windows Phone 7 app that displays the area and perimeter for rectangles, and write a `Rectangle` class that performs the calculations. Instantiate a `Rectangle` object based on user-entered length and width values.

3.   Create a Windows Phone 7 app that converts temperature from degrees Fahrenheit to degrees Celsius. Ask users for the temperature in degrees Fahrenheit. Write a `TempConverter` class to perform the calculations, and instantiate a `TempConverter` object with the user input. Use the following formula for the conversion:

$C = 5/9(F - 32)$

4.   Create a Windows Phone 7 app that converts temperature from degrees Celsius to degrees Fahrenheit. Ask users for the temperature in degrees Celsius. Write a `TempConverter` class to perform the calculations, and instantiate a `TempConverter` object with the user input. Use the following formula for the conversion:

$F = 9/5 * C + 32$

5. Combine Programming Exercises 3 and 4 so that users can choose between converting Fahrenheit to Celsius and vice versa. Be sure to include the `TempConverter` class and instantiate a `TempConverter` object for each calculation.

6. Create a Windows Phone 7 app that calculates payroll. Allow the user to enter the number of hours worked and an hourly wage. The wage should be "time and a half" for hours worked over 40 in a week. Display the amount to be paid to the user.

Web Applications

CHAPTER 8

Web Applications

In this chapter, you learn to:

◎ Determine when users access your Web pages with a mobile device

◎ Choose tools for creating Web page files

◎ Use File Transfer Protocol to upload files to a Web server

◎ Use JavaScript as the programming language for Web pages

◎ Design and create JavaScript objects

◎ Use HTML and CSS as the view layer in Web pages

◎ Test Web pages in different emulators

Web applications are a collection of resources on a publicly accessible server that provide some sort of functionality. Users access them by using a Web browser, which is responsible for downloading any code needed for the Web application, interpreting the code, and displaying the results to users. The standard types of files you create when building a Web application are Hypertext Markup Language (HTML), Cascading Style Sheets (CSS), and JavaScript files. Taken together, these types of files enable you to build powerful Web applications.

Generally, smartphones are capable of rendering pages intended for the desktop with no problems, and the devices covered in this book have excellent browsers that can render Extensible HTML (XHTML) with CSS and run JavaScript code. Both iOS and Android devices use the WebKit browser engine. **WebKit** is an open-source rendering engine developed by Apple as a derivative of the Linux Konqueror browser's KHTML engine. Windows Phone 7 devices use a version of Internet Explorer (IE), Microsoft's Web browser.

Almost any application you develop on the Web for the desktop can be rendered on a smartphone browser, with the exception of Adobe Flash content. For a number of reasons, including security and battery drain, Apple has rejected including support for any Flash content on iOS devices; instead, it targets the newest HTML 5 specification. Both Android and Windows Phone 7 support versions of Flash.

 For the complete story on why Apple doesn't support Flash on iOS devices, go to *www.apple.com/hotnews/thoughts-on-flash/*.

 Adobe announced recently that it will no longer release Flash resources for any mobile devices; instead, it plans to focus on HTML 5. To view the Adobe release, go to *http://blogs.adobe.com/conversations/2011/11/flash-focus.html*.

Developing for Mobile Browsers

Usually, Web sites designed for mobile devices are—and should be—different from their desktop counterparts. Mobile browsers have much less screen space for you to use, and connection speeds are usually slower than desktop speeds. Most important, mobile users have a different mindset than desktop users do. Mobile Internet users are generally looking for something specific when they browse. Current usage data indicates that mobile users spend 3 to 5 minutes per session on their browsers. Your site designs must accommodate this usage pattern and be fast loading and easy to navigate.

Most large Web sites have separate versions: one for desktop browsers and one for mobile browsers. Some sites route mobile browsers to the mobile version automatically. Better sites display the mobile version but ask users whether they'd prefer to use the desktop version. There are a few ways to add this feature:

- Put a link at the top of the page asking mobile users whether they'd like to use the mobile version. This approach is the easiest because you just need to create a link. Of course, the caveat is that *all* users see the link, even those who aren't mobile users.

- Use CSS, and specify which style sheet to use for your pages based on the user's browser. In the HTML declaration, you can add `media="handheld"` to indicate that a specific style sheet should be used for handheld or small devices. Testing to make sure the browser loads the correct style sheet is then the only concern.

- Use JavaScript on the client. This solution is viable, depending on how you do it. You can try to have your code detect each browser variation (but there are many), or you can use object detection to see whether a browser supports a certain object before your code uses it. Object detection is the preferred approach by far.

- Use a server-side solution. You can use the Web server to determine the client by using server-side technologies, including PHP, Java Server Pages (JSP) and Java servlets, and Active Server Pages (ASP) or ASP.NET. These technologies give you control over the server configuration, which you can modify to suit your needs.

The examples in this chapter use JavaScript on the client to create and deliver Web content to smartphones.

Choosing an Editor

So far, you have had little choice of tools for smartphone development because of the binary nature of the files needed to run apps on certain devices. So you have used tools that can create the correct file types for your app on a specified platform.

When developing for the Web, however, the choices are more plentiful. All the files needed for Web apps to run are text based, meaning you need just a text editor to create files. In addition, there's no compilation stage when writing Web apps, so you don't need a compiler, either. The browser is responsible for downloading the necessary files, interpreting the code in them, and acting on the code.

Having said that, dedicated Web editors are available for all platforms. Which one you use is a matter of preference. Choices range from simple text editors, such as Notepad for Windows, to software packages, such as Adobe Dreamweaver. You can even use some tools you already know, such as Microsoft Visual Studio or MOTODEV Studio, to create Web apps. The trick is to find the tool that best fits your needs.

 When developing Web apps for smartphones, using a bare-bones editor—one that simply does syntax highlighting for Web files—is often better. The file types needed for Web development are HTML, CSS, and JavaScript, so find an editor that can color-code these file types at least. That way, when you make a mistake—as you no doubt will—finding it will be easier.

The Web file editor used for these projects is JXEd, which includes editors for XHTML, XML, CSS, and JavaScript. It has syntax highlighting for all supported file types and even offers basic code completion. In addition, it has a dedicated editor for CSS files (see Figure 8-1).

 You can download JXEd at *http://jxed.bright-moments.com.*

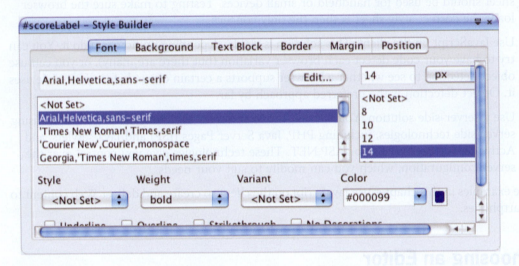

Figure 8-1   JXEd showing the CSS editor

A few other components are needed for a Web development environment. First, of course, you need a browser, and you should try to test in as many browsers as possible. Translating this guideline to smartphones, you should test on as many devices or emulators as possible, too. The four main browsers to use for testing are Firefox, Safari, Chrome, and Internet Explorer. Generally, the recommended testing strategy is to run your app in Firefox, and make sure it works in this browser first. If you're creating a desktop version of a Web site, test in IE next. If you're creating a mobile version, test in Chrome and Safari next. These decisions are based on market share of these browsers.

 You can download these browsers for testing at the following sites: Apple Safari, *www.apple.com/safari/*; Google Chrome, *www.google.com/chrome*; Microsoft Internet Explorer, *http://windows.microsoft.com/en-US/internet-explorer/downloads/ie*; and Mozilla Firefox, *www.mozilla.org/en-US/firefox/new/*.

Two add-ons are useful when testing in Firefox: Firebug and Web Developer (see Figure 8-2). **Firebug** is a JavaScript debugger. **Web Developer** is an environment manipulator, and you can use it to simulate different user environments. To install these add-ons, select Tools, Add-ons from the Firefox menu. Click Get Add-ons, and do a search for these tools.

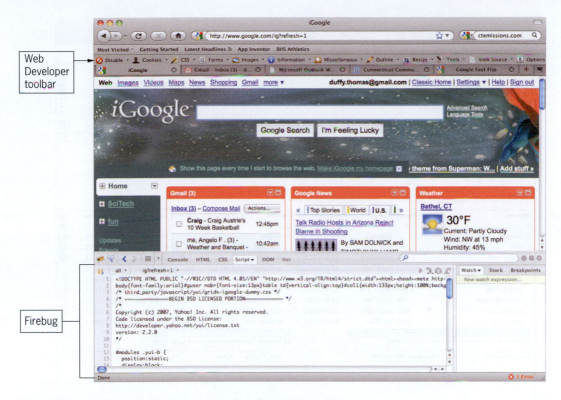

Web
Developer
toolbar

Firebug

Figure 8-2 Firefox with Firebug and the Web Developer toolbar

Finally, you need a tool to transfer files from your local machine to the Web server. Most Web servers use **File Transfer Protocol (FTP)** to transfer files. Stand-alone tools are available, too. FileZilla, for example, has versions for Mac, Windows, and Linux. Like other FTP clients, it connects you to a Web server after you enter your username and password. It displays two lists of files: On the left is your local file system, and on the right is the server's file system (see Figure 8-3). You use commands to move files from the local server to the remote server or simply drag and drop files. When developing Web apps, you're trying to duplicate your local file system on the remote file system.

You can download FileZilla free at *http://filezilla-project.org/download.php?type=client*.

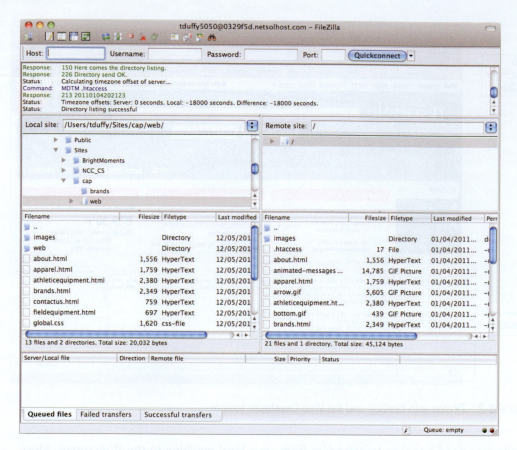

Figure 8-3   The FileZilla FTP tool

More complex tools dedicated to Web development include site management features. With Dreamweaver, for example, you can connect to a remote server by FTP, Web Distributed Authoring and Versioning (WebDAV), or Relational Database Service (RDS) and upload files without using a third-party tool. Microsoft Expression Web is another tool with similar capabilities.

To find a list of free Web editors, visit *www.thefreecountry.com/webmaster/htmleditors.shtml*.

Detective Work

1. Set up your Web development environment. It must include an editor for HTML, CSS, and JavaScript files as well as an upload mechanism. Write a short description of your environment, and explain why you chose the tools you did.

2. Get a Web address. You can use the free developer package at Brinkster.com. To sign up, go to *www.brinkster.com/FreePkgLanding.aspx*.

3. Familiarize yourself with the upload process for your Web address. You must be able to upload and edit files.

A Quick Look at Web Technologies

To create Web apps, you need to combine three types of files: HTML, CSS, and JavaScript. Each file type handles a different part of the app. Although the lines between MVC tiers can be blurred at times, especially on a client-side app, the MVC design pattern can help when thinking about file types. HTML and CSS provide the View tier for a Web app. HTML supplies the structure of a document, and CSS provides the formatting. The Controller tier is written in JavaScript combined with event attributes in HTML. The Model tier for an app changes based on the nature of the app. It might be just the text on the page, or it might be data entered by a user for a calculation.

HTML

Hypertext Markup Language (HTML) is a markup language consisting of tag pairs that tell the browser how to handle the content the tags enclose. Most tags contain data as well as attributes. In general, data is displayed onscreen, and attributes are information about the data. HTML elements are the combination of the tag, any attributes, and the data between the opening and closing tags.

HTML tags are enclosed by angle brackets. The opening tag declares what the tag is, and the closing tag indicates the end by prefacing the tag name with a forward slash (/). So the opening tag for a paragraph is <p>, and the closing tag is </p>. The browser displays data between the <p> and </p> tags in a paragraph structure.

All HTML files start and end with <html></html> tags, and the data between them is the Web page. In addition, all HTML files have <head></head> and <body></body> elements. The head contains metadata, which is information about the page, and is where you can declare external scripts and CSS rules. The body holds all the information that's displayed onscreen.

HTML is a **structure-based language**, so its elements describe the parts of a document, not the document's content. Elements such as headings, paragraphs, and tables make sense as part of the document displayed onscreen. Browsers understand how to render each element onscreen and are consistent in how this rendering is done.

Aside from the usual document-centered elements, two elements warrant special attention: <div></div> and <span></span>. Both <div> (short for "division") and <span> are container elements that make it possible for you to group elements and treat them as a single entity, so you can manipulate the group with code or style it as a single entity. The only difference between these elements is that <div> is a block-level element, and <span> is an inline element. Block-level elements represent blocks onscreen and include white space above and below the element. Inline elements display their content next to whatever content surrounds them.

Without hyperlinks, there wouldn't be a World Wide Web. The Web is a collection of documents connected by hyperlinks and accessible via a browser. Originally, the Web was intended for users to be able to jump back and forth between related documents. The Web's hyperlink function is provided by the `<a></a>` element. It includes an `href` attribute (for hypertext reference) that points to an external resource. When a user clicks the link, the browser navigates to the resource the `href` attribute specifies.

Here's a short example that uses some common tags.

```
<html>
<head>
  <title>The Art of Noise</title>
</head>
<body>
  <h1>
    <img src="http://www.bright-moments.com/webdeveloper/images/
artofnoise.jpg" alt="Art of Noise" width="125" height="125">
    <a href="http://www.theartofnoiseonline.com/">The Art of Noise</a>
  </h1>
  <h3>Computer Enhanced Music Lives</h3>
  <p>The Art of Noise is a techno-pop group whose music is an amalgam
of studio gimmickry, tape splicing, and synthesized beats.
  </p>
  <hr />
  <p>Some of their works:</p>
  <ol>
    <li>Who's Afraid</li>
    <li>Daft</li>
    <li>Sirius Sounds</li>
  </ol>
  <hr />
  <p>Some of my Favorite Songs:</p>
  <ul>
    <li><a href="http://www.bright-moments.com/webdeveloper/sound/
daftpunk.mp3">Daftpunk-world</a></li>
    <li>Beat Box (Diversion 1)</li>
    <li>Close (to the Edit)</li>
  </ul>
</body>
</html>
```

The `<html>` element contains data for the page, and the `<head>` element describes the Web page and includes the `<title>` element. The browser displays the `<title>` element at the top of the window or as the text for a tab.

The `<body>` element contains the data shown onscreen. `<h1>` is a first-level header and, in this case, contains an `<img>` element and an `<a>` element. The `<img>` element specifies which image to load in the `src` attribute; it's a "replaced" element, meaning the image file replaces the tag in the document. Note the `href` attribute in the `<a>` element. That's where the user jumps to when The Art of Noise link is clicked.

The rest of the tags are easy to understand. `<h3>` is a third-level header, `<p>` is a paragraph, and `<hr>` stands for horizontal rule. `<ol>` is an ordered list, containing a collection of `<li>` (list item) elements. The browser numbers the list for you by default. `<ul>` is an unordered list (bulleted by default), also containing a collection of list items.

Notice the hyperlink pointing to the `.mp3` file. Hyperlinks can point to a variety of resources on the Web. When a browser doesn't know how to handle a specific file type, it hands the task over to the OS, which looks for a registered program for the file type.

Figure 8-4 shows the HTML file loaded in Chrome.

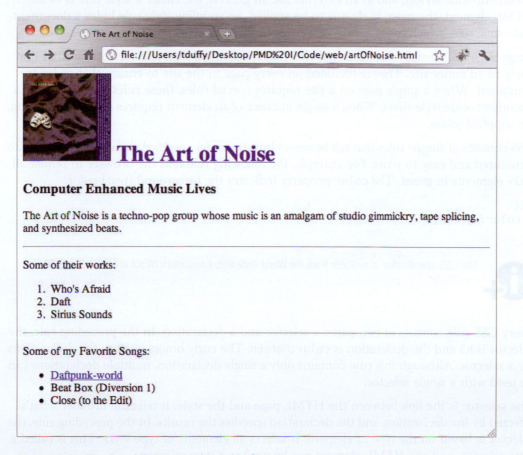

Figure 8-4   The Art of Noise page loaded in Chrome

For a complete HTML tutorial, visit the W3 Schools site at *www.w3schools.com/html/default.asp*.

CSS

Web designers learned they could use HTML components as formatting instructions in the early days of the Web, but you should use CSS for all formatting because it's a much better tool that separates data from how it's viewed. You can supply separate style rules for pages viewed with a desktop browser and pages viewed with a smartphone browser, for example.

The "cascading" part of CSS works much like dynamic method invocation. You can supply CSS style rules in three ways: as a `style` attribute for a single HTML element (called inline styles), as the content of a `<style>` element in a document's `<head>` element (called document-wide styles), and as an external file. In general, the closer a style rule is to an HTML element, the more likely it is to be applied. So an inline style rule hides a document-wide style rule, which hides a style rule declared in an external file.

Large Web sites usually have external CSS files specifying design and formatting rules that apply to an entire site. They're included on every page in the site to ensure that styles are consistent. When a single page on a site requires special rules, these rules are supplied in a document-wide style sheet. When a single instance of an element requires special formatting, it's supplied inline.

CSS consists of simple rules that tell browsers how to render specified elements. The rules are structured and easy to write. For example, the following rule tells the browser to render all `<h3>` elements in green. The `color` property indicates the foreground (text) color.

```
h3{
   color: green;
}
```

The CSS specification is available from the World Wide Web Consortium (W3C) at *www.w3.org/TR/css-2010/*.

Every CSS rule consists of two parts: a selector and a declaration. In the preceding rule, the selector is `h3` and the declaration is `color: green`. The curly braces enclose the declarations for a selector. Although this rule contains only a single declaration, multiple declarations can be used with a single selector.

The selector is the link between the HTML page and the style. It tells the browser what's affected by the declaration, and the declaration specifies the results. In the preceding rule, the selector is based on the type of element: It selects all elements of type `<h3>`. This is called a type selector, and any HTML element can be used as a type selector.

CSS declarations also have two parts, separated by a colon: a property and a value. If you're thinking this sounds like attributes and values in HTML, you're correct. The concepts are nearly identical except for how they're written. So in the previous rule, the declaration includes the property named `color` and the value `green`. The property is a characteristic that the selector possesses, and the value is the precise specification of the property.

To add the style rule to the HTML document as a document-wide style, the following code is added to the `<head>` section just after the `<title>` line. Figure 8-5 shows the result in Safari.

```
<style>
  h3{
    color: green;
  }
</style>
```

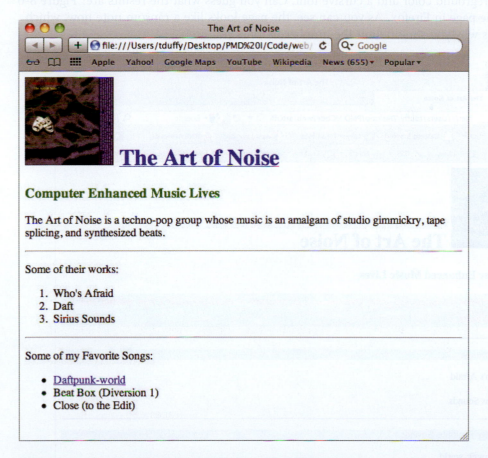

Figure 8-5   The Art of Noise file with the style rule added

To show cascading in effect, a second document-wide style is added after the first one. This rule states that all `<p>` elements on the page should use gray as the foreground color and light blue as the background color and use a sans-serif font.

```
p{
  color: gray;
  background-color: lightblue;
  font-family: sans-serif;
}
```

Then an inline style element is added to the paragraph beginning with "The Art of Noise is a techno-pop group"; the bold code shows what's been added:

```
<p style="color:red;font-family:cursive">The Art of Noise is a ↵
 techno-pop group...</p>
```

This inline style specifies that the `<p>` element containing the `style` attribute should use red as the foreground color and a cursive font. Can you guess what the results are? Figure 8-6 shows the page in Firefox. As you can see, the page looks like a ransom note now, which illustrates why you should limit the number of fonts you use!

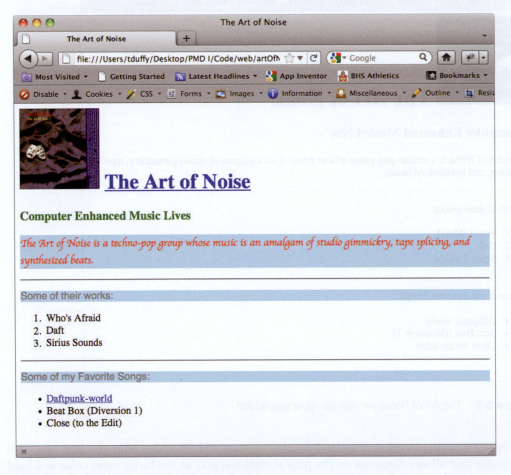

Figure 8-6   The CSS cascade shown in Firefox

Because the inline style doesn't specify a background color, the one specified in the document-wide style rule is applied.

For the most part, elements on a Web page are positioned next to or below each other, depending on their order and whether they're inline or block level. The distances and alignment of these elements are given by properties such as margin, padding, and width. An element might use the float property occasionally to shift it to one side, but generally, the browser fills the canvas with elements in the order they're received. This process is called relative positioning, as each element gets its placement relative to others on the canvas. CSS supports relative positioning and adds the capability to make corrections to an element's position without affecting other elements.

CSS also supports the concept of absolute positioning, which is entirely different. Absolute positioning takes an element out of the rendering sequence and places it at the onscreen location you specify by using the top and left properties combined with the position property set to absolute. The top and left attributes specify the coordinates of the element's top-left corner with pixel-level control. Using these properties along with the width and height properties can produce interesting effects. Here's an example:

```
<html>
<head>
  <title>Positioning</title>
</head>
<body>
  <div style="background-color:lightgray;height:250px;width:325px;↵
position:absolute;top:0px;left:0px;">
  </div>
  <div style="position:absolute;top:50px;left:100px;">
  <img src="http://www.bright-moments.com/webdeveloper/images/artofnoise.jpg"↵
alt="Art of Noise" width="125" height="125">
  </div>
</body>
</html>
```

This code draws a light gray rectangle in the top-left corner of the browser window and then places the Art of Noise image 50 pixels from the top and 100 pixels from the left edge. The image is drawn on top of the gray rectangle because it's declared after the rectangle in the HTML file. Figure 8-7 shows the results in Safari.

The coordinate system places (0,0) in the top-left corner of the browser window. As you go from left to right, the left property's value increases; as you move from top to bottom, the top property's value increases. You can assign negative values, but doing so moves the element outside the window's viewable area.

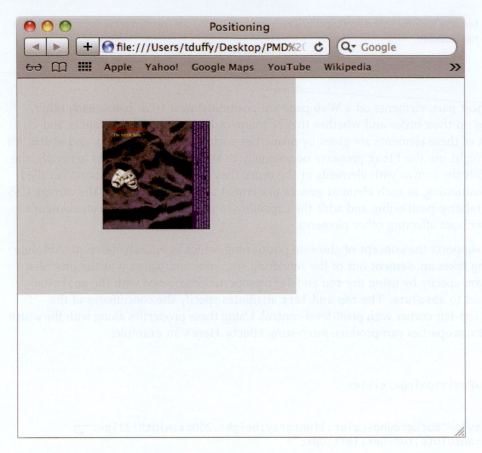

Figure 8-7   The `positioning.html` file shown in Safari

The W3 Schools site offers an excellent tutorial on CSS at *www.w3schools.com/css/default.asp*.

JavaScript

JavaScript is the standard programming language for running code on a client's machine. It's supported in all major browsers on the desktop and, more important, in all the default browsers for each smartphone platform discussed in this book. A quick look at JavaScript is a good idea, especially if you haven't done any JavaScript development.

What JavaScript Is Not

Starting with what something isn't rather than what it is can be easier. JavaScript isn't a subset of the Java programming language in the way VBScript is a subset of Microsoft Visual Basic. Java is a full-strength, **compiled language**, meaning it's translated from English-like commands to a machine language only once—at compile time. JavaScript, on the other hand, is an **interpreted language**, which must be translated into machine code each time the program runs. Java is an object-oriented language, but JavaScript is an object-based language, so it doesn't have some of the features that a true object-oriented language does (discussed in more detail in "Is JavaScript Object Oriented?"). It helps, however, to think in terms of objects when you write JavaScript.

What JavaScript Can Do

So what can you do with JavaScript? A lot! You can manipulate the browser itself, play sounds, create animations, perform calculations, and even have Web pages created on the fly. It includes a fairly complete set of functions and commands to manipulate the Document Object Model (DOM), and it can make your Web pages seem more alive, compared with static HTML pages.

If you've done any programming at all, especially in C derivatives such as Java, Objective-C, and C#, JavaScript will seem familiar. Many of the same programming constructs used in other languages are present, such as loops, conditional statements, assignment, arrays, functions, methods, and variables. Here are a few simple rules for JavaScript:

- JavaScript is case sensitive.
- JavaScript ignores white space.
- JavaScript uses curly braces ({ }) to group statements.
- JavaScript uses dot (.) notation to access properties and methods. For example, to access the firstName property of an object representing a person, you write myAunt.firstName.

Is JavaScript Object Oriented?

When considering OOP languages, JavaScript is often excluded from this group. It does, however, make use of some object-oriented principles. To see how JavaScript fits with other OOP languages, this section compares it with Java because it's available on all platforms covered in this book.

One reason JavaScript isn't considered a true object-oriented language is that, unlike Java, it isn't strongly typed. JavaScript variables don't have specified data types; instead, data type depends on the value you assign to a variable. This means JavaScript is a **weakly typed** language. To change the data type, you simply assign a different kind of data to the variable or treat the data in a different way. For example, in JavaScript you can write:

```
var myVar = "a string";
myVar = 4;
alert("myVar = " + myVar);
```

This code creates the myVar variable as a string, but in the second line, it becomes an integer by assigning a numeral (4) to it instead of text. When the script displays the value, it casts the integer value of the myVar variable back into a string, this time containing a string representation of the integer value. This is perfectly legal in JavaScript. In fact, it's one of the reasons JavaScript is easier to write than Java: You don't have to worry about what type of data you're dealing with. In Java, the compiler would raise an error for this code. The equivalent Java code is as follows:

```
String myString = "a string";
int myInt = 4;
System.out.println("myInt = " + myInt);
```

In Java, you must declare the data type with the variable, and in this case, you need two variables, one for each data type. If you want to change a variable's data type in Java, you create a new variable of the correct data type and then cast the variable from one type to the other. However, sometimes casting just isn't possible.

Another reason JavaScript isn't considered an OOP language is that it doesn't use class-based inheritance. In Java and other true object-oriented languages, class-based inheritance means you define objects in a logical hierarchy, with more abstract objects at the top and more concrete objects at the bottom. This top-down design makes it easy to say, for example, "A four-wheeled vehicle is an object, and a car is a specific kind of four-wheeled vehicle." That way, cars inherit all the things that come with four-wheeled vehicles and add information specific to cars. Class-based inheritance is a powerful mechanism because the hierarchy can have many levels, each added to all objects farther down the hierarchy. In essence, you design objects in Java by determining how they're different from other existing objects.

JavaScript doesn't support class-based inheritance. However, it does support **prototype-based inheritance**, which differs from class-based inheritance in that properties and methods are inherited from a constructor only, not from a class higher up in the hierarchy. All object constructors in JavaScript create objects with properties and methods that are inherited from the prototype's properties and methods.

Building JavaScript Objects

Suppose you want to create an object in JavaScript modeled after a person. This person object has two properties for now: a last name and a first name. First, you create the prototype function, as shown in this example:

```
function person() {

}
```

Next, add the parameters for initializing properties:

```
function person(first,last){

}
```

Finally, assign the parameters to property placeholders in the prototype:

```
function person(first,last) {
  this.firstName = first;
  this.lastName = last;
}
```

Notice that the properties `firstName` and `lastName` are nested inside the prototype. The `this` keyword seems to associate them with the object, but as you see later, it also makes the properties publicly available to outside routines. In fact, just nesting properties makes them local to the object.

Later in your code, you can create as many `person` objects as you like, each of which has `firstName` and `lastName` properties automatically:

```
var tDuffy = new person("Tom","Duffy");
```

JavaScript and the Document Object Model

Most practical applications of JavaScript involve manipulating an HTML page's elements. Each element on the page is converted into an object by the browser, and your JavaScript code can access these objects. Objects are organized into a logical hierarchy called the **Document Object Model (DOM)**, which specifies a standard for accessing data in documents, such as HTML and XML documents.

 The DOM hierarchy isn't an inheritance hierarchy. It's more of an object composition model.

The DOM includes a `document` object you can use to access Web page elements. The browser creates a `document` object for every page. The `document` object, among others, has a `getElementById('id')` method for referring to any HTML element on the page that you've assigned an `id` attribute.

To see how the DOM works, the same example used to illustrate positioning is used here. In the positioning example, the Art of Noise album cover image was placed at coordinates (100,50). Say you want to write a simple script that waits 5 seconds after the page loads and then moves the image to the top-left corner at coordinates (0,0). First, an `id` attribute (shown in bold code) is assigned to the `<div>` element containing the image:

```
<div id="image" style="position:absolute;top:50px;left:100px;">
```

Then a `<script>` element is added in the `<head>` element with the following code shown in bold:

```
<head>
<title>Positioning</title>
<script type="text/javascript">
function moveImage(top,left){
  document.getElementById('image').style.top = top;
  document.getElementById('image').style.left = left;
}
</script>
</head>
```

You supply new `top` and `left` values to the `moveImage()` function, and it assigns these new values to the `top` and `left` properties of the element whose id attribute is specified as `image`. `getElementById()` takes a string as a parameter and creates an HTML object corresponding to the HTML element with the specified id attribute. HTML objects have a `style` object that enables you to manipulate an object's CSS properties.

To get the function to execute 5 seconds after the page loads, the `<body>` element must be modified to include an `onload` event that fires when all the page's content has finished loading. Using this event is a convenient way to make sure you don't try to access something on the page that hasn't loaded yet. Then the built-in `setTimeout()` function is used to call `moveImage()` after a 5-second delay:

```
<body onload="setTimeout('moveImage(0,0)',5000)">
```

The `setTimeout()` function takes two parameters: the code to run and the delay. In this case, it calls `moveImage(0,0)`, which changes the `top` and `left` properties of the `<div>` element containing the image and waits 5000 ms (5 seconds). Figure 8-8 shows the results in Safari.

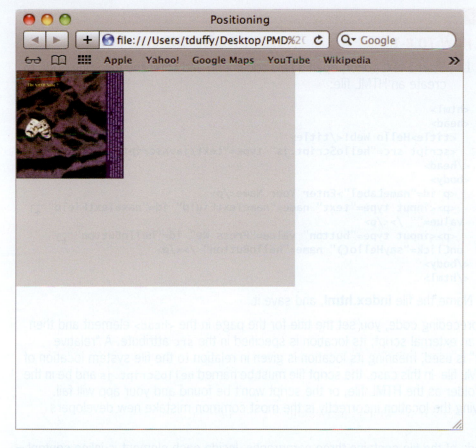

Figure 8-8 Moving the image with JavaScript

The browser creates a `window` object for every page, too. This object is where `setTimeout()` is defined and is used when you call a built-in function without an object. In other words, you can safely omit the `window` object reference. The `document` object is actually a child of the `window` object. Because `getElementById()` is defined in the `document` object, not the `window` object, you must call it from the `document` object.

For more information, try the W3 Schools DOM tutorial at *www.w3schools.com/htmldom/dom_intro.asp* and the JavaScript tutorial at *www.w3schools.com/js/default.asp*.

Your First Web App: Hello Web!

Now that you know enough HTML, CSS, and JavaScript to be dangerous, it's time to write the traditional "Hello World" app by using Web technologies. This project requires two files: an HTML file to store the app's objects and a JavaScript file containing the code needed to get objects to work together.

HOW-TO 8-1

1. Start a text editor, open a new document, and enter the following code to create an HTML file:

```html
<html>
<head>
  <title>Hello Web!</title>
  <script src="helloScript.js" type="text/javascript"></script>
</head>
<body>
  <p id="nameLabel">Enter Your Name</p>
  <p><input type="text" name="nameTextField" id="nameTextField"
 value="" /></p>
  <p><input type="button" value="Press Me" id="helloButton"
 onClick="sayHello()" name="helloButton" /></p>
</body>
</html>
```

2. Name the file **index.html**, and save it.

In the preceding code, you set the title for the page in the `<head>` element and then attach an external script; its location is specified in the `src` attribute. A "relative locator" is used, meaning its location is given in relation to the file system location of the HTML file. In this case, the script file must be named `helloScript.js` and be in the same folder as the HTML file, or the script won't be found and your app will fail. Specifying the location incorrectly is the most common mistake new developers make.

The body of the file contains three paragraphs. Inside each element is inline content data. The first paragraph is where the Hello message is displayed. The `id` attribute in this paragraph enables you to change its content in the script later.

The second paragraph contains an `<input>` element of type `text`, and its `id` attribute is `nameTextField`. Notice that it has a `name` attribute, too. This attribute is identical to the `id` attribute, but it's for older browsers. Input elements are "replaced" elements, meaning that when the browser encounters them, the place where they're declared in the document is replaced with a graphical representation pulled from the attributes. In this case, a text field is drawn onscreen, and users can type inside it.

You've already seen replaced elements, such as `<img>` elements. The browser takes the file associated with the `src` attribute and replaces the `<img>` element with the file's contents.

(continues)

(continued)

Assign an `id` attribute to every HTML element that's accessed in code.

The final paragraph contains the button that triggers the app. The `onClick` attribute is the event associated with the button. When the user clicks the button, the browser looks for a function named `sayHello()` declared in the script. You write the `sayHello()` function in the next step.

HTML isn't case sensitive, but JavaScript and CSS are. However, treating every language as though it's case sensitive makes coding much easier.

3. Create a second text file, enter the following JavaScript code, and save the file as **helloScript.js** in the same folder you saved the HTML file:

```
function sayHello(){
  var nameText = document.getElementById("nameTextField").value;
  var displayString = "Hello, " + nameText + "!";
  document.getElementById("nameLabel").innerHTML = displayString;
}
```

Notice that the filename matches the name declared in the HTML file's `<script>` element, and the function name matches the function declared in the button's `onClick` event. The first line of code creates the `nameText` variable and assigns it the value stored in the `nameTextField` HTML object.

The second line of code creates the `displayString` variable and assigns its value based on the `nameText` variable. Finally, the `nameLabel` object's `innerHTML` property is set to the `displayString` value, which causes the browser to redraw the `nameLabel` element and display the greeting.

Although JavaScript is a weakly typed language, try to avoid changing a variable's data type by assignment. Doing so makes code harder to read and maintain.

To test your app, you must upload the files to a Web server. This example shows uploading files at Brinkster.com. If you have an account with Brinkster, you can follow along with the steps. If not, upload your files with the FTP tool you're using.

(continues)

(*continued*)

4. After logging into Brinkster.com, open the File Manager. Then click the **Options** button (with the gear icon) on the left side of the toolbar, point to **New**, and click **Folder**. In the New Folder Name dialog box, type **HelloWeb**, and click **Ok**.

5. Double-click the **HelloWeb** folder and click the **Upload** button (black arrow on a white rectangle) on the right side of the toolbar. Navigate to where you stored the two files you created earlier, select them, and then click **Open**. After the upload is finished, your window should look like Figure 8-9.

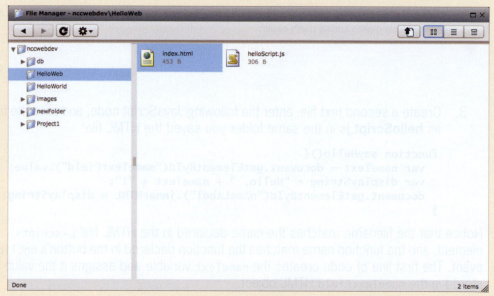

Figure 8-9 Uploaded files on Brinkster.com

6. To load your files in the browser, navigate to your Web address, or click **Settings** on the top toolbar. Figure 8-10 shows the Website Settings page. Copy the Default Web Address link, and paste it in the browser address bar. Type /**HelloWeb** at the end of the address, and press **Enter**.

 It can take 24 to 48 hours for Brinkster to set up your free account.

(continued)

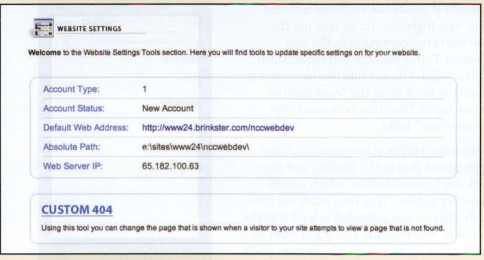

Figure 8-10   The Website Settings page

7. Enter your name and click the **Press Me** button. Your page should look similar to Figure 8-11.

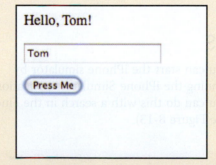

Figure 8-11   Clicking the button yields good results

Testing Web Apps in Emulators

Testing a Web app in smartphone emulators is a bit more difficult. In general, the process is as follows:

1. Start the emulator for the platform.

2. Click the Home button and then the browser button.

3. Type the URL and click Enter or Go.

The Web page should load, and you should be able to interact with it.

Android

The easiest way to test your Web pages in Android is to use the emulator included with App Inventor. To do this, use the `run-emulator` command in the App Inventor Extras package you downloaded and installed. You can find this command by searching for it or in the "AppInventor Extras Install Directory/commands-for-Appinventor" folder.

Unlock the phone, if necessary, click the applications grid at the bottom, and then click the browser button, which usually looks like a globe. Type the URL of the Hello Web app you just uploaded to load it in the emulator (see Figure 8-12). If you want to use the files for this chapter's example, point the emulator's browser to *www24.brinkster.com/nccwebdev/HelloWeb*.

iOS

You can start the iPhone simulator by running the iPhone Simulator application. You can do this with a search in the Finder (see Figure 8-13).

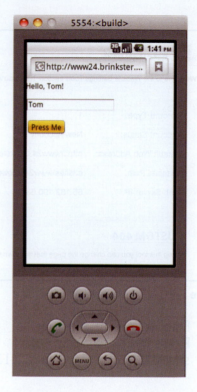

Figure 8-12 Testing in the Android emulator

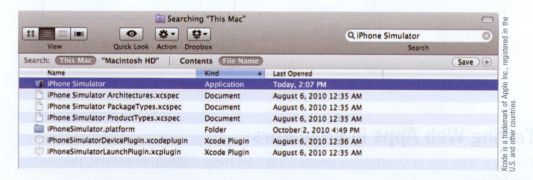

Figure 8-13 Search results for iPhone Simulator in the Finder

278

Next, click Safari to load the browser, and enter the URL of the files you just uploaded. Again, if you want to use the sample files, the URL is *www24.brinkster.com/nccwebdev/ HelloWeb*. Figure 8-14 shows the results.

Windows Phone 7

For Windows Phone 7, start the Windows Phone Emulator from the Start menu. Click the Internet Explorer button to load the browser, and type the URL of the files you just uploaded. (Again, to use this chapter's sample files, use the URL *www24.brinkster.com/ nccwebdev/HelloWeb*.) Figure 8-15 shows the results.

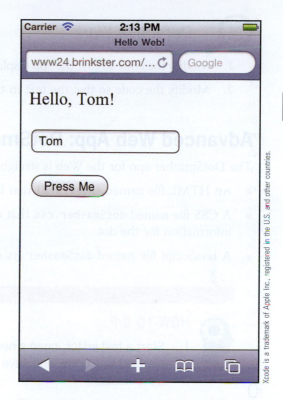

Figure 8-14   Testing in the iOS simulator

Figure 8-15   Running in the Windows Phone 7 emulator

Detective Work

1. Modify the code so that the app displays the correct text when no username is entered.

2. Modify the code so that the text in the button's label is "Thank you."

Advanced Web App: DotSmasher

The DotSmasher app for the Web is straightforward. It consists of three files:

- An HTML file named `index.html` that loads the CSS and JavaScript files

- A CSS file named `dotSmasher.css` that contains formatting instructions and positioning information for the dot

- A JavaScript file named `dotSmasher.js` containing functions for the app's events

HOW-TO 8-2

1. Start a text editor, open a new document, create the HTML file by entering the following code, and save the file as **index.html** in a new folder named DotSmasher:

```html
<html>
<head>
<title>DotSmasher</title>
  <link rel="stylesheet" href="dotSmasher.css" type="text/css"/>
  <script type="text/javascript" src="dotSmasher.js"></script>
</head>
<body onLoad="setGameAreaBounds()" onResize="setGameAreaBounds()">
  <div id="scoreLabel">Score: 0</div>
  <div id="pageTitle">DotSmasher</div>
  <div id="gameArea">
    <button id="dot" onClick="detectHit()"></button>
  </div>
</body>
</html>
```

Two events are specified in the body element: `onLoad` and `onResize`. The `setGameAreaBounds()` function is called in both events. The `onLoad` event fires when the page content loads. The available height and width must be calculated after the page loads, or the values always return as 0. The `onResize` event fires when the user resizes the browser window. More important, from the perspective of mobile devices, `onResize` fires when the user rotates the device. Because the available height and width change when the device is rotated, these values should be recalculated whenever this event fires.

(continues)

(continued)

2. Open a new text document, enter the following code, and save it as **dotSmasher.css** in the DotSmasher folder:

```css
#scoreLabel{
    font-family: Arial,Helvetica,sans-serif;
    font-size: 14pt;
    color: #000099;
    font-weight: bold;
    position: absolute;
    top: 10px;
    left: 10px;
    height: 25px;
}
#pageTitle{
    font-family: Arial,Helvetica,sans-serif;
    font-size: 24pt;
    font-weight: bold;
    color: #000099;
    position: absolute;
    top: 35px;
    left: 10px;
    height: 25px;
}
#gameArea{
    position: absolute;
    top: 75px;
    left: 10px;
    border: 1px #000099 solid;
}
#dot{
    position: absolute;
    top: 25px;
    left: 25px;
    background-color: #000099;
    width: 64px;
    height: 64px;
}
```

In this code, the # sign refers to the `id` attribute of elements in the HTML file. So the declarations in the `#scoreLabel` rule are applied to the HTML element with an `id` attribute set to `scoreLabel`. The rest of the rules in this file apply to the other elements.

(continues)

(continued)

All the CSS rules use absolute positioning. Absolute positioning works in the context of a container, and coordinates originate at the top-left corner of the surrounding element. In this example, the dot is initially positioned at top: 100, left: 35 because it's a child of the `gameArea` element, which has its own positioning information.

If you use absolute positioning for one page element, you should use it for all page elements. Unless you're adept at CSS, mixing absolute and relative positioning can sometimes produce undesirable results.

3. Open a new text document, enter the following code, and save it as **dotSmasher.js** in the DotSmasher folder:

```
var score = 0;
var aWidth;
var aHeight;
var timer;
function detectHit(){
  score += 1;
  scoreLabel.innerHTML = "Score: " + score;
}
function setGameAreaBounds(){
if(document.all){
  aWidth = document.body.clientWidth;
  aHeight = document.body.clientHeight;
}else{
  aWidth = innerWidth;
  aHeight = innerHeight;
}
aWidth -= 30;
aHeight -= 95;
document.getElementById("gameArea").style.width = aWidth;
document.getElementById("gameArea").style.height = aHeight;
aWidth -= 74;
aHeight -= 74;
moveDot();
}
```

(continues)

(continued)

```
function moveDot(){
    var x = Math.floor(Math.random()*aWidth);
    var y = Math.floor(Math.random()*aHeight);
    if(x<10)
      x = 10;
    if(y<10)
      y = 10;
    document.getElementById("dot").style.left = x;
    document.getElementById("dot").style.top = y;
    clearTimeout(timer);
    timer = setTimeout("moveDot()",1000);
}
```

The `detectHit()` function increments the score by 1 when the button is clicked. Then the `scoreLabel` object's `innerHTML` property is updated to reflect the new score.

The `setGameAreaBounds()` function sets the `gameArea` element's size dynamically. The first conditional statement is a good example of object detection. IE is the only browser that supports the `document.all` object. When you're trying to get the screen's height and width in IE, you use the `clientHeight` and `clientWidth` properties of the `document.body` object. Safari, Chrome, and Firefox use the W3C standard `innerWidth` and `innerHeight` properties of the `window` object.

After getting the available width and height of the canvas, some space is subtracted for a horizontal margin and then for a vertical margin that includes the height of the `pageTitle` and `scoreLabel` objects. The `gameArea` element's width and height are set, and then the dot's width and height are subtracted from the `innerWidth` and `innerHeight`, plus a little margin.

Then the `moveDot()` function is called, which uses the `aWidth` and `aHeight` variables to calculate maximum values for the dot's top and left coordinates. This function does most of the work in the app. First, random values are calculated by using the `Math` object; `aWidth` and `aHeight` represent maximum values for x and y coordinates. Conditional statements are used to make sure the dot doesn't disappear off the top or left edge of the game area. If the value of the x or y coordinate is less than 10, part of the dot is drawn offscreen, so the conditional statements make sure this doesn't happen. Then the dot's `top` and `left` properties are set to move it onscreen.

Next, the `clearTimeout()` function is called to clear the timer. (Remember that it's a function of the `window` object.) Finally, the `setTimeout()` function is called. This function expects two arguments: the code to run (usually a method) as the first argument and the delay in milliseconds as the second argument. The return value of `setTimeout()` is assigned to the `timer` variable.

(continues)

(continued)

4. To test your code, upload it to your Web server and open it in a browser. Figure 8-16 shows the results in Firefox.

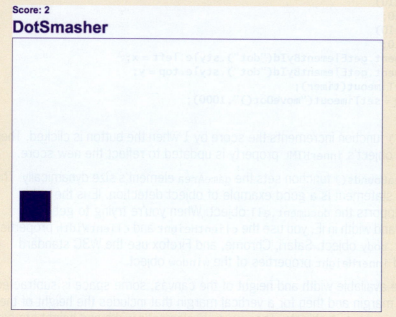

Figure 8-16 DotSmasher running in Firefox

5. You still need to test your app in all the emulators/simulators. Start each emulator/simulator and enter the URL of the files you just uploaded (or the URL for this chapter's example, *www.bright-moments.com/dotSmasher*). Figure 8-17 shows the results.

If you're having trouble clicking the button, increase the delay in `setTimeout()` or make the dot larger by increasing the width and height properties in the CSS file.

(continues)

(continued)

Xcode is a trademark of Apple Inc., registered in the U.S. and other countries.

Figure 8-17 DotSmasher running in each emulator/simulator

The benefit of doing Web development for small devices is that if you're careful, your app will look the same on all devices. You can also use the same code on all devices, meaning you need to maintain only one set of files. The same applies when you want to add new features: You need to do it only once.

Although developing Web apps for smartphones sounds great, especially from a code maintenance perspective, there are two glaring problems. First, getting a Web app to look like a native app on multiple devices isn't easy. You need to supply multiple style sheets and have the JavaScript code determine which device is being used before your app displays anything onscreen. Second, and more important, you don't have the benefit of selling your app in online marketplaces. Getting users to pay you for an app they can browse to isn't likely.

 ## Detective Work

1. Create a start/stop mechanism for the app. (*Hint*: Use `clearTimeout()`.)

2. Force the game to end after 30 seconds, and inform the user that the game has ended.

3. Create a way for users to select a difficulty level. You might want to give them the choices Easy, Medium, and Hard. Then you need to determine what defines the level of difficulty. You might increase the speed at which dots move or make dots smaller, for example.

286

Chapter Summary

- Both iOS and Android devices use the WebKit browser engine, an open-source rendering engine developed by Apple as a derivative of the Linux Konqueror browser's KHTML engine. Windows Phone 7 devices use a version of Internet Explorer.

- Apple doesn't support Flash content on iOS devices; instead, the newest HTML 5 specification is targeted. Both Android and Windows Phone 7 support versions of Flash.

- Most large Web sites have separate versions of their Web sites: one for desktop browsers and one for mobile browsers.

- All the files needed for Web apps to run are text based and include HTML, CSS, and JavaScript files.

- HTML is a structure-based language used to describe the parts of a Web page.

- CSS is a formatting language used to style and position elements on a Web page.

- JavaScript is the scripting language used to manipulate the elements of a Web page.

- The browser is responsible for downloading necessary Web files, interpreting the code in them, and acting on it.

- Web apps should be tested in as many browsers and on as many devices as possible.

Key Terms

compiled language—A programming language that's translated from English-like commands to a machine language only once, at compile time.

Document Object Model (DOM)—A standard for accessing objects in documents, such as XML and HTML documents. It's a hierarchical, treelike structure that represents a document's objects.

File Transfer Protocol (FTP)—The protocol used to transfer files to and from Web servers.

Firebug—A Firefox add-on that provides JavaScript debugging capabilities.

interpreted language—A programming language that must be translated into machine code each time a program runs.

prototype-based inheritance—A programming technique in which properties and methods are defined in a constructor, not from a class higher up in the hierarchy.

structure-based language—A language that describes an entity's structure, such as HTML describing the structure of a Web page.

weakly typed—A programming language characteristic in which data types are determined by assignment.

Web Developer—A Firefox add-on for manipulating the browser environment.

WebKit—An open-source rendering engine developed by Apple as a derivative of the Linux Konqueror browser's KHTML engine.

Review Questions

1. iOS and Android devices use which browser engine?

   a. Internet Explorer
   b. WebKit
   c. Mosaic
   d. Safari

2. Which of the following file types isn't typically used in a Web application?

   a. HTML
   b. CSS
   c. JavaScript
   d. Objective-C

3. Which step in the development process is unnecessary for Web apps?

   a. Write
   b. Compile
   c. Debug
   d. Deploy

4. Which of the following statements about JavaScript is true? (Choose all that apply.)

   a. It's an object-based language.
   b. It's compiled before running.
   c. It's a subset of the Java language.
   d. It's a derivative of the C language.

5. What is it called when properties and methods are inherited only through constructors?

   a. Class-based inheritance
   b. Polymorphism
   c. Prototype-based inheritance
   d. Encapsulation

6. An HTML attribute is which of the following? (Choose all that apply.)

   a. Information about the HTML data
   b. A character trait of the entire file
   c. A key/value pair
   d. Case sensitive

7. An interpreted language:

    a. Is compiled before it's run
    b. Must be interpreted each time it's run
    c. Is written in a foreign language
    d. Is more efficient than compiled languages

8. Which of the following is the de facto programming language for running scripts on the client's browser?

    a. AppleScript   c. Perl
    b. VBScript   d. JavaScript

9. A weakly typed language means:

    a. Typing commands is easy.
    b. The code contains a lot of special characters.
    c. The data types can't change.
    d. The data types can change based on assignment.

10. Which platform currently supports Flash? (Choose all that apply.)

    a. iOS
    b. Android
    c. Windows Phone 7

11. Which of the following is typically a file needed for Web apps to run? (Choose all that apply.)

    a. HTML   c. JavaScript
    b. CSS   d. Objective-C

12. HTML is which of the following? (Choose all that apply.)

    a. A markup language   c. A structure-based language
    b. A scripting language   d. A formatting language

13. Which of the following represents a Web page's objects?

    a. JavaScript   c. DOM
    b. HTML   d. CSS

14. You use which of the following to format elements of Web pages?

    a. JavaScript   c. HTML
    b. CSS   d. XML

Up for Discussion

1. Apple doesn't support Adobe Flash technology on iOS devices. Why did it make this decision? Do you agree with it? Explain your answer.

2. Discuss HTML, CSS, and JavaScript in terms of the MVC design pattern. Which language fits each tier? Explain your answer.

3. Is JavaScript object oriented? Explain your answer.

4. What are the pros and cons of developing Web apps for smartphones compared with native apps?

5. Compare compiled languages and interpreted languages, and give examples of both. Which language is better, and why?

Programming Exercises

1. Create a Web app that displays the area and circumference for circles. Create a `Circle` object that performs the calculations, and instantiate this object based on a user-entered radius.

2. Create a Web app that displays the area and perimeter for rectangles. Create a `Rectangle` object that performs the calculations, and instantiate this object based on user-entered length and width values.

3. Create a Web app that converts temperature from degrees Fahrenheit to degrees Celsius. Ask users for the temperature in degrees Fahrenheit. Create a `TempConverter` object to perform the calculations, and instantiate this object with the user input. Use the following formula for the conversion:

   $C = 5/9(F - 32)$

4. Create a Web app that converts temperature from degrees Celsius to degrees Fahrenheit. Ask users for the temperature in degrees Celsius. Create a `TempConverter` object to perform the calculations, and instantiate this object with the user input. Use the following formula for the conversion:

   $F = 9/5 * C + 32$

5. Combine Programming Exercises 3 and 4 so that users can choose between converting Fahrenheit to Celsius and vice versa. Be sure to include the `TempConverter` object and instantiate this object for each calculation.

6. Create a Web app that calculates payroll. Allow the user to enter the number of hours worked and an hourly wage. The wage should be "time and a half" for hours worked over 40 in a week. Display the amount to be paid to the user.

Cross-Platform Development with PhoneGap

In this chapter, you learn to:

◎ Create cross-platform smartphone apps with PhoneGap

◎ Create PhoneGap projects for Android and iOS

◎ Use different strategies for PhoneGap development

◎ Use existing Web projects to create native apps built with PhoneGap

◎ Create Web files in MOTODEV Studio and Xcode

◎ Add existing files to projects in MOTODEV Studio and Xcode

◎ Use the PhoneGap Geolocation API

◎ Use an Android handset in MOTODEV Studio

As you've seen, developing apps for the three major smartphone platforms can be frustrating. You need to be proficient in three different object-oriented languages, master three different IDEs, and maintain three different codebases (code versions) for Android, iOS, and Windows Phone 7. You've also learned that by using Web technologies, you can write a single app that works for all platforms. With Web apps, you can manage a single codebase, and when modifications are necessary, you need to make them in only a single location.

Of course, the problem is that users want native apps, and they want to shop in an app store or marketplace. They also want the ease of updating apps via their phones, not over the Web.

Each platform includes a Web browser component. You could add this component to your app and then load Web pages into it, which would certainly alleviate the problem of having to know multiple programming languages. You could then use HTML, CSS, and JavaScript in your Web app. In theory, you could access each platform's technologies from the browser component, but this method isn't practical.

Introducing PhoneGap

PhoneGap seeks to address these problems by including a unified API for using Web technologies in native apps as well as project templates developers can use for Android and iOS apps. As of this writing, Windows Phone 7 isn't supported, but support for this platform is forthcoming. By the time you read this, it might already be available.

PhoneGap was developed by Nitobi, Inc., which was recently acquired by Adobe Systems, Inc. It's open source and available to developers free under an Apache Software Foundation license. This license allows you to do almost anything with the code as long as you include Nitobi's copyright notice. To view details of the license, go to *www.phonegap.com/about/license*.

This tool also has a unified API for accessing **native device capabilities**, which are built-in features of the device. These capabilities include Accelerometer, Camera, Capture, Compass, Connection, Contacts, Device, Events, File, Geolocation, Media, Notification, and Storage. You have access to all these capabilities through JavaScript.

The end product of a PhoneGap project is an app that looks and behaves like a native app. You can deploy it to any marketplace and be confident it will be approved, as long as you adhere to the marketplace rules.

Apple is notorious for rejecting apps that use external Web content because they can eat up users' data allowances. PhoneGap addresses this problem by storing your Web content on the device. This solution is not only more cost efficient for users, but also much faster.

The steps in this chapter aren't quite as detailed as in previous chapters. If you need a reminder, refer to Chapter 5 for working with MOTODEV Studio and Chapter 6 for working with Xcode. In addition, refer to Appendix A, if necessary, for PhoneGap installation instructions.

Your First PhoneGap App: Hello PhoneGap!

In PhoneGap, you can not only maintain a single codebase for your app, but also choose how you develop your app. There are two general strategies. First, use whatever editor you like to create Web files, test in Chrome and Safari, and then copy the Web files to the www folder of your PhoneGap project. Second, create your PhoneGap project first and use the tools built into MOTODEV Studio and Xcode to create your Web content. Both strategies are shown for each platform. Enough chitchat—it's time to build your first PhoneGap app!

Creating the Project Files in MOTODEV Studio

HOW-TO 9-1

1. Start Studio, and create a new Android project. In the New Android Project dialog box (see Figure 9-1), type **HelloPhoneGap** in the Project name text box, and then click **Finish**.

(continues)

(*continued*)

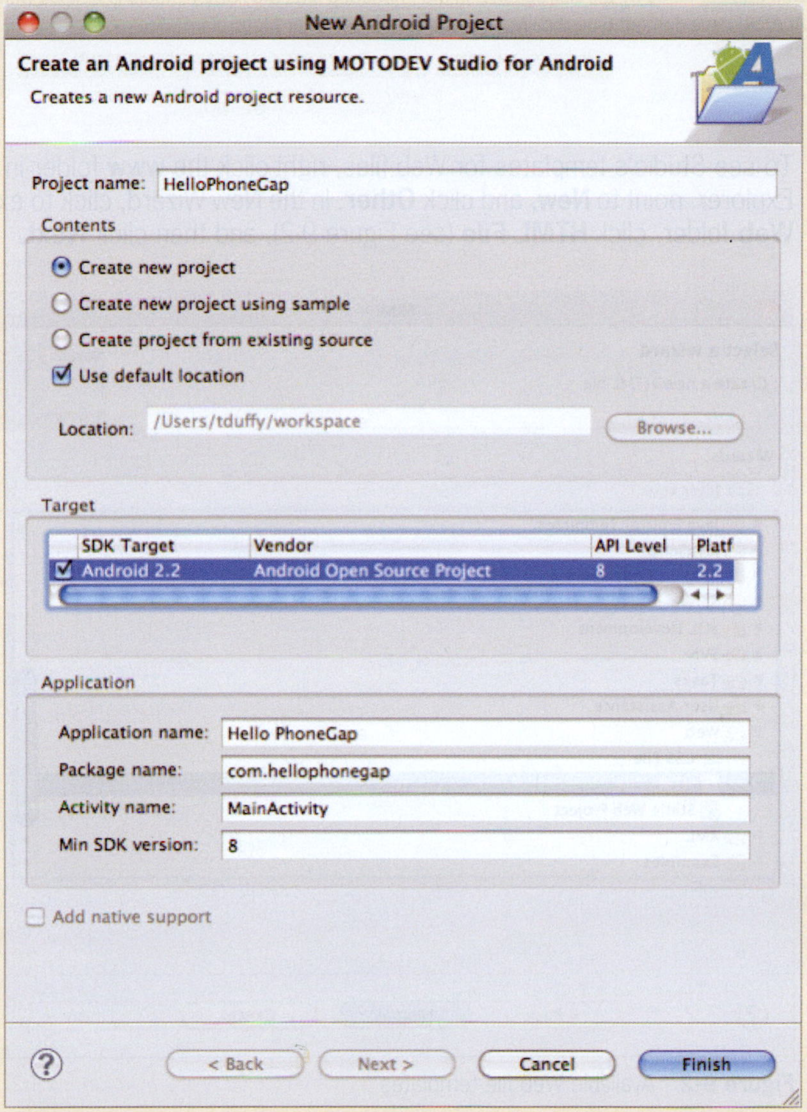

Figure 9-1 The New Android Project dialog box

To use PhoneGap in an Android project, follow the instructions in Appendix A. (You can also refer to *www.phonegap.com/start#android*.) The instructions include creating specific folders and copying PhoneGap files to certain locations in the project.

(*continues*)

(continued)

Don't be confused by the instructions on the PhoneGap site. MOTODEV Studio *is* Eclipse with plug-ins for Android development (specifically, Android development for Motorola devices).

2. To see Studio's templates for Web files, right-click the **www** folder in Package Explorer, point to **New**, and click **Other**. In the New Wizard, click to expand the **Web** folder, click **HTML File** (see Figure 9-2), and then click **Next**.

Figure 9-2 Available Web file templates

3. Make sure the **www** folder is selected in the list box for the parent folder, name the file **index.html**, and click **Finish** to open the file in the code editor.

4. Replace the existing code in `index.html` with the following:

```
<!DOCTYPE html PUBLIC "-//W3C//DTD HTML 4.01 Transitional//EN"
 "http://www.w3.org/TR/html4/loose.dtd">
```

(continues)

(continued)

```html
<html>
<head>
  <title>Hello Web!</title>
  <script src="helloScript.js" type="text/javascript"></script>
</head>
<body>
  <p id="nameLabel">Enter Your Name</p>
  <p><input type="text" name="nameTextField" id="nameTextField"
  value=""/></p>
  <p><input type="button" value="Press Me" id="helloButton"
  onClick="sayHello()" name="helloButton"/></p>
</body>
</html>
```

 The files used in this chapter are the same ones you used in Chapter 8. You can copy the code from the Chapter 8 files and use it for the files in this chapter.

5. Right-click the **www** folder again in Package Explorer, point to **New**, and click **Other**. This time, click to expand the **JavaScript** folder, click **JavaScript Source File**, and then click **Next**.

6. Name the file **helloScript.js**, and click **Finish** to open the file in the code editor. Replace the existing code, if any, in the helloScript.js file with the following:

```javascript
function sayHello(){
  var nameText = document.getElementById("nameTextField").value;
  var displayString = "Hello, " + nameText + "!";
  document.getElementById("nameLabel").innerHTML = displayString;
}
```

7. Save your work, and then run the project in the Android emulator. Enter your name in the text box and click the button to see the app work. Figure 9-3 shows the results.

(continues)

(continued)

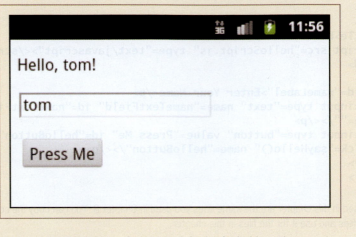

Figure 9-3   HelloPhoneGap at work in the Android emulator

Creating the Project with Existing Files in Xcode

HOW-TO 9-2

1.   To build the iOS app, start Xcode, and click **Create a new Xcode project**. Click the **PhoneGap-based Application** template (see Figure 9-4), and then click **Next**.

To use the PhoneGap template, you must install PhoneGap first. Follow the instructions in Appendix A or at *www.phonegap.com/start#ios-x4*.

(continues)

296

(continued)

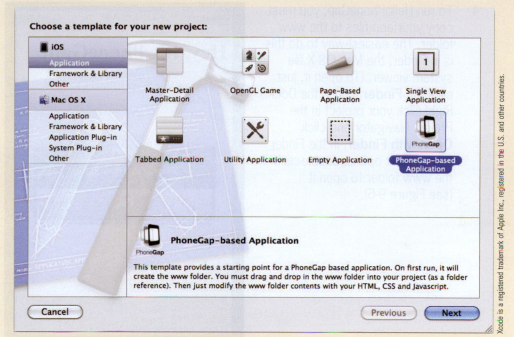

Figure 9-4 Creating a new PhoneGap project in Xcode

2. Name the project **HelloPhoneGap**, and save it in a location of your choice.

PhoneGap installs a project template for you in Xcode that includes the files needed for your PhoneGap project to run. You don't need to copy files and configure the project, as you did with MOTODEV Studio.

3. Xcode creates the project for you. After running the project, it populates the www folder with the PhoneGap JavaScript file and an `index.html` file. You can use these files to test your PhoneGap installation. Click **Run** on the Xcode toolbar to see the default project in action (see Figure 9-5).

(continues)

(continued)

4. To run HelloPhoneGap, you must copy your app files to the www folder. The easiest way to do this is in Finder, the Mac OS X file system viewer. (To open it, just click the **Finder** icon in the Dock.) Right-click your project in the Project Navigator and click **Open with Finder**. In the Finder window that opens, double-click the **www** folder to open it (see Figure 9-6).

Figure 9-5   Testing PhoneGap

Figure 9-6   The Finder window for the www folder

(continues)

(continued)

Depending on the version of PhoneGap you installed, your files might differ from what's shown in Figure 9-6.

299

5. Open a second Finder window for the folder containing the HelloPhoneGap project files.

The files for this project are the same files you created for the Android project. You can find them in your MOTODEV Studio workspace folder—for example, users/*username*/workspace. To open a new Finder window, click the Finder icon in the Dock again.

6. Drag the **index.html** and **helloScript.js** files to the HelloPhoneGap project's www folder. When the Copy message box opens, click **Replace**.

You can also right-click any project folder, point to Add, and click Existing Files to add files to your project, but you can't replace any files Xcode has created. For example, `index.html` and `phonegap-1.0.0.js` are grayed out in Figure 9-7.

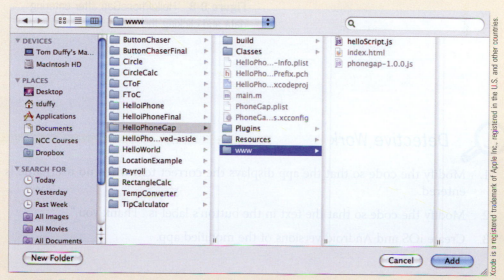

Figure 9-7 Files created by Xcode can't be replaced

(continues)

(continued)

7. Back in Xcode, click **Run** on the toolbar to open the app in the simulator. Enter some text and click the button to test the app. Figure 9-8 shows the results.

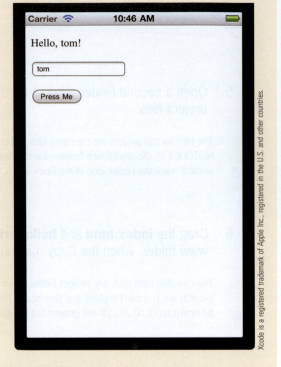

Figure 9-8   HelloPhoneGap after entering data and clicking the button

Detective Work

1. Modify the code so that the app displays the correct text when no username is entered.

2. Modify the code so that the text in the button's label is "Thank you."

3. Create iOS and Android versions of the modified app.

Advanced PhoneGap Apps: DotSmasher

For the DotSmasher app, you create a PhoneGap project in Xcode and then copy the Web files to the www folder in MOTODEV Studio to create the Android version. The files for this project are identical to those you created in Chapter 8.

Creating the Project Files in Xcode

HOW-TO 9-3

1. Start Xcode, if necessary, and create a new PhoneGap project in Xcode. Name the project **PhoneGapDotSmasher**, and save it in a location of your choice. Run the project to create the www folder.

2. Expand the **www** folder in the Project Navigator, and click **index.html** to open it in the code editor. Replace the existing code with the following:

```html
<!DOCTYPE HTML PUBLIC "-//W3C//DTD HTML 4.01 Transitional//EN">
<html>
<head>
   <title>DotSmasher</title>
      <link rel="stylesheet" href="dotSmasher.css" type="text/css"/>
      <script type="text/javascript" src="dotSmasher.js"></script>
</head>
<body onLoad="setGameAreaBounds()" onResize="setGameAreaBounds()">
   <div id="scoreLabel">Score: 0</div>
   <div id="pageTitle">DotSmasher</div>
   <div id="gameArea">
      <button id="dot" onClick="detectHit()"></button>
   </div>
</body>
</html>
```

3. Then right-click the **www** folder in the Project Navigator, and click **New File**. Click **Other** in the list of templates on the left, and on the right, click **Empty File** (see Figure 9-9). Click **Next**.

(continues)

(continued)

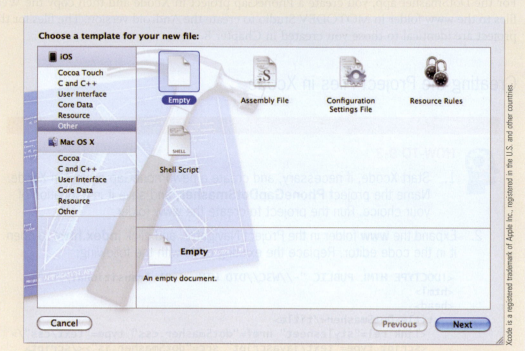

Figure 9-9   Selecting a template

4. Name the file **dotSmasher.css**. Click the **www** folder to save the file there (see Figure 9-10), and then click **Create**.

(continues)

(continued)

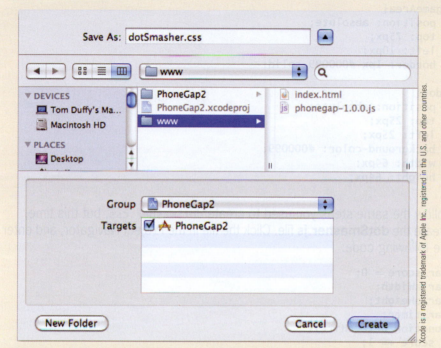

Figure 9-10 Creating **dotSmasher.css** in the www folder

5. In the Project Navigator, click **dotSmasher.css**, and enter the following code:

```
#scoreLabel{
    font-family: Arial,Helvetica,sans-serif;
    font-size: 14pt;
    color: #000099;
    font-weight: bold;
    position: absolute;
    top: 10px;
    left: 10px;
    height: 25px;
}
#pageTitle{
    font-family: Arial,Helvetica,sans-serif;
    font-size: 24pt;
    font-weight: bold;
    color: #000099;
    position: absolute;
    top: 35px;
    left: 10px;
    height: 25px;
}
```

304

(continued)

```
#gameArea{
   position: absolute;
   top: 75px;
   left: 10px;
   border: 1px #000099 solid;
}
#dot{
   position: absolute;
   top: 25px;
   left: 25px;
   background-color: #000099;
   width: 64px;
   height: 64px;
}
```

6. Follow the same steps you used to create dotSmasher.css, but this time, create the **dotSmasher.js** file. Click the file in the Project Navigator, and enter the following code:

```
var score = 0;
var aWidth;
var aHeight;
var timer;
function detectHit(){
   score += 1;
   scoreLabel.innerHTML = "Score: " + score;
}
function setGameAreaBounds(){
if(document.all){
   aWidth = document.body.clientWidth;
   aHeight = document.body.clientHeight;
}else{
   aWidth = innerWidth;
   aHeight = innerHeight;
}
aWidth -= 30;
aHeight -= 95;
document.getElementById("gameArea").style.width = aWidth;
document.getElementById("gameArea").style.height = aHeight;
aWidth -= 74;
aHeight -= 74;
moveDot();
}
```

(continues)

(continued)

```
function moveDot(){
    var x = Math.floor(Math.random()*aWidth);
    var y = Math.floor(Math.random()*aHeight);
    if(x<10)
        x = 10;
    if(y<10)
        y = 10;
    document.getElementById("dot").style.left = x;
    document.getElementById("dot").style.top = y;
    clearTimeout(timer);
    timer = setTimeout("moveDot()",1000);
}
```

7. Save your work, and click **Run** on the toolbar to load the app in the simulator (see Figure 9-11).

 If you're having trouble clicking the button, increase the delay in the `setTimeout()` function.

 The IE-specific code was left in `dotSmasher.js` to be used when PhoneGap adds support for Windows Phone 7.

Figure 9-11   Running the PhoneGap version of DotSmasher in the simulator

Xcode is a registered trademark of Apple Inc., registered in the U.S. and other countries.

Creating the Project with Existing Files in MOTODEV Studio

HOW-TO 9-4

1. Start Studio, if necessary, and create a new PhoneGap project. Name the project **PhoneGapDotSmasher**, and save it in a location of your choice.

2. You can copy files to the www folder in MOTODEV Studio. Copy **index.html**, **dotSmasher.css**, and **dotSmasher.js** from the www folder of the Xcode project to the www folder in Studio. You can also use the files you created in Chapter 8.

3. Run the project in the emulator. Figure 9-12 shows PhoneGapDotSmasher running.

Figure 9-12   Running PhoneGapDotSmasher in the Android emulator

Detective Work

1. Implement a start/stop mechanism for the app. (*Hint*: Use the `clearTimeout()` method.)

2. Force the game to end after 30 seconds, and inform the user that the game has ended.

3. Devise a way for users to select a difficulty level. You might want to give them the options Easy, Medium, and Hard. You need to determine what defines the level of difficulty. You might increase the speed at which the dot moves, make the dot smaller, and so forth.

4. Create iOS and Android versions of the modified app.

Using PhoneGap's Geolocation API

So far, you've been writing your own scripts for use in PhoneGap apps. PhoneGap includes libraries you can use to incorporate the built-in functions in devices. The PhoneGap libraries give you a way to access location services, and the following project makes use of this feature.

 For a complete list of PhoneGap functions, visit *http://docs.phonegap.com*.

 HOW-TO 9-5

The project contains two files: `index.html` and `geoLocation.js`. For this project, you should choose how you want to create the files. You can create them in Xcode or MOTODEV Studio, or you can use the editor you selected in Chapter 8 to create the files. No matter how you create the files, they must be copied to the www folder of your PhoneGap project.

1. Create the `index.html` file and add the following code:

```
<!DOCTYPE html PUBLIC "-//W3C//DTD HTML 4.01 Transitional//EN"
 "http://www.w3.org/TR/html4/loose.dtd">
<html>
<head>
<meta http-equiv="Content-Type" content="text/html; charset=UTF-8">
  <title>PhoneGap GeoLocation Example</title>
  <script src="phonegap-1.0.0.js"></script>
  <script src="geoLocation.js"></script>
</head>
```

(continues)

(continued)

```
<body>
<h3>PhoneGap GeoLocation Example</h3>
  <p>Click the button to display Location data</p>
  <p><input type="button" onClick="showLocation()" ↵
 value="Show Location"/></p>
  <p id="display"></p>
</body>
</html>
```

This code provides a Show Location button that calls the `showLocation()` function (written next) when it's clicked. Notice the reference to the `phonegap-1.0.0.js` file. It's where links to the native OS are stored. If you're using a different version of PhoneGap, make sure you refer to the correct file. A paragraph element is added to display the location data. It's empty when the page loads but is populated after the user clicks the button.

2. Following is the code to add for `geoLocation.js`:

```
// Variables to hold values for the button click
var latitude = "Latitude: ";
var longitude = "Longitude: ";


// Event handler for button click
function showLocation(){
  navigator.geolocation.getCurrentPosition(onSuccess, onError);
}
// onSuccess() Geolocation receives a Position object
function onSuccess(position){
  latitude = "Latitude: " + position.coords.latitude;
  longitude = "Longitude: " + position.coords.longitude;
  document.getElementById('display').innerHTML = latitude ↵
+ '<br />' + longitude;
}

// onError() callback receives a PositionError object
function onError(error){
  document.getElementById('display').innerHTML = 'code: ' ↵
    + error.code    + '<br />' + 'message: ' + error.message;
}
```

First, this code creates variables to hold the latitude and longitude. The `showLocation()` function gets the device's current location by accessing the `geolocation` object's `getCurrentPosition()` function. Then you provide callback handlers to `getCurrentPosition()`. In this case, the `onSuccess()` function is called when `getCurrentPosition()` is successful. The `onError()` function is called if there's a problem.

(continues)

(continued)

PhoneGap supplies the onSuccess() function with a Position object. The function then uses the coords property to access the latitude and longitude and stores the values in the corresponding variables. An HTML string is created from the latitude and longitude variables and then shown in the display <div> element, using the innerHTML property. The onError() function is supplied an Error object and displays any problems reported.

3.   You still need to create PhoneGap projects in Xcode and MOTODEV Studio to test the app. If you haven't done that yet, you should now. When you run the app in the iOS simulator, the simulator notifies you that the app wants to access your location. Click **OK** to grant permission and view your location, as shown in Figure 9-13. You can set the simulator's location as you did in Chapter 6.

4.   Next, copy the **index.html** and **geoLocation.js** files to an Android project, and run it in the Android emulator.

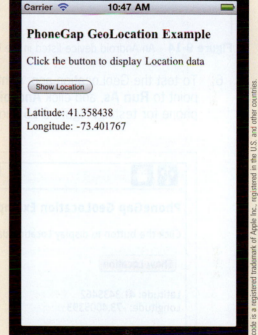

Because the location permissions are set in the PhoneGap project, there's no notification that the location services are being accessed. When you click the Show Location button, nothing happens. This is a known bug in PhoneGap. Simply put, the Geolocation API just doesn't work in the Android emulator, which is evident in the onSuccess() and onError() functions not being called. If either function had been called, the display would have been set.

Figure 9-13   The PhoneGap GeoLocation app running in the iOS simulator

5.   If you have an Android device and want to test a workaround solution, connect the device to your PC. In Studio, it should be listed in the Device Management view under Android Handset (see Figure 9-14).

(continues)

(continued)

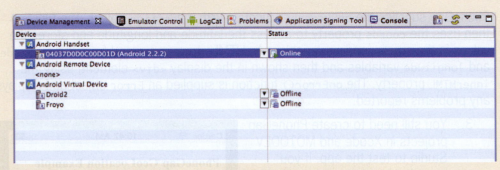

Figure 9-14   An Android device listed in the Device Management view

6. To test the GeoLocation app, right-click the project in the Package Explorer, point to **Run As**, and click **Android Application** to install the app on your phone for testing. Figure 9-15 shows the results of clicking the button.

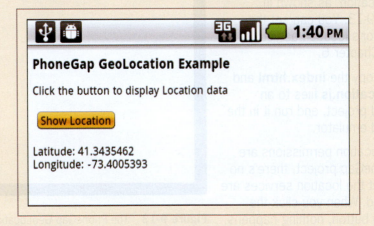

Figure 9-15   The PhoneGap GeoLocation app running on an Android device

311

Chapter Summary

- PhoneGap is an open-source library that provides a unified API for accessing native device capabilities, using HTML, CSS, and JavaScript. It includes project templates for Android and iOS apps.

- There are two general strategies for creating PhoneGap apps: Use an external editor to create project files and copy them to a PhoneGap project, or create a PhoneGap project and create the files in MOTODEV Studio or Xcode.

- PhoneGap allows you to access native device capabilities, including Accelerometer, Camera, Capture, Compass, Connection, Contacts, Device, Events, File, Geolocation, Media, Notification, and Storage.

- Both MOTODEV Studio and Xcode are capable of editing HTML, CSS, and JavaScript files.

Key Terms

native device capabilities—Built-in device features, including Accelerometer, Camera, Capture, Compass, Connection, Contacts, Device, Events, File, Geolocation, Media, Notification, and Storage.

PhoneGap—An open-source library that provides a unified API for accessing functions built into devices, using HTML, CSS, and JavaScript.

Review Questions

1. Which of the following describes PhoneGap?

   a. The distance between phones

   b. A cross-platform smartphone development solution

   c. A proprietary OS

   d. A cellphone accessory store

2. PhoneGap uses which programming language?

   a. Java   c. Objective-C

   b. C#   d. None of the above

3. With PhoneGap, you can access native device capabilities. True or False?

4. PhoneGap development strategies include which of the following? (Choose all that apply.)

   a. Creating Web files and copying them to the www folder of PhoneGap projects
   b. Creating PhoneGap projects and adding Web files to them
   c. Using the WebView component in each platform
   d. Building a custom JavaScript interpreter

5. Access to which of the following isn't available with PhoneGap?

   a. System settings   c. Geolocation
   b. Accelerometer   d. Compass

6. Which kind of file is typically *not* used in PhoneGap development? (Choose all that apply.)

   a. HTML   c. C#
   b. C++   d. Objective-C

7. PhoneGap makes it possible for developers to do which of the following? (Choose all that apply.)

   a. Maintain a single codebase for smartphone apps.
   b. Use Web technologies to develop smartphone apps.
   c. Target multiple platforms.
   d. Access native device capabilities.

8. PhoneGap addresses the problem of apps with external Web content being rejected by storing your app's Web content on Web servers. True or False?

9. You can replace project files Xcode has created. True or False?

Up for Discussion

1. Discuss the pros and cons of using PhoneGap to develop smartphone apps.

2. Discuss when using PhoneGap is clearly not the best option for developing apps. Explain your answer.

3. Rhodes and Appcelerator Titanium are also cross-platform development tools for smartphone apps. Discuss the capabilities of each tool and compare them with PhoneGap. Which tool is best, and why?

Programming Exercises

1. Create a PhoneGap app that displays the area and circumference for circles. Create a `Circle` object that performs the calculations, and instantiate this object based on a user-entered radius.

2. Create a PhoneGap app that displays the area and perimeter for rectangles. Create a `Rectangle` object that performs the calculations, and instantiate this object based on user-entered length and width values.

3. Create a PhoneGap app that converts temperature from degrees Fahrenheit to degrees Celsius. Ask users for the temperature in degrees Fahrenheit. Create a `TempConverter` object to perform the calculations, and instantiate this object with the user input. Use the following formula for the conversion:

    $C = 5/9(F - 32)$

4. Create a PhoneGap app that converts temperature from degrees Celsius to degrees Fahrenheit. Ask users for the temperature in degrees Celsius. Create a `TempConverter` object to perform the calculations, and instantiate this object with the user input. Use the following formula for the conversion:

    $F = 9/5 * C + 32$

5. Combine Programming Exercises 3 and 4 so that users can choose between converting Fahrenheit to Celsius and vice versa. Be sure to include the `TempConverter` object and instantiate this object for each calculation.

6. Create a PhoneGap app that calculates payroll. Allow the user to enter the number of hours worked and an hourly wage. The wage should be "time and a half" for hours worked over 40 in a week. Display the amount to be paid to the user.

Installation and Setup

This appendix explains how to install all the tools needed to complete the projects in this book. As with any technology, tools get updated, often at the most inopportune moment! The good news is that you usually have time to finish the project you're working on before updating your development tools. In other words, unless you're waiting for a new API to be released, the tools you're using are almost certainly adequate.

As of this writing, MOTODEV Studio is at version 3.0.2. The latest version of the Android SDK is version 4.0, code-named Ice Cream Sandwich (ICS). This book uses MOTODEV Studio 3.0, but the projects are targeted to version 2.2 of the Android SDK, code-named Froyo. The simple fact is no ICS devices are available yet. The good news is that Froyo apps can run on versions 2.2 and 2.3.3 (code-named Gingerbread) as well as ICS. Targeting Froyo makes sense because your apps can run on nearly every current Android device.

Gingerbread is the last version of Android designed exclusively for cellphones. Google released Android 3.0 (code-named Honeycomb), but it's meant for tablet computers, and Honeycomb apps can't run on Android phones. ICS represents the convergence of cellphone and tablet versions of Android. By targeting ICS, you can support cellphones and tablets with a single codebase. In addition, all new devices will run ICS or later, so targeting ICS is a good way to look to the future.

For iOS development, Xcode and Interface Builder are included with OS X on Mac computers. The version on your Mac depends on the OS X version. The newest version of OS X (10.7, code-named Lion) includes Xcode 4 and the iOS SDK 5. Xcode 4 and the iOS SDK 5 can also be downloaded for OS X 10.6 (code-named Snow Leopard).

If you have an older Mac running OS X 10.5 or earlier, you aren't out of luck. Xcode 3 and the iOS SDK 4 are available free. Xcode 3 isn't compatible with OS X 10.7 but works beautifully on OS X 10.6 and earlier versions. If you're using Xcode 3, the screenshots and steps will be slightly different from what's in this book. With the exception of automatic reference counting, the code you write to create apps in this book is compatible with iOS 4.

The current version of the Windows Phone SDK is 7.1. It has all the tools needed to create apps for both Windows Phone 7.0 and Windows Phone 7.5 (code-named Mango) devices.

The current PhoneGap version is 1.x, but PhoneGap version 1.0, the first official release, is used in this book because it includes support for both Android and iOS projects as well as others. Later versions might include support for Windows Phone 7. For the most part, if you download and install a version of PhoneGap later than 1.0, the only thing that will be different from what's shown in this book is that the name of the PhoneGap JavaScript file you include in HTML documents must match what you've installed.

 When asked to enter a project name in these instructions, stick with Java naming conventions. (For example, no spaces or special characters should be used, and each word in a multiple-word name is capitalized.) Even when other programming languages are used in these IDEs, follow these conventions to make finding your files easier. For more information on Java naming conventions, go to *www.oracle.com/technetwork/java/codeconventions-135099.html#367*.

Android

To do the projects in this book, you need to install two tools for developing Android apps: App Inventor and Motorola's MOTODEV Studio.

App Inventor

You must be signed in with your Google account to use App Inventor.

 For up-to-date information on where to find this tool, visit *www.cengagebrain.com* and search by ISBN for this book. Select Access Now, and click Updates in the left navigation bar. Depending on the version you use, steps and screens might differ slightly from what's shown in this appendix.

1. Open a browser and go to **www.appinventorbeta.com/learn/setup/index.html**. Two steps for setting up App Inventor are listed:

   - Set up your computer.

   - Set up your Android phone (optional) or use the emulator.

 You don't need an Android phone to develop apps, so you don't need to follow the steps for setting up your phone. All the apps you develop in this book can run in the emulator included with App Inventor. Of course, if you have an Android device and want to test your apps on it, follow the instructions in that section. Regardless, you must install the App Inventor Extras Software for your OS to test apps because it includes tools to make App Inventor work.

Should things go wrong during the installation, check *www.cengagebrain.com*, as described previously, to look for troubleshooting tips.

2. After you have installed and tested the software as specified in the setup instructions, open a supported browser and go to **www.appinventorbeta.com**. The My Projects page should be displayed, as shown in Figure A-1. If it's not, click the **My Projects** link at the top of the page.

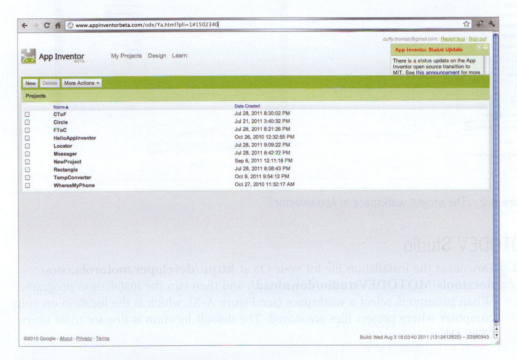

Figure A-1   The My Projects page in App Inventor

3. Click the **New** button. Enter a name for your project, and then click **OK**. The App Inventor workspace opens with your project loaded (see Figure A-2).

318

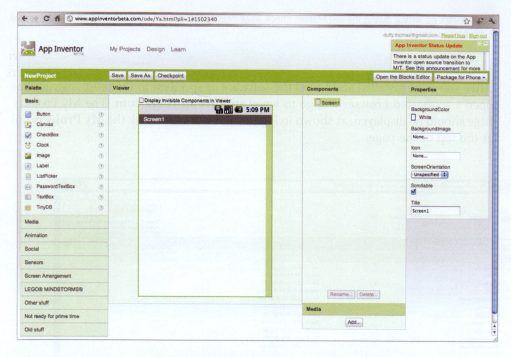

Figure A-2   The project workspace in App Inventor

MOTODEV Studio

1. Download the installation file for your OS at **http://developer.motorola.com/docstools/MOTODEVstudio/download/**, and then run the installation program. When prompted, select a workspace (see Figure A-3), which is the location on your computer where project files are stored. The default location is fine for most users. Click **OK**.

 You can have multiple workspaces, but if you need to have multiple projects open, they must be in the same workspace. You can import projects from another workspace into the current workspace.

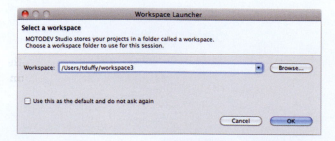

Figure A-3   The Workspace Launcher dialog box

2. Next, you need to install the Android SDK Tools. Click **Yes** to start the process.

3. In the Android SDK and AVD Manager window, click **Available packages** on the left. On the right, click the **Android Repository** check box (see Figure A-4), and then click the **Install Selected** button. Then click **Install** to install the platforms. If you're prompted to restart ADB (Android Debugger), click **Yes**.

 You must be connected to the Internet to install platforms and tools.

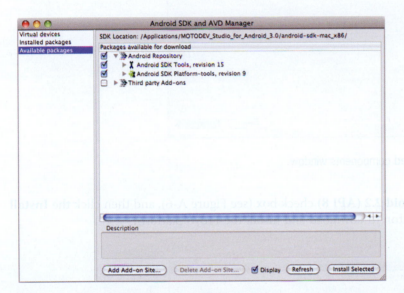

Figure A-4   The Android SDK and AVD Manager

4. If you're prompted to create a virtual device, click **Cancel**. You have installed the Android tools, but you haven't installed any working platforms yet. The next step is to update MOTODEV Studio to make sure you have the most recent version. Click **Update MOTODEV Studio** from the MOTODEV menu. If prompted to enter your credentials, enter the username and password you created when downloading Studio. When any necessary updates have been installed, you might need to restart MOTODEV Studio.

5. Next, you download and install components. Click **Download components** from the MOTODEV menu. In the window that opens, click the **Download platforms, non-Motorola add-ons and samples** link (see Figure A-5).

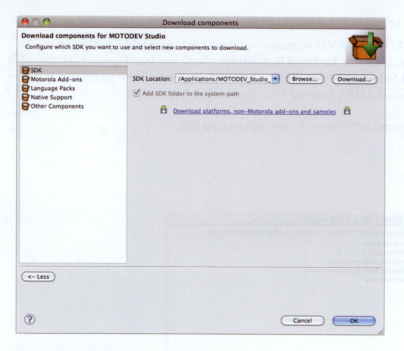

Figure A-5 The Download components window

6. Click the **Android 2.2 (API 8)** check box (see Figure A-6), and then click the **Install 2 packages** button to download and install the Froyo platform.

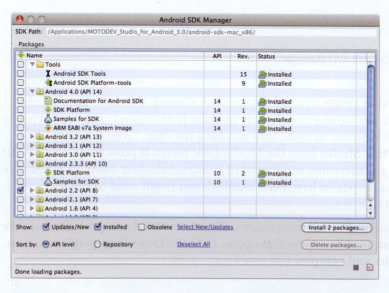

Figure A-6 Downloading the Froyo platform in the Android SDK Manager

7. Accept the license agreement. MOTODEV Studio downloads and installs the components. After all the software has been installed, you need to create an Android Virtual Device (AVD). If you aren't prompted to create an AVD, click **New Android Virtual Device** from the MOTODEV menu. Name the device **Froyo**, and then click **Next**.

8. In the AVD Target drop-down list, click **Android 2.2**. In the SD Card section, create a 16 GB SD card by clicking the **New** option button and entering **16000** MB in the text box next to it (see Figure A-7). Click **Finish** to create the AVD.

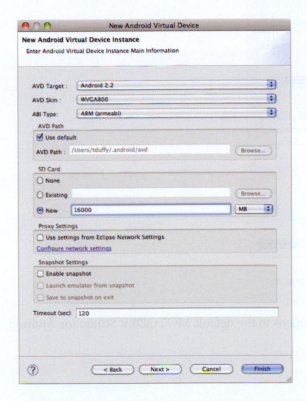

Figure A-7 Creating a new Android Virtual Device (AVD)

 All the platforms installed on your system are available as targets. In addition, you can create multiple virtual devices, each with its own platform, if you want to test on more than one platform. Just repeat Steps 5 through 8 for other platforms. Figure A-8 shows the Gingerbread and Ice Cream Sandwich platforms installed in addition to Froyo.

9. Click **File** on the menu, point to **New**, and click **Android Project Using Studio for Android**. Name the project, leave the default settings shown in Figure A-8, and click **Finish**.

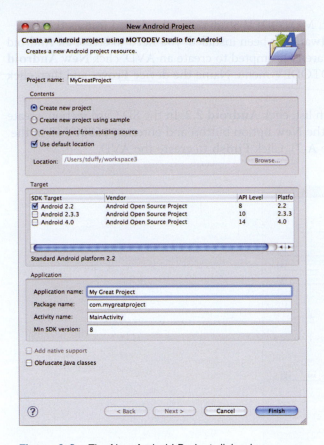

Figure A-8 The New Android Project dialog box

As shown in Figure A-9, the workbench opens to the default MOTODEV Studio for Android perspective (discussed in Chapter 5).

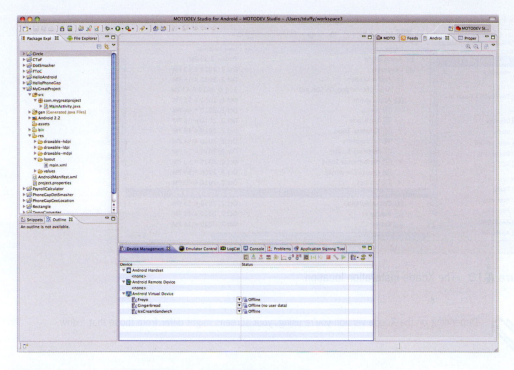

Figure A-9 The MOTODEV Studio for Android perspective

Apple iOS

To develop iOS apps, you use Xcode and Interface Builder coupled with the iOS SDK. You need an Intel-based Mac to use the iOS SDK.

1. Go to **http://connect.apple.com/cgi-bin/WebObjects/MemberSite.woa/wa/ getSoftware?bundleID=20792**, and download Xcode 4. If you're running OS X 10.5 or earlier, install Xcode 3 from your OS X installation disc.

2. Run the installation program; if prompted, enter your password. The software is installed in the Developer folder in your root directory of your hard drive, and development applications (Xcode and Interface Builder) are installed in the Applications subfolder (see Figure A-10).

Figure A-10 The Xcode installation location

Depending on the Xcode version you're using, your screens might differ from those that follow.

3. Start Xcode by double-clicking it in the Finder. The Welcome window displays the options shown in Figure A-11.

Figure A-11 The Xcode Welcome window

4. Click **Create a new Xcode project**. In the next window, click **Application** in the iOS section on the left, click the **Empty Application** template on the right (see Figure A-12), and then click **Next**.

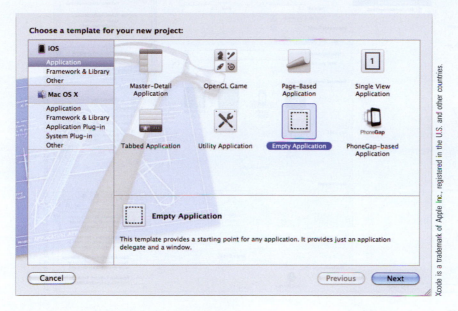

Figure A-12 Selecting a project template

5. Name the project, and specify where to save it. The workspace opens with your project loaded (see Figure A-13).

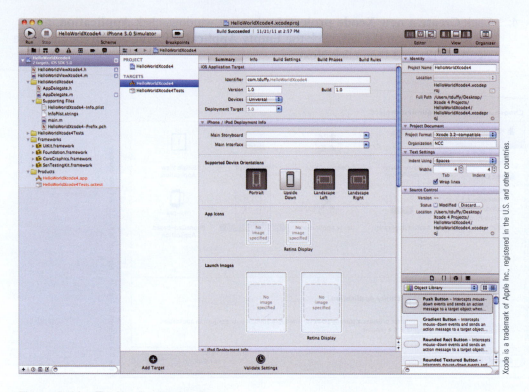

Xcode is a trademark of Apple Inc., registered in the U.S. and other countries.

Figure A-13   The Xcode user interface

Windows Phone 7

1. Download Visual Studio 2010 Express for Windows Phone at **http://create. msdn.com/en-us/resources/downloads**. Run the installation program. When prompted for a registration key, click **Obtain a registration key online**, and then click the **Register Now** button.

2. Enter your information in the online registration form. When you're finished, Visual Studio 2010 for Windows Phone 7 should start and display the Start Page, shown in Figure A-14. If Visual Studio doesn't start automatically, click it in the Start menu.

Figure A-14 The Visual Studio Start Page

If the Start Page isn't visible, click File, New Project from the menu or click the New Project toolbar icon.

3. Click the **New Project** link on the left. Double-click **Windows Phone Application**, and enter a name and location for the app. If prompted to select a platform, click **Windows Phone OS 7.1**. The solution name is filled in automatically (see Figure A-15).

Figure A-15 The New Project dialog box

Visual Studio displays the project workspace and loads your project, as shown in Figure A-16.

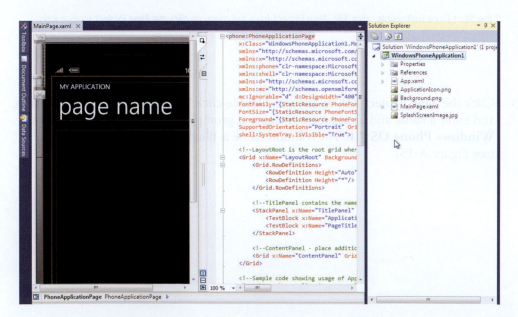

Figure A-16 The Visual Studio default workspace

PhoneGap

Download the latest build of PhoneGap at *www.phonegap.com/home/*, and unpack the contents of the download. Because PhoneGap works in multiple IDEs, you need to install it on each platform.

Using PhoneGap with Xcode 4

1. Navigate to the iOS folder from your PhoneGap download, and run the installation program. Start Xcode, and then click **Create a new Xcode project** in the Welcome window. In the iOS section on the left, click **Application**, and on the right, click **PhoneGap-based Application** (see Figure A-17).

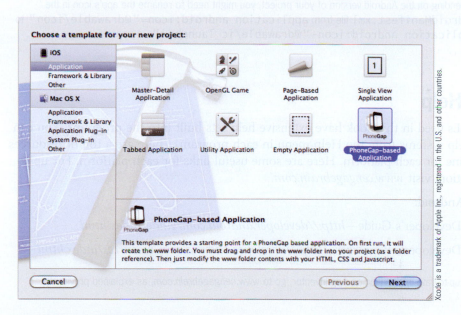

Figure A-17   Selecting the PhoneGap template

2. Click the **Next** button, name your project, and select the location for the new project, as described previously. Follow the instructions for using PhoneGap with Xcode 4 at *http://phonegap.com/start#ios-x4*, and then you're ready to create iOS apps with PhoneGap in Chapter 9.

For information on using PhoneGap with Xcode 3, go to *http://wiki.phonegap.com/w/page/16494778/ Getting%20Started%20with%20PhoneGap%20%28iOS%29%20-%20Xcode%203*.

Using PhoneGap with MOTODEV Studio

Using PhoneGap to build Android apps isn't as easy as using it to build iOS apps. In addition, the instructions change periodically. For the newest, detailed instructions, refer to *http://phonegap.com/start#android*. Because you've already installed MOTODEV Studio, you have done Steps 1 and 2. Start the process of building a PhoneGap project beginning at Step 3.

 You must follow these steps for each PhoneGap app you create in MOTODEV Studio.

 Depending on the Android version of your project, you might need to rename the app's icon in the `AndroidManifest.xml` file from `application android:icon="@drawable/icon"` to `application android:icon-"@drawable/ic_launcher"`.

Getting Help

All of the IDEs used in this book have extensive help sets built into the programs. You can access the help systems from the Help menu in each program. There are a ton of resources available online for each platform. Here are some useful links for each platform. For up-to-date information, visit *www.cengagebrain.com*.

For Google Android:

- Android Developer's Guide—*http://developer.android.com/guide/index.html*
- Android Developer's Resources—*http://developer.android.com/resources/index.html*

 For up-to-date information on App Inventor, go to *www.cengagebrain.com*, as explained previously.

- App Inventor Learning Pages—*http://AppInventor.googlelabs.com/learn/*
- App Inventor for Android Blog—*www.AppInventor.org*
- MOTODEV Studio for Android Documentation—*http://developer.motorola.com/docstools/MOTODEVstudio/*
- MOTODEV Help Set—*http://127.0.0.1:50427/help/index.jsp* (*Note*: This local address runs on your machine, and MOTODEV Studio for Android must be running for it to work.)

For Apple iOS:

- iOS Dev Center—*http://developer.apple.com/devcenter/ios/index.action*
- iOS Developer Library—*http://developer.apple.com/library/ios/navigation/index.html*

For Windows Phone 7:

- Windows Phone 7 Forum—*http://forums.create.msdn.com/forums/default.aspx? GroupID=19*

- Windows Phone Development on MSDN—*http://msdn.microsoft.com/library/ff402535% 28VS.92%29.aspx*

- Windows Phone Developer's Hub—*http://create.msdn.com/en-US/*

For PhoneGap:

- PhoneGap Docs—*http://docs.phonegap.com*

- PhoneGap Wiki—*http://wiki.phonegap.com/w/page/16494772/FrontPage*

Glossary

A

accessor methods Methods for making instance variables private and providing mechanisms for accessing and setting data values and handling errors; often called "getters" and "setters."

Activity An Android component that represents a single screen with a user interface.

Android Google's open-source OS for smartphones and similar devices. It includes a free SDK that integrates with various IDEs for creating native apps, which are written in Java.

Android Package (.apk) A file used as a deployment bundle for installing Android apps.

App Inventor Google's Web-based IDE for creating Android apps. It includes a user interface designer and a code block editor.

application delegate In iOS, this object is where you write code to interact with the OS and the user; it's also where life cycle events occur.

application layer The highest level in a platform architecture; includes third-party apps that interact with core libraries to provide functionality. *See also* core libraries layer.

B

best practices Accepted ways of doing things that result in favorable outcomes.

blocks Graphical representations of code snippets that snap together to form an app's logic.

Broadcast Receiver An Android component that responds to systemwide broadcasts.

bundle An abstraction of a file system location that groups code and resources to be used in an application.

C

C# The programming language used to create Windows Phone 7 apps.

category An Objective-C mechanism for adding methods to an existing class, even if you don't have the source code for the class.

application programming interface (API) A collection of public data and behaviors made available to outside programs.

arrays Collections of data, usually of the same type. Array members are accessed by index (place in the collection).

attributes Key/value pairs stored in XML elements.

class A template for creating objects; classes are the fundamental constructs of object-oriented programming. *See also* object-oriented programming (OOP).

code folding An IDE feature used to show or hide blocks of code with a click.

Common Language Runtime (CLR) The virtual machine used in Windows Phone 7.

compiled language A programming language that's translated from English-like commands to a machine language only once, at compile time.

conditional statements Tests in a program that evaluate to true or false.

constructors Methods that supply data at creation time and initialize objects.

Content Provider An Android component that manages a shared set of application data.

core libraries layer A platform architecture level that represents functions the platform makes available for apps.

D

Dalvik virtual machine A specialized Java virtual machine designed to run on Android.

Delegate design pattern A mechanism whereby an object hands off some of its work to another object, called a delegate. *See also* design patterns.

design patterns Best practices for structuring an application.

device convergence The concept that users no longer need separate devices to perform multiple tasks.

Document Object Model (DOM) A standard for accessing objects in documents, such as XML and HTML documents. It's a hierarchical, treelike structure that represents a document's objects.

dynamic method invocation The process by which the system first looks locally for code to execute then looks up the class hierarchy if code is not found.

E

emulator A program for testing code that can be used if an Android phone isn't available. The emulator is a software-based phone that makes almost the entire Android OS available for testing.

encapsulation The process of bundling data and behavior into discrete units and protecting them from outside programs.

event delegates Objects that handle interactions between data and the component firing the event.

Extensible Application Markup Language (XAML) An XML vocabulary designed to contain and describe user interface components.

Extensible Markup Language (XML) A tag-based language designed to store information.

F

File Transfer Protocol (FTP) The protocol used to transfer files to and from Web servers.

Firebug A Firefox add-on that provides JavaScript debugging capabilities.

framework A collection of classes, used for performing certain tasks.

functions Blocks of code in a program that run when called; can be thought of as the verbs in a program and represent what a program does.

334

G

game loop Code that manages data processing and rendering the display in a game app.

H

hardware layer A platform architecture level that represents physical components, such as memory, the screen, and so forth.

header file A file with an .h extension in Objective-C that's used to declare a class's public API.

I

implementation file A file with an .m extension in Objective-C that's used to define class behavior.

infix notation A notation system used in Objective-C code that intertwines the method name and parameters.

inflating The process of instantiating objects created in the form designer.

inheritance A prerequisite for any OOP language that makes it possible for classes lower down a hierarchy to have automatic access to classes higher up the hierarchy.

instance variables Data members whose scope is the entire class.

instantiation The process of creating objects from classes.

integrated development environment (IDE) A collection of tools programmers use for writing, compiling, running, and debugging code and deploying apps; usually has graphical tools and includes extensive documentation to help developers build apps.

IntelliSense The code-completion feature in Visual Studio.

Intent A piece of information used to activate an Activity, Service, or Broadcast Receiver in an Android app.

Intent Filters Objects that inform the system about the kinds of Intents a component can handle. *See also* Intent.

interpreted language A programming language that must be translated into machine code each time a program runs.

iOS Apple's OS for mobile devices.

J

Java Micro Edition (ME) This platform, intended to address the concerns of multiple small-device platforms, uses Java as its programming language.

Java Web Start A technology that enables developers to deploy full-strength applications without the installation problems of typical desktop applications.

join The process of concatenating strings in App Inventor.

L

launcher An object that starts a system service.

life cycle The series of events from an app's launch to its destruction.

literal A piece of immutable data stored in memory.

loop invariant A quantity that doesn't change inside a loop.

loops Programming mechanisms for repeating a set of programming instructions until some end condition is met.

M

marketplace An online location hosted by platform providers where programmers can sell apps.

memory leak When an object exists in a program that can't be accessed by the running code, a memory leak occurs when the program no longer needs an object but its reference count is greater than 0. Memory leaks result in slower programs and possibly system crashes.

method overriding A programming technique used to make a method's implementation appear in the subclass.

methods *See* functions.

Model-View-Controller (MVC) A design pattern that represents a structure in which each program task is in a different tier. *See also* design patterns.

MOTODEV Studio The Motorola IDE for developing Android apps.

N

namespace A C# feature used to bundle assets for reuse.

native app An application compiled for a specific platform's architecture.

native device capabilities Built-in device features, including Accelerometer, Camera, Capture, Compass, Connection, Contacts, Device, Events, File, Geolocation, Media, Notification, and Storage.

non-visible components Objects that have no user interface and are used to access Android system services, such as location and messaging services.

O

object composition An aspect of the Delegate design pattern that represents a "has a" relationship rather than the "is a" relationship denoted by inheritance. Objects that make use of object composition contain other objects that perform some task. *See also* Delegate design pattern.

Objective-C The programming language used to develop apps in both Mac OS X and iOS.

object-oriented programming (OOP) A programming model in which programs are built by creating objects that interact with each other. Each object possesses its own data, and access to data is granted by writing methods stored in the object.

operating system layer A platform architecture level that represents the platform's interface between programs and the device's underlying hardware.

optimization Techniques for making programs run faster or on less memory.

outlet An instance variable that can be connected to a UI component.

P

parameters Data values passed to other parts of a program, usually methods and functions. *See also* functions.

perspective An editor in Eclipse that enables you to work with specific file types.

PhoneGap An open-source library that provides a unified API for accessing functions built into devices, using HTML, CSS, and JavaScript.

polymorphism An object's capability to be treated as more than one type. It can be achieved through inheritance or the interface/protocol mechanism of C#, Java, and Objective-C.

procedural language A programming language that executes instructions as a series of commands, one after the other.

properties Data associated with the objects of a program. They can be thought of as adjectives, describing what an object is and does.

property list (plist) The file used to set global parameters for an app.

protected data members Data members available to classes in the same package and to all subclasses.

prototype-based inheritance A programming technique in which properties and methods are defined in a constructor, not from a class higher up in the hierarchy.

R

refactoring The process of rewriting code to make it better without changing its behavior.

reference A collection of assets stored in a Dynamic Link Library (.dll) file.

S

Service An Android component that runs in the background to perform long-running operations.

Silverlight A development platform for creating interactive apps for the Web, desktop, and mobile devices.

single inheritance model A model in which a class can have only one superclass. C#, Java, and Objective-C use this model.

smartphone A handheld computer integrated with a cellphone; it runs native apps. *See also* native app.

software development kit (SDK) A collection of platform libraries, tools, and documentation that developers use for building applications.

solution A group of files in Visual Studio containing one or more projects.

string buffers Objects that hold character data but are mutable.

strings Collections of character data. Strings are immutable in Java, Objective-C, and C#.

structure-based language A language that describes an entity's structure, such as HTML describing the structure of a Web page.

subclass A class below another class in an inheritance tree. It's defined by adding functionality to an existing superclass. *See also* inheritance.

superclass A class above another class in an inheritance tree. It contains information common to all subclasses beneath it in the hierarchy. *See also* inheritance.

T

target A set of instructions for building a product.

tombstones A term used in Windows Phone 7 to describe deactivating an app.

V

variable A named pointer to data in a program that can change.

view A window in Eclipse that displays a certain aspect of a project.

view controller An object, usually a subclass of UIViewController, that's responsible for setting up and configuring the view when asked and for brokering requests between the model and view.

virtual machine A collection of resources used to run applications on a host OS.

Visual Studio 2010 The IDE used to create Windows Phone 7 apps.

W

weakly typed A programming language characteristic in which data types are determined by assignment. In Objective-C, a weakly typed object means you don't have to determine its type at design time.

Web Developer A Firefox add-on for manipulating the browser environment.

WebKit An open-source rendering engine developed by Apple as a derivative of the Linux Konqueror browser's KHTML engine.

Windows Phone 7 The Microsoft platform for developing smartphone apps. Its IDE is Visual Studio 2010, and Windows Phone 7 apps are written in the C# programming language.

workbench An arrangement of specific windows in Eclipse.

workspace In Eclipse, a set of files on disk used to help organize development projects.

Index

353